D0108831

Praise for

Five Easy Theses

"*Five Easy Theses* sets out key issues of public policy easy to identify in concept but long unresolved in practice. Stone proposes sensible approaches to breaking the long-standing political deadlock. The specific measures to deal with budgetary balance, income inequality, public education, health care, and financial reform should provide a guide for constructive debate as we choose our next president."
—**Paul A. Volcker,** chairman of the Federal Reserve (1979 to 1987) under Presidents Carter and Reagan, and currently chairman of the Volcker Alliance

"An extraordinarily impressive and important book. Stone is smart, balanced, and sensible, three traits that are in desperately short supply in our discourse about the future of the country. His analysis is penetrating, logical, and powerful, without ideological spin. Every policy idea he presents follows from that logic. You don't have to agree with all of his proposals to realize his book's value to politicians, policymakers, and citizens everywhere."
—**Norman Ornstein,** author, political scientist, and resident scholar at the American Enterprise Institute

"This book is a recipe for restoring America's greatness. Stone offers thoroughly persuasive solutions to five economic and social problems we often consider insoluble. The more closely we follow his prescriptions, the brighter our national future will be."
—**Stephen Kinzer,** author of *All the Shah's Men* and *The Brothers*

"James Stone's *Five Easy Theses* is masterfully written, straightforward, and free of jargon. The marvelous chapter on income and wealth distribution presents a compelling essay on inequality in the United States. Stone speaks with particular and rare authority on these issues. People should listen to what he has to say."

—**Janet Gornick,** director, Luxembourg Income Study, and professor of political science and sociology, Graduate Center, City University of New York

"Well crafted and highly engaging, James Stone's *Five Easy Theses* takes on five of the nation's biggest problems and offers solutions that are as simple and accessible as they are illuminating. Particularly at a time of intense partisan polarization, *Five Easy Theses* is refreshingly honest—a model of straight talk. Readers may not agree with everything Stone proposes, but they'll marvel at his command of the issues and finish the book with a new sense of possibility and much to cheer about."

—**David A. Moss,** John G. McLean Professor of Business Administration, Harvard Business School

"A pithy, well-documented distillation of pressing public policy issues, including the causes of America's annual trillion-dollar overspend on health care—and what, in practical terms, we could do as a nation to substantially lower costs and perhaps even improve outcomes. In vivid prose that combines convincing evidence and compelling stories, Stone persuasively argues that a universal, single-payer system should replace our highly inflationary patchwork of private insurance and government programs."

—**Jonathan D. Quick,** MD, MPH, president and CEO, Management Sciences for Health; chair, Global Health Council; and faculty member, Harvard Medical School

Five Easy Theses

Commonsense Solutions to America's Greatest Economic Challenges

James M. Stone

Houghton Mifflin Harcourt
BOSTON NEW YORK
2016

www.hmhco.com

Library of Congress Cataloging-in-Publication Data is available.
ISBN 978-0-544-74900-9

Printed in the United States of America
DOC 10 9 8 7 6 5 4 3 2 1

Contents

Introduction and Foundations

LET ME EXPLAIN the title of this book. Americans, on the whole, are deeply dissatisfied with the inability of our government to solve a host of obviously consequential problems. Some are genuinely hard to solve because they don't have solutions that equitably resolve nasty tradeoffs between winners and losers. But the paralysis today is worse than that. Our system can't even seem to deal with eminently solvable problems.

This book is about five of those. It presents straightforward answers to several of today's most important public policy issues. Or, more precisely, it asserts that straightforward logical answers to some issues are staring us in the face, yet there seems to be no political path to their resolution. I hope you will declare this an unacceptable state of affairs. Worse still, the key issues are too seldom part of what passes for political debate these days. Politicians in both parties steer away from exactly the subjects they ought to be addressing in favor of sound bites, "gotchas," and mini-matters. My book title, I admit, is slightly facetious because the logic of the five issues is not entirely beyond debate and the politics may appear hopeless. But I wanted to make the point that these are issues politicians should stop running from. An alternative title for the book was *Too Big to Touch*. Please don't mistake the conversational tone or intentional lack of bombast in what follows for a belief that the recommendations offered here are of small consequence or could be readily enacted. Together, they are transformative and thus would be heartily resisted.

Americans disagree about many things, and so it shall always be, but I would wager at pretty good odds that most of you share the concerns embodied in these five questions:

- Are you confident that Social Security and Medicare will be solvent enough to meet their promises when you and your children need them?
- Do you want to live in a society in which a tiny fraction of the public and a few corporations hold a greater share of the wealth and influence than has ever been the case in America before? Can a society so tilted be as productive and stable, not to mention pleasant, as the America you grew up in?
- Must your health care cost almost twice as much as it costs your counterparts in every other advanced nation, while our health system delivers objectively worse results than most of the others?
- Why can't the schools of this affluent and admired nation train students not headed to college for realistic careers and stop busting the budgets and burdening the futures of so many who do go on to university?
- Did we learn anything from the Crash of 2008? How have we allowed our financial sector to accumulate even greater derivatives positions than prior to the crash, to concentrate

> its assets in even fewer institutions than before, and to take home a massive and unprecedented share of the economy's profits?

I am a Democrat, but this is not a partisan book. Americans of every political stripe — the Right, the Left, the Center, the not-sures, and even the don't-cares — share these concerns. Many talk about our nation as adrift, with hazardous rapids not necessarily around the next bend but maybe the one right after that, and surely somewhere ahead. I am not so pessimistic, but it is true that you are not getting the deal you had counted on, and that your children have even slimmer prospects of getting it in the future. We are still the most affluent and powerful nation the world has yet produced, and at little risk of losing that status anytime soon. But most Americans today believe that we are leaving our rising generation a society in worse shape than the one we inherited. If you believe that, you are probably right . . . but it doesn't have to be.

As the problems grow larger, alas, it seems that our politics become smaller. It is standard fare in civics classes to describe democracy's requirement that officeholders find a balance between representing and leading, between following the wishes of their constituents and acting on their convictions. Similarly, there is a recurrent debate in campaigns for office between those who want to follow the polls at some critical moment and those who want the candidate to demonstrate courage and philosophical consistency. These tensions are inevitable, but today's balance is way out of whack. Few current politicians dare to go beyond nearsighted polls, and those who do are often dismissed in the media as hopelessly outside the mainstream.

Scanning this forbidding landscape, many of you may have concluded that issues like those I have listed cannot be solved in ways that will provide any genuine benefits to you and your families. Perhaps you feel that a better life for your children has rather unexpectedly moved out of reach. America is in decline, some can be heard to complain; the century of America is in the past. To this, I say nonsense. I could hardly disagree more. This is, in fact, exactly the attitude I wish to challenge. That America has passed its peak is far from an inevitability. Ours is still the country that most favors, at least in the private and academic sectors, intellectual challenge to the established ways of doing things. And from this spring innovation and creativity no other society can match. The advantage, moreover, is proving robust. I will try to persuade you that the public sector can tap into this energy and become a worthier partner for the rest of the country—if only it would adopt some specific, commonsense policies. Only the will to act is missing; the course is relatively clear.

The course corrections I advocate are largely off the table in contemporary politics. There are three ingredients of serious political progress, and all three are currently missing. The first is clarity of vision—pragmatic thinking about courses of action that will really work. I hope to provide a bit of that here. The second ingredient I cannot provide. This ingredient is political leadership, at an opportune moment for change, imbued with the unusual guts, charisma, and communications talent to champion a bold change, even if it risks defeat and the polls suggest the public isn't ready to follow yet. Politics is a tightrope for an elected official. You fall off to one side if you don't get elected. You fall off as well, though, if you waste your opportunity to lead. An election to office is a chance to demonstrate leadership, in both philosophy and action, to advance the values you believe in. Public servants without idealism, politicians who don't care about improving their slice of the world or promoting values to which they are committed, are little more than career freeloaders.

This is not, on the other hand, to suggest that all those who fail to bring about transformative change are parasites. Some of the best in public life will try and fall short. It takes more than intellect, vision, and personal courage, however admirable, to produce great leadership success. Timing counts, too. In the history of any nation, there will be moments that particularly call for tilting toward compromise and moments that call for leaning toward courage. This country has been remarkably lucky to have great statesmen who have chosen a bold leadership path and rallied public opinion in times of obvious crisis. That's why we remember them as great. Ours are times of less apparent crisis. It remains to be seen whether, in the absence of charismatic events, leaders will rise — or the times will allow them to rise — to galvanize public opinion and act boldly in the common interest.

Clarity of vision and leadership, the first two ingredients required for change, are necessary but not sufficient. The third ingredient of change is a countervailing force to set against the well-armed protectors of the status quo. Constructive change will always find opponents in those campaign contributors and lobbyists whose goals are antithetical to the public interest on any issue. This is an inherent quality of democracy. Even in the best of times, the hand-to-hand political combat of reform has been an uphill battle. And these are not the best of times in that regard by a long shot. The recent tide has favored the already powerful. Of the three ingredients of change, winning the battle against entrenchments is the hardest to count on. Ideas, even clear ideas, will certainly be offered from time to time. History has provided the occasional brave and talented change agent. The battle against the interests is more formidable. But I am sure it *cannot* be won without a clear agenda and the emergence of courageous leaders to precede that battle.

An astute friend told me years ago that the United States is ruled by a bicameral government, but it's not the one described in civics books. He said we have a House of Money and a House of Votes, where the former is in charge day to day and even year to year but the latter is a sleeping dragon that could rise up and take control briefly when properly stirred. I'll be proud if this work contributes even a jostle to awaken the dragon from its sleep.

As a Democrat, I considered at one point writing a book addressed mainly to members of my own party. Much of what I propose, though, ill fits the political mainstream for both major parties at the moment. I have more hope that Independents and open-minded people more generally can make progress than I have for the most partisan factions of either party. At this juncture, the Democrats are weak in both clarity and farsightedness, and the Republicans are disinclined to change what must be changed. Too many Democrats have fallen into espousing bland policies that voters see as unlikely to bring any major improvement to their lives and finances. Republicans have not broken free from wealthy interests with manifestly narrow objectives.

The Democrats are hurt nowadays by the natural pendulum of politics writ large. Left-of-center ideas had held sway from the time of Franklin D. Roosevelt until the Reagan Revolution. Lofty expectations proved unmet, and the pendulum swung. An even grander pendulum was simultaneously in sweep. From the time of Karl Marx until recently, idealistic egalitarian thinking was in vogue worldwide. Many intellectuals around the world looked forward to the near-perfectibility of their societies; this was a futile notion from the start. The harsh truth is that we humans are an imperfect species by our evolutionary nature, forever to be conflicted between altruism and selfishness, warlike and peaceful urges, competition and cooperation, hierarchy and rebellion, empathy and antipathy. The Left has never recovered from the embarrassment of having fallen in love with a disillusioning dream. As the reigning giant of evolutionary biology E. O. Wilson likes to say, "Great idea. Wrong species."

We are destined to continue with little concept of what an ideal society would look like. That's why cartoonists envision heaven as a place where souls with little winglets sit on clouds strumming harps. Try to picture what you would like to do every day in blissful eternity, and you will come up short, too. For that reason, this book makes no attempt to lay out universal advice applicable across time or place. I have, however, a predilection for free enterprise democracy. Properly regulated market economies have proven themselves beyond reasonable doubt. Pluralistic democracy, even if not as robust, has proven itself as well. The invisible hand is a powerful idea. Enlightened self-interest is good for the economy, and with a level enough playing field, it can contribute to sound governance. This agenda is not, therefore, a call to sacrifice, debilitating austerity, or the nobility of adherence to some rigid ideology. Instead, it offers solutions that deliver tangible benefits for the majority of us today and, all the more so, for future American generations. I will not be asking Americans to search for their better angels. More emphatically, I'm not counting on any alteration of human nature. I do ask the reader to think logically and try to put aside political categories and opportunities for sophistry in favor of the national interest. The alternative is a less pluralistic, less democratic, and less prosperous future America.

I offer at this point a bit of personal history and a presentation of credentials. It is optional for appreciating the rest of the book, so skip it if you like, and I won't be a bit offended. Better yet, I won't even know. I was born in New York City; grade-schooled in the bedroom suburb of Pelham, New York; and then attended college and graduate school at Harvard. Otto Eckstein was the professor who sparked my interest in economics and mentored me most generously. He showed me that economics needn't ever be a dismal science. The course that introduced me to Bayesian decision making under conditions of uncertainty, taught by Howard Raiffa, made almost no sense at the time — and has shaped my approach to virtually every job and intellectual challenge I have had since. An unanticipated rant that same year from Nobel laureate Wassily Leontief fortuitously confirmed the waning of my desire to become a full-time academic economist. Leontief tearfully told me that he was quitting Harvard economics because the field had become obsessed with small, unimportant questions that could be definitively answered through mathematics. At the same time, he said, economics was pounding out of its most talented young people the ambition to examine the larger questions that mattered more to mankind but defied precise proofs. Years later, when Leontief was nearly ninety, I saw him at a cocktail party and he asked me what I was doing. When I said I had started an insurance company, he hugged me tightly and declared triumphantly, "You listened!"

I am now in my third career. My first career, immediately following the award of my PhD, was teaching the Economics of Securities Markets to Harvard undergraduates. As Leontief would have urged, I sought a part-time appointment as a Lecturer rather than a tenure-track professorship and simultaneously began my business career. Then, in 1975, I switched entirely. Having worked in my non-teaching days as a consultant in the insurance industry, I had quickly developed a nice set of paper credentials in that field. I had also devoted a good deal of time to local politics. That combination brought me an appointment as Commissioner of Insurance under the new Governor of Massachusetts, Michael S. Dukakis. The Governor had promised to find someone for the job with expertise in the business of insurance who was not beholden to the industry. The field was narrower than he probably expected, and I fit the bill. I looked so young that when I paid the Senate President a courtesy call, his assistant announced me as a visiting high school Insurance-Commissioner-for-a-Day. After four years in that job, and a veteran public servant at the age of thirty-one, I was ready to return to an academic-business mix. A semester at the London School of Economics was arranged for me, but luck again intervened and I went to Washington instead.

Jimmy Carter was the President of the United States then, and he interviewed me personally for the job of Chairman of the Commodity Futures Trading Commission. I survived a tough confirmation process, about which I could relate more stories than space here allows. A *New York Times* piece soon thereafter said that my new position came with a crown of thorns, which has proven to be prophetic of its burden for all those who have tried to do it right. My tenure there was more instructive than successful. "Character-building" is the phrase that comes to mind when I think of those years. The CFTC holds principal regulatory jurisdiction over the trading of the complex derivatives instruments that were to play a calamitous role in the Crash of 2008, but the agency has been hamstrung from the start by a halfhearted mandate from Congress and a powerful, politically sophisticated body of regulatees. Many resisted the whole notion of restrictions on their Wild West practices as a matter of principle. Financial derivatives were just coming into their own in 1979, with the force of a tidal wave, and I didn't like their lack of customer protections or their excessive leverage. Commanding tidal waters to retreat has never been an especially rewarding mission, and it worked for me no better than for King Canute. In fact, it worked less well — since Canute was actually trying to show court sycophants that he could *not* command the tides. I briefly thought I could command those waters and stop overly leveraged financial derivatives from becoming a hazard to the country.

Instead, I set a different standard of rare accomplishment. I may be the only federal agency head in history to have spoken tirelessly on a major policy issue and failed to convince anyone at all, possibly not even my own staff, that I was right. More important, I persuaded not one of my fellow commissioners or the leaders of the other financial regulatory agencies that overleveraged and underregulated derivatives trading could reap a tsunami. After the Crash of 2008, I received a generous note from the redoubtable Paul Volcker, who had served as the Chairman of the Federal Reserve Board during my D.C. tenure, saying that he wished I had persuaded him back then of the dangers of leverage. I served a few years into the Reagan administration and left the CFTC in early 1983.

Eight years out of academia, I was no longer qualified to teach economics without relearning the literature. Government was in the hands of the other party, and the Democrats were racing to ape the winners in both denouncing regulation and raising as much Wall Street money as possible. The private sector held all of the appeal. Cleansed of revolving-door syndrome by four years in Washington in a different field, I founded an insurance company in Massachusetts. This fit an old self-awareness of mine beautifully. I recall having told my parents, when I was a teen and they spoke admiringly of someone they knew who had achieved senior executive status at a giant corporation, that I would rather sell apples from my own cart on the streets of New York than hold a top position at a large, well-established company. I was warned that insurance was not an entrepreneurial field, and it didn't escape anyone's notice that I lacked experience leading a private business, but the die was cast.

In the earliest moments of January 1, 1984, my soon-to-be wife, Cathy, and I were returning from a New Year's Eve party when I called her attention to the fact that two thousand people had driven to parties that evening sober — and duly insured by someone else — but were now returning from parties mainly drunk and insured by our brand-new company. Plymouth Rock Assurance Corporation was born that midnight. My idea from the start was to build a company a few inches better than its competitors along three dimensions. First, since it seemed that the largest insurers took their customers and agents for granted, better and more respectful service would be rewarded. To accomplish that, I knew we would have to treat our own people better as well. A strong service culture requires leadership by example, not just command, and a minimum of the office politics that can undermine a high-service attitude. Second, perhaps because my background was analytical, I wanted to build a company more mathematically sophisticated than the others. Math and statistics underlie the auto and homeowners insurance business. This insight, although correct, was soon shared by the top performers in the industry. Luckily, though, those companies that outdistanced us in the early years tended not to be active in our two major states.

Finally, I resolved to operate a company without a hatred of regulation. When the government tells consumers to buy a product as a precondition of driving a car, it has an obligation to assure affordability and accessibility. When people pay for a financial product, of value to them only if the seller performs honestly and fully at some future point, regulation must protect integrity and solvency as well. In auto insurance, moreover, market pricing forces a product offering that is inherently and severely income regressive. The poorer, more crime-plagued, and crowded your neighborhood, the more you pay to insure a car. This is another solid basis for regulation. Plymouth Rock has never been opposed to a legitimate regulatory role in our industry, something many of our competitors waste energy in fighting as though it were a religious imperative.

Plymouth Rock Assurance has never sought a grand innovation meant to revolutionize auto and homeowners insurance. There's an old joke about two campers in the woods. One sees a fierce and hungry-looking bear headed for their campsite. He warns the other camper of the bear's approach, and his buddy grabs his sneakers. "What are you doing?" asks the first camper. "You can't outrun a hungry bear." "I know," replies the other, "but I only have to outrun you." In business, it is not necessary to create a perfect company, just a company inches better than the competition. It has worked pretty well for Plymouth Rock. It is not the biggest auto and homeowners insurer in the country, but it's in the top few dozen. It now has revenues in excess of a billion dollars a year, with something like a million homes and autos insured. The company, which I still lead, employs 1,400 men and women and has returned to its stockholders an average of 17 percent per year on their money over a period of thirty years now. In 2014, Plymouth Rock's employees voted it one of Boston's best places to work. And it has created more jobs within the City of Boston than any other company established and headquartered in Boston during the past forty years. A foe at the CFTC told me that my views wouldn't be worth much until I had met a private payroll. Those are stripes I have now earned.

I can claim some partial credentials from work outside of Plymouth Rock as well, in business and the nonprofit sector. I was an active member of the board of directors of the *Boston Globe* for six years. My interest in the press is expressed today by my service as Vice Chairman of Global Post, an award-winning worldwide Internet news service based in Boston. About a dozen years ago, I helped to create a private-equity fund in New York, where I still serve as an adviser and a member of the general partnership that manages the fund. That fund has now raised a total of $13 billion for its investments. I was a founder of three insurance companies other than Plymouth Rock; all three had Wall Street funding, and, as a result, all three were sold to larger corporations as they matured — an inevitability that privately held Plymouth Rock does not have to face.

On the nonprofit side, I work with an organization that helps secure private funding for public schools in Boston. In that role, I serve as chairman of a panel that awards a substantial cash prize every year to the most-improved public school in the city. To forward our knowledge of education, my wife and I each chose one school with which to get more deeply and directly involved. Cathy joined the board of the most impressive charter school in Boston, and I picked the public high school with the lowest standardized test scores. Cold Spring Harbor Laboratory on Long Island in New York State is probably the most prestigious genetics research center in the world. I have been a trustee of the lab since 1983 and serve on its Executive Committee, and I chair its Academic Affairs and Commercial Relations committees. Finally, I am the Chairman of the Board of Management Sciences for Health, a large humanitarian nonprofit organization in the Boston area whose 2,500 staffers reinforce basic public health infrastructure in about forty of the world's neediest countries. Cathy and I, as a shared passion, have visited over seventy countries by now, including some where MSH has projects.

There are a number of credentials I cannot hope to claim. This book will focus on domestic economic issues rather than national security and foreign policy. It will also go light on issues of moral, cultural, and social policy, except where they directly intersect with economic issues. And, although there is no denying their importance, it will touch only peripherally on environmental issues, because many better-prepared authors are tackling that subject now. Just as important, solutions to many issues in the environmental realm actually *are* hard. More generally, this is not a book with ambitions to describe the operational details of the remedies it suggests or anticipate all of the future bumps on the roads I suggest taking. It makes no claim of original academic research. Rather, it is a short collection of public policy essays, aimed at convincing you that the adoption of a few familiar, commonsense ideas could make this country operate more effectively in your interests. Remember the title of this work. Mine are the easy theses.

ONE
Fiscal Balance

It is perfectly proper for a country like ours to finance investments in its future through borrowing. It is senseless, however, to keep expanding an already worrisome national debt for purposes inconsistent with our common goals. While there is room for legitimate debate about what represents an optimal bottom line for the annual federal budget, and plenty of room for debate over priorities, no one wants to see taxpayer money spent wastefully. Yet the hunt for current savings is largely misdirected. The least justifiable expenditures arise not from excessive programmatic spending but from unproductive tax subsidies. The official recording of the national debt, moreover, wholly omits the most threatening future obligations: those we are incurring at an accelerating pace in the entitlement programs for seniors. Social Security's shortfalls can be cured in a straightforward manner, but only if we act decisively and soon to restore the program's balance. The fiscal house should be, and can be, put in order—both short-term and over the long horizon.

"NEITHER A BORROWER nor a lender be," said Shakespeare's Polonius. But economists of every stripe concur that some use of debt can be helpful to a household, a corporation, or a country. It is certainly the case that most households, businesses, and countries ignore Polonius and actually carry debt all the time. The question of how much debt a responsible entity of each sort should carry is harder to answer than whether debt should be carried at all. The literature on optimal corporate capital structure is rich, and there is endless, though much looser, discussion about how much debt a household can responsibly incur. I have seen nowhere, though, a convincing theory of just how much debt a nation ought to have.

The right answer for a government has something to do with its aptitude for creating future wealth by borrowing and spending. It has something to do with its ability to service the debt from available revenues even if rising interest rates increase its cost. It has something to do with the expanding temptation to pay off obligations by inflating the currency as the debt load increases. And it has something to do with what economists call "crowding out," which occurs when public debt markets divert money from the private investment required for healthy economic growth. I have no unified theory of the ideal national debt burden to offer here.

Instead, we can just agree that many Americans are worried that the country has too much of a debt burden already, and that its debts are growing too fast for them to feel good about the future. I am agnostic on that score but count myself among the worried for a related reason. The United States is accumulating its debt — and, more important, its unfunded future entitlement commitments — too mindlessly. We are incurring it for purposes beyond its principal justification, which is to build wealth and opportunities for our future generations.

I might confess that I come with a bias against debt. My parents, Henry and Babette Stone, fretted about the monthly mortgage bill, and early on I felt that a care worth avoiding. While I borrowed for education early in life, and later for a mortgage, I have shunned debt ever since. My principal business, Plymouth Rock Assurance, has been debt free for most of its existence as well. This may not be the strategy that maximizes profit, but the extra sleep is often worth more than the extra wealth. A mentor once told me that the best rule of personal debt is "Never borrow money when you need it, only when you don't." A different rule might apply to government borrowing: a country should never borrow to postpone political discomfort, only when its next generation will be grateful that it did.

The national debt keeps expanding, and the accumulation of future obligations excluded from the debt calculation should be a source of greater concern. There is surprisingly little to cut from current or future spending if programs for the elderly and national security are off the table.

Common sense tells us that there should be some years over the economic cycle in which the national debt increases and some in which its accumulation slows or falls. That's how a sound household is run. In the past forty years, however, the federal budget has recorded only five surplus years, one of which can be more accurately described as break-even — and not one in which the magnitude of the surplus was nearly as large as the average year's shortfall.[1] The rest of the forty years were in deficit, and often substantial deficit. The actual numbers are too large, abstract, and mind-numbing for most people to absorb. The federal deficit was $680 billion in 2013 and $486 billion in 2014; it is expected to be similar in 2015.[2] The good news is that these magnitudes and trends represent a return to historical normalcy from deficits of over a trillion dollars in each of the prior four years.[3] The bad news is that this still means that the Treasury has incurred in this relatively decent year about $1,500 in new debt for every man, woman, and child in the country.

The deficit each year, of course, adds to the national debt, representing the total indebtedness incurred over the years and not yet paid off. The national debt, inclusive of intergovernmental holdings, has now passed $18 trillion, more than $55,000 for each American.[4] If instead of all Americans, one looks only at working Americans, the obligation exceeds $100,000 each.[5] This debt is owed to whoever is holding the government's bonds. The largest holders of United States debt other than our government itself are Japan and the People's Republic of China.[6] Other foreign governments and private entities abroad taken together hold roughly as much as China and Japan. Theirs are legitimate claims on the future productivity of the United States. One might argue that debt issued by Americans and held by other Americans is a harmless wash. To owe one another money within the same family may not make the family as a whole any poorer, but that is certainly not the case when future debts are incurred to someone outside the family in order to pay for something enjoyed today. That a substantial portion of our national debt is owed to foreign entities means that others in the world are entitled to take, and remove from our economy, a meaningful cut of America's future prosperity.

Expressed as a fraction of gross domestic product (GDP), which is probably more meaningful than the absolute dollars, the national debt is less weighty than it was at the close of World War II.[7] But that fraction is higher than at any other time since the Civil War and rising. And it does not include the huge entitlements that have been promised but have not yet come due. You have probably read dire predictions about the prospective weaknesses of Medicare and Social Security in store as the baby boomers continue to age into their governmentally expensive years. This is where your concern about fiscal imbalance should be greatest.

Meanwhile, the political system has proven unable to address these present and potential imbalances. The ideological biases of both major parties preclude responsible compromise. Republicans who decry the debt are sometimes more interested in just cutting programmatic spending. Their calls for cutting taxes tend to worsen the imbalances, an extreme example of this being the revenue cuts in the early part of the millennium. In good economic times, tax reductions are demanded on the grounds that households, rather than the government, should decide what to do with the money. In less propitious times, tax cuts are seen as the best tool for stimulating the economy. A logician would describe this as "If A, then B. If not A, then B anyway." When taxes are so oppressive as to restrain economic activity, a case can be made for expanding the economy by reducing taxes, but there is no evidence at all that this is the case today in America. Mark these words. The country will not restore fiscal balance with further tax cuts.

The Democrats are also rigid. In good times, they say we can afford to exercise more compassion by increasing spending on social programs. In tough times, liberal economists want to boost the economy and ease people's pain through greater deficit spending. They seek in both environments a course that leads to higher taxes or greater deficits. This logic is equivalent to that of the Republicans, but with stimulative or empathetic spending substituted for tax cuts as the preferred answer. In candid settings, many leading Democrats confide that they understand the peril faced by Social Security and Medicare, but they feel we must wait for an unabashed crisis for our political process to reach a solution. They too often see any entitlement cutting undertaken as an invitation to dismantle the entire social safety net.

It may be helpful to clarify here the distinction between the national debt and the burden of future obligations. The federal government uses a definition of the deficit that is perfectly valid but importantly narrow. The official debt and deficit numbers you read about regularly in the newspapers ignore predictable and accrued liabilities of Social Security, Medicare, and the federal pension system. The result can be deceptive unless you keep in mind that the published numbers are only part of the federal fiscal picture. If counted the way private-sector financial statements are produced, the national debt would be far greater.

A corporation, like Plymouth Rock, must record in its financial statements *accrued* income and expenses. Accruals are identified items that will predictably turn into cash in or cash out sometime in the future. Under corporate accounting, a reader of financial statements can see not only what is happening in the immediate present, but also a bit of what is anticipated to happen in the future. There is no useful way to predict in my company's case whether Plymouth Rock customers will still like its products, prices, and service in a few years, or to forecast weather catastrophes that might arise, so the glimpse into the future is necessarily incomplete. Nonetheless, recording what is ascertainable about the future, and estimating accruals, is far more revealing than simple cash accounting could ever be. The official government budget is closer to a cash budget. It works the way you compute your income taxes, tracking money flowing in and out within a year.

Think about your household budget, which is probably constructed on a similar cash basis. If the amount of cash coming into your bank account is larger than the amount going out, you find yourself saving. If it's less, you dip into previous savings or borrow money from other sources. The government is in a similar position. When cash going out is greater than cash coming in, the Treasury must borrow, which it does by issuing bills and bonds payable in the future and bearing interest along the way. In some countries, the central authorities have solved imbalances by simply printing money, which can lead to hyperinflation and other miseries. We can count our blessings that the United States has been relatively free from that plague, but nowhere in our government's accounting is there any provision for commitments to pay out entitlement cash in the future. The books are accurate enough, but the story is incomplete.

Think again about your household. Let's say you are prudent about cash in and cash out, and you never have a shortfall. Unlike the federal government, your income every recent year has exceeded your spending. Your cash budget and your balance sheet are in great shape. Can you now relax and call yourself prosperous? Well, that depends. You can't if you promised your three children that you'd pay for the eight grandkids' college educations and don't have enough savings to make good. Maybe on top of that you have an elderly mother, and she is either going to move in with you or require long-term nursing home care. A balanced cash budget does not assure prosperity.

Accrued obligations do not increase your immediate cash needs. That the pledged outflows are in the future, though, doesn't make them any less real. The federal government is in the same situation, where most of the future commitments are to the elderly, and the government is essentially saying that it will cross those bridges when it comes to them. Both you and the federal policymakers should construct present and future budgets if fiscal soundness is a goal. If your household, or your government, makes no provision for future costs known to be around the corner, it invites a crisis when that corner is turned. It may have to renege on its promises, suddenly find new sources of income, cut other expenses, or end up broke.

Even if accurate future cash flows could be incorporated into the federal accounts, of course, this wouldn't produce a sketch of the entire government sector, since it would still omit state and local income and spending. This omission is anything but negligible. State and local expenditures represent nearly half of the grand total of government spending, and those governments have serious overhanging problems of their own to confront in future entitlements, especially with respect to pensions.[8] But state and local spending is not the subject of this particular work.

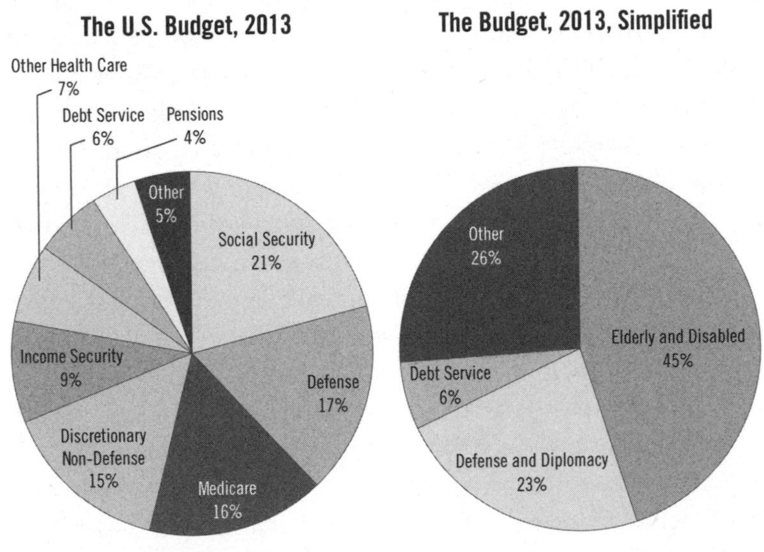

Figure 1.1

Figure 1.2

The pie chart in Figure 1.1 depicts the current federal budget, using the official categories and sums.[9] The chart in Figure 1.2 breaks the same total into a different set of categories you may find more intuitively informative. It won't match any official report that I am aware of, but it highlights an important story.

There is no attempt in these charts to project the numbers into the future. In many budget categories, and especially Defense, projections would be only the roughest of estimates — on which experts would surely disagree. A reckoning of accrued liabilities and estimates of future trends would be meaningful mainly in the entitlement programs. If these were built into the simplified pie diagram, you would see the Elderly and Disabled pie slice swell to more than half of the total. That slice and Defense and Diplomacy, taken together, would likely constitute more than three-fourths of the whole. Elements of the category labeled Other that are related to health care would also expand. This is the core reality of the fiscal picture. Without considering future entitlement burdens or estimating future defense needs, any fiscal soundness forecast is grossly incomplete . . . yet the most important point comes through plainly nonetheless.

The fact is that only a relatively small fraction of federal spending is devoted to all of the various programs Congress so contentiously argues about. The big dollars are virtually all in programs generally considered off the table for cuts. The category called Elderly and Disabled in Figure 1.2 is dominated by Medicare, Social Security, and federal pensions, including the railroad pensions the federal authorities long ago absorbed. Military pensions could be in that slice, too, but they are grouped with Defense and Diplomacy for clarity. Increased precision would require removing non-elderly Social Security beneficiaries from the Elderly and Disabled slice and adding back payments to older veterans. For an intuitive grasp of where the money goes, though, we can consider these two potential adjustments a wash.

The Defense and Diplomacy pie slice includes the armed services and the State Department, as well as other foreign policy institutions. The Debt Service item is straightforward enough. It represents the interest on the national debt, a class of spending anything but optional once the debt is issued. This is a category to watch carefully. A weak economy and Federal Reserve easy-money policies have kept the interest rate on the debt so low that the normal pain signal is barely present. The cost of interest on the debt would more than double if interest rates were to return to their levels of not very long ago.

The lesson here is that talk of meaningful change in expenditures, while exempting the elderly and defense along with debt service, is mainly election rhetoric. Little is on the table except the Other pie slice in Figure 1.2, and it contains numerous items, such as the FBI, the food inspection program, the Centers for Disease Control and Prevention, and the national parks — governmental services that no sensible person really wants to do without. Even within what would be left of that slice if the indispensables were removed, several points of the total represent spending that the Office of Management and Budget classifies as nondiscretionary. This categorization is not always governed by a useful bright-line test since some of what is called nondiscretionary can be altered by changes in law, but the distinction is widely used in Washington, and some items are genuinely beyond simple discretion. My guess is that the debate you hear so much about covers no more than one-eighth of all spending, and that two-thirds or more of that eighth would be restored by nearly unanimous consent if cut.

In the present, Social Security is not a substantial contributor to the deficit. In fact, 2010 was the first year in which benefit outgo exceeded tax income in the Social Security Trust Fund, where its partially funded reserves sit.[10] If interest on the trust fund is considered as income, that flow won't turn negative until 2020. Medicare has no deficit yet. The frightening imbalances projected for these programs lie ahead of us.

Some of the largest expenditures go unnoticed and unchallenged. These are not appropriations but tax expenditures in the form of deductions and exemptions from taxes. Among these are some budget busters that provide little or no public benefit. Interest deductions taken by both individuals and corporations, while seldom questioned, should lead the short list for repeal.

Although imbalances arising from future commitments should worry you more than the current deficits, the annual shortfalls are worth addressing as well. More income all along will help in both time frames, and some of the causes of the current deficit are little short of irrational waste. The political debate on this topic focuses only on expenditures, but the more wasteful extravagance is actually on the revenue side. The money the government pays out by writing checks to the assistance recipient, the defense or highway contractor, the soldier, and the civil servant defines only one kind of spending. The component I urge you to turn your focus toward is what economists call "tax expenditures." These are the deductions, exemptions, and statutory loopholes that Congress has created to allow certain taxpayers to pay less than they would otherwise pay—presumably in order to further some worthwhile goals for your benefit. This is the honey pot at which shrewd lobbyists have long aimed a disproportionate share of their efforts because the rewards are so generous and the scrutiny so scant. Some of the same politicians who claim to fight hardest against every alleged dollar of waste, fraud, and abuse in direct expenditures are soft touches for these less scrutinized tax expenditures.

Tax expenditures are every bit as costly to you as other types of spending. There is no real difference between taxing all of us and spending the proceeds on Congress's favored projects and, alternatively, taxing entities that run favored projects at reduced rates, while making up the lost revenue by taxing the rest of us more. Lobbyists advising Congress know well that this type of subsidy is easier to obtain and keep than a direct payment. Where spending programs require repeated reauthorizations, Congress doesn't even sunset most of the tax expenditures. That's the very least that could be done in this arena. The oil depletion allowance, which just celebrated its one hundredth birthday, is among the better-known tax expenditures. Eliminating it and its companion breaks would be the equivalent of cutting up to $8 billion in spending.[11] The subsidies for growing tobacco carry direct costs with a digit less than that, but if the incremental costs of health care from the encouraged smoking are counted as well, they may be in the same range. Subsidies of all kinds from the U.S. Department of Agriculture, including insurance, for other agricultural crops and dairy products have averaged more than $15 billion annually for the past decade.[12] There are at least two hundred other tax expenditures. The total cost of tax expenditures has about doubled since 1991, even after adjusting for inflation.[13] Please try to remember that you are borrowing from other nations, and incurring debts for your kids to pay, when you permit this. Tax expenditures are not harmless to your pocketbook.

Given the lack of sunlight, you should be skeptical of all tax expenditures. Charitable deductions are among the very few that make indisputably good sense. Almost all presumably have some vaguely colorable justification on the merits, but I doubt many would pass the test that you'd willingly write a personal check to help finance them. Their degrees of public popularity run across a broad spectrum, but unfortunately the spectrum does not match up particularly well with a careful assessment of their actual benefits. The one I would most like to delete is one of the most popular. When a tax expenditure helps throw the budget out of balance and its broader economic consequences are on the whole negative, it ought to be repealed. This is the case however popular it may be. The deductions taken by both individuals and businesses for payment of interest are popular, but they are costly and wasteful tax expenditures. And, yes, that includes the seductive deduction for home mortgage interest that many of you think you love.

Payments of interest, other than for homes, are not deductible for most taxpayers. Personal interest payments in connection with business activities are deductible on individual tax returns only to the extent of profits from the same activity. Credit card interest and auto loan interest are not deductible at all. The deduction for credit card interest, once considered a sacred cow on Capitol Hill, was repealed in 1986, and there is no hue and cry for its return. The student loan interest deduction applies only to certain loans and is capped at $2,500. Even home mortgage interest is deductible only for the one-third of taxpayers who itemize their deductions, a subset of the population with income far above the median American income.[14] The deduction, though, has an impressive provenance. Congress enacted it early in the twentieth century at the request of homebuilders and banks. At the time, it seemed of little consequence since only about 350,000 households paid taxes at all.[15] The deduction today excludes interest on mortgage amounts over $1 million, but it has become a whale of an item. The Joint Committee on Taxation estimates that the deduction costs it close to $100 billion a year in revenue.[16] This is about one-third of the average federal deficit over the past two dozen years and roughly one-fifth of the current deficit.[17]

It is far from obvious that this incentive boosts the percentage of people who own their own homes. The homeownership percentage has not increased in close to forty years.[18] While it is possible that this percentage would have fallen were it not for tax incentives, I frankly doubt that. It has proven a pretty intransigent statistic. The banks and homebuilders still swear by the home mortgage deduction, though they may be unaware of how little it moves the aggregate needle. Among taxpayers, its main effect is to redistribute money from the lower middle class to more prosperous taxpayers — a dubious goal at best. The bottom economic quartile pays too little in taxes to be much affected as payers, and people who don't itemize deductions or who rent get no benefit from this subsidy. Only 16 percent of taxpayers in the lower tax brackets itemize their deductions, while 90 percent of taxpayers in the top brackets itemize.[19] That's the group eligible to benefit from this subsidy and likely to have the largest homes. A typical taxpayer earning $50,000 a year saves about $600 from the deduction. At earnings of $200,000 and above, the number is more like $5,000.[20] And there is no wealth created here. Wealthier middle-class taxpayers gain relative to working-class taxpayers, whereas renters, those with the greatest need for housing subsidies, get nothing at all while contributing to make up the revenue shortfalls.

The political sky might fall in if anyone in power proposed the repeal of this regressive tax giveaway program, but certainly not the economic sky. Australia, Canada, and New Zealand have all done without the home mortgage interest deduction for some time, and all have higher percentages of homeownership than the United States.[21] Great Britain abolished the deduction in 2000, and even the political sky stayed in place.[22] In 2005, an expert panel set up by President George W. Bush proposed further restricting the home mortgage deduction in this country. Even some supporters of the tax break for mortgages concur that it would be fairer to substitute a tax credit for a deduction, so that it could be available to everyone and not just those prosperous enough to itemize. If repeal isn't possible, this would be a useful step, perhaps accompanied by a tighter limit on the size of mortgages to which the deduction applies. Any step in the direction of saving the Treasury this $100 billion improvident cost and reversing the income transfer from lower middle class to upper middle class would represent a welcome step in the right direction, but the best case is plainly for outright repeal.

The deduction by corporations for interest paid is all the more wasteful. This one, however, is seldom questioned. The corporate interest deduction dates back to 1918, the year before the individual interest deduction was born. Its original goal was merely to offset the impact of an excess profits tax following World War I.[23] The cost today of the corporate interest deduction is many times the cost of the personal income tax deductions for mortgages. One public policy observer has suggested that disallowing just 30 percent of this deduction would save the Treasury about $120 billion each year.[24] The whole of the corporate interest deduction removes from the Treasury each year an amount in excess of 80 percent of the entire annual budget deficit.[25]

The Treasury revenue benefit, moreover, wouldn't be the only gain from repealing the corporate borrowing subsidy. The interest deduction is a driver of the use of debt to enlarge corporate balance sheets in the normal course of business and the financing of takeovers. Not all corporate takeovers are harmful to the country, and maintaining both debt and equity on a balance sheet is hardly an evil. Takeovers can be useful when they remove a complacent or inept management of a business in favor of a more ambitious, able, and innovative team. Buyouts can be similarly valuable when an ownership team knows it has run out of steam, or a second generation of owners prefers liquidity to a continued corporate role. There is an economic cinch of an argument, moreover, for carrying some debt on a balance sheet in the normal course of business, or to borrow money for expansion when the interest charge is less painful than the potential dilution to the shareholders from issuing more stock. The case for the availability of debt to complement corporate equity is rich and convincing. The issue here is whether you, as a taxpayer, need to subsidize the debt — and, if so, how much.

The usual case for a subsidy from you to a business stems from an assertion that there is not enough of its product or service. This situation might arise from a market failure or the need to encourage early action and research before a socially useful activity can be viable. So, please ask yourself whether anyone has recently convinced you that there is too little debt on American corporate balance sheets or that the economy needs more corporate takeover activity. If you are, in fact, persuaded that you are financially better off with corporations and buyout firms having below-market access to debt, borrowing with federal help not offered to you, and you want to reach into your wallets to help them out, then all is as it ought to be. But be careful. Those of you who find discomfort in the deficit or the national debt should think twice about tacitly accepting corporate interest rate subsidies. Merely having survived for a century does not render a dubious policy sound.

Profits, in general, are not subsidized. Equity, usually raised through the issuance of stock, is not subsidized. Some would say it is actually penalized, since the dividends paid to shareholders come out of already taxed net income and then are taxed again when paid out. Interest on debt is tax deductible for a corporation, but dividend payouts are not. Debt is the only major form of corporate capital favored by the tax code. I would urge you to frame the debt subsidy issue this way: You answer a knock on your door and find an agent of the federal government outside. He seeks a voluntary contribution on the part of taxpayers like you of several thousand dollars annually to help some of America's corporations borrow money and assist some Wall Street buyout funds in financing corporate takeovers. I would decline, and I am guessing you would, too.

Perhaps you feel unqualified to decide whether the economy needs debt or takeover subsidies. You want to hear what experts think. If so, it might help to know that the Federal Reserve and the Office of the Comptroller of the Currency recently warned Wall Street banks to reduce the volume of risky loans they are making to finance private-equity takeovers.[26] In 2014, they issued guidance urging banks to avoid financing leveraged buyouts in most industries that would put debt on a company of more than six times its earnings, yet 40 percent of U.S. private-equity deals in that year used leverage above that six-times ratio — the highest percentage since the pre-crisis peak a decade ago.[27] It is fair to assume that the banks and private-equity firms ignore the regulators' softball guidance precisely because it is so rewarding to finance takeovers with your tax subsidy.

Consider a simple example in which a corporation is for sale for $1 billion. The buyer, most likely today a private-equity firm or a competitor, might put up $300 million in cash, and take on $700 million in debt, to complete the transaction. If the value of the business rises over time by 60 percent after considering its new debt load, the buyer has tripled the original investment before considering interest costs. The heavy debt load was attractive for multiple reasons. One is your subsidy for the debt. If the money was borrowed at 4 percent, the annual interest cost is $28 million. That, however, is before taxes. You, the taxpayers, will give the buyer back over $9 million of this every year in tax benefits, and more if the buyer is a partnership taxed at individual rates. Second, if the buyer is a private-equity firm, the debt lies in the acquired company. Should the acquired firm fail, perhaps because of its new debt load, the private-equity fund itself loses only reputation. If my business, Plymouth Rock, wanted to borrow for an acquisition, our company itself, and not the target company, would be on the hook. But, then again, we can never be as valuable a customer as a private-equity firm that will borrow time and time again. The third reason the debt is so attractive is simply that today's interest rates are being kept at historically low levels. Remove the subsidy and the low interest rates, and the volume of takeovers would be closer to what a free market ought to have. You can't easily change the interest rates, and banks may continue to favor their repeat customers, but your representatives in Congress could surely ditch the tax subsidy if you told them to.

There are other parts of the tax laws that could be changed to reduce your burden. I will describe another gaping tax hole in the next chapter, and surely there are some wasteful expenditures in the appropriated budget as well. The goal here, though, is just to persuade you that whether or not large deficits are useful, the maintenance of home mortgage and corporate interest deductions is not a valid reason to incur those deficits. The most salient lesson from examining today's budget is that if you want it better balanced, don't spend too much time looking for massive savings through cutting investments for the next generation, essential oversight tasks, or basic government services. That's not where the money is. A better case can be made for *more* government expenditures on infrastructure, research, and other public investments. But you'll have your choice if we can get our act together to stop unproductive tax expenditures. We should all be deficit hawks of that breed.

The most serious long-term imbalances are in Medicare and Social Security. Medicare cannot be repaired without basic changes in the U.S. health-care system, but Social Security's strength can be easily protected if we act soon enough.

The short-run budgetary imbalance story is largely one of opportunities. The longer run is characterized more by dangers, and Social Security funding is among the most important to defuse. Many people believe that Social Security is a true insurance program, operating just like a private insurer that collects periodic premiums from a cohort of working people, invests the money, and then gives most of the principal and interest back to that same cohort on retirement. The purity of this notion is a useful myth for political purposes, but the reality is that it is at best a half-truth. A private insurer would be required to keep actuarially sound reserves such that at reasonable rates of investment return, the reserves would grow to cover all expected payouts. And, in a private insurer, each participant would be a potential source of profit.

The Social Security system is more complex than that. Its insurance nature is contradicted by its largely pay-as-you-go funding and its intentional absence of actuarially sound reserves. Benefits to retirees are financed mainly through payroll taxes on current workers. There is unspent money from prior contributions, the so-called Social Security Trust Fund, but no one relies on this source of savings to cover all of the future costs. That's fortunate, because the fund trustees have predicted that the trust fund will exhaust its cash in 2033.[28] This wouldn't be so bad if revenues at that time were expected to be greater than benefit payouts, but nobody seriously believes that will be the case, absent serious changes in its outflow or inflow streams.

You are not wrong to wonder how the country's major retirement safety net will be kept intact when you and your children retire.

The 2014 trustees' report suggests that the ratio of incoming payroll taxes to benefits will soon be 75 percent.[29] This alarm is not the first warning, of course. The extent of the problem was well laid out in an advisory committee report in 1996. President George W. Bush established the President's Commission to Strengthen Social Security in 2001, chaired by the late Senator Daniel P. Moynihan. Commission members plainly saw the need for changes in Social Security's costs or funding.[30] Nine years later, President Barack Obama set up the bipartisan National Commission on Fiscal Responsibility and Reform, known more widely as the Simpson-Bowles Commission, and charged it with putting together a comprehensive remedy for the nation's future fiscal issues. That team reached similar conclusions about both the scope and immediacy of the issues.[31] The inescapable problem is that there will be more retired people (to be paid) for every working person (paying) as time goes on. This trend will be amplified by past and present birth demographics and increasing life expectancies.

The Social Security program (or, more formally, Old-Age, Survivors, and Disability Insurance) was proposed by President Franklin D. Roosevelt during the depths of the Great Depression. It passed Congress overwhelmingly in 1935.[32] The public was ready for it. In the earlier days of the republic, a large proportion of the population lived on family farms where custom provided that the elder generation would live at home, or nearby, to help with the upcoming generations. This had been the way of our species from humanity's most primitive days. The nation, however, had changed by the time of FDR. Over half the people were living in cities, and many had hourly wage employment in manufacturing. The support provided by cohesive extended families gradually fractured. A few workers received livable pensions from their employers, but few indeed. Social Security was designed as a compulsory savings program requiring employee and employer contributions, which could grant the broader population a privilege only the most enlightened employers were already providing. Early on, the objective was summarized this way: "The practical objective is to pay benefits that provide a minimum degree of social security—as a basis upon which the worker, through his own efforts, will have a better chance to provide adequately for his individual security."[33] It was certainly made to sound like an insurance program.

Social Security has been wildly popular—and for good reason. And it has long been political quicksand for politicians who have dared to question its benefits. Social Security, moreover, has always been efficient. Quite unlike our health-care system, it operates at an administrative cost of less than 1 percent of revenues.[34] For more than seventy-five years now, it has operated without scandal or serious misstep, and its role in society has grown with the prevalence of independent senior lifestyles. Studies indicate that half of all elderly married couples and three-quarters of elderly individuals depend on Social Security checks for at least half of their income.[35] The average monthly check is a little over $1,300, and the maximum benefit for someone retiring at the full retirement age is about $2,700 per month.[36]

Since inception the Social Security Trust Fund has collected $8.7 trillion in payroll taxes and disbursed $7.4 trillion in benefits, with the surpluses invested in Treasury bills.[37] The trust fund, clearly, would have earned more if the trustees had invested it in the stock market, but that course was ruled out early on. One reason for sticking with Treasuries was the inherent volatility of equity investments, but there is another reason. Depending on the mix of equities and debt it held, even a partially funded national pension plan could have quickly become one of the nation's largest, and most powerful, investors in American business. That's a dangerous role for the government of a free enterprise society.

The financial history of Social Security has been superficially comforting. Even now, payroll taxes approximate annual payouts. The future course, though, will be unambiguously rockier. In the first years of the program, there were a great many workers paying in and few eligible retirees. Time alone, bringing maturity to the program, ended that deceptively cash-rich era. Then came the baby boom and an inflection point in life expectancies. Either one of these phenomena would by itself have doomed Social Security's ability to simultaneously maintain the current eligibility age, tax rates, and benefit levels. When the program was first established, the experts looked at the retirement ages used by the thirty states that had already set up rudimentary systems. About half used sixty-five as the retirement age, and the others mostly used seventy. The choice of sixty-five was a decision that fit the 1930s better than the 2010s.

Congress had no idea at the time that life expectancy was about to turn dramatically upward. When Franklin Roosevelt was elected president for the first time, the average life span at birth in the United States was just below sixty.[38] Now it is over eighty.[39] More to the point, in 1940 an average male worker who started collecting benefits at sixty-five had about thirteen more years to live.[40] Today the expected retirement life span of a male at sixty-five is over nineteen years.[41] Females were a small part of the work force in 1940, but that has changed, and the trend in their life expectancies has been about the same as for males. A female at sixty-five in 1940 could expect almost fifteen more years of life;[42] today that expectation approaches twenty-two years.[43] You can thank better drugs, better public health practices, healthier lifestyles, reduced poverty, and more active care of elderly patients for that. What is good for longevity, though, is not as good for the Social Security Trust Fund.

The other element of the demographic shift toward an older population is a comparably irresistible force. During the decade from the Depression trough to the end of World War II, there were about two and a half million live births a year in the United States.[44] People hesitated to start families in the Depression years, and a great many young men were inconveniently located for that purpose in the war years. During the fertile decades that followed, from 1946 to 1964, the average annual number of live births was more like four million.[45] My own parents married as soon as my dad completed his army service and made me a contributor to the baby-boom statistics. Then, with the catch-up completed, births dropped back into the threes of millions again for much of the remainder of the millennium.[46] Having annual cohorts of four million working-age people pay for cohorts of two and a half million was relatively easy. As the numbers shift and the boomers retire, asking a cohort three million a year strong to pay for a retiring annual cohort of four million will become increasingly tough. Ten thousand baby boomers are now signing up for benefits every day,[47] and that number is unlikely to taper for several decades.

The candle is burning at both ends. The clearest way to put all this may be to say that in 1950, there were 7.1 workers available to pay for each retiree in the country,[48] and a full 16 workers for each retiree actually eligible for Social Security,[49] while now there are 2.8 workers per eligible retiree.[50] That ratio is expected to dip to 2.1 within the next twenty years.[51] It should not be surprising on an intuitive level that the equilibrium ratio should tend over time toward a number more like 2 than 7 or 16. If everyone lived to be a uniform eighty-five and birthrates were constant over time, the number of people between twenty-five and sixty-five would be exactly twice the number of those between sixty-five and eighty-five.

Congress has not been entirely idle as these realities have emerged. The maximum taxable income was once only $3,000; today it is $118,500.[52] The tax rate in the early years was 2 percent for employee and employer combined; today the tax rate for the retirement and disability programs under the Social Security mantle is 12.4 percent.[53] The age for full-benefit retirement, moreover, is being adjusted gradually upward. For workers born in 1960 and later, the minimum age for full-benefit eligibility will be sixty-seven.[54] There have been changes, however, in the opposite direction as well. To maximize constancy in the ratio of benefits to preretirement income, the dollar value of benefits has been raised annually for many years as wages have risen,[55] while longer life spans further raised program costs. The annual dollar increases in benefits, aimed at sustaining the replacement ratio, have cumulatively exceeded inflation as measured by the Consumer Price Index, because wages have risen faster than prices. Stated in constant dollars, the average lifetime benefit is almost 66 percent greater than it was in 1970, and 33 percent higher than in 1990.[56]

The arithmetic simply won't work much longer without politically painful changes. Robert Pozen, an influential Moynihan Commission member, has urged that low-wage workers continue to see benefits rise in the current manner, while higher earners would see a smaller annual increase tied to the Consumer Price Index. This could be a helpful patch, as would incremental changes to the payroll tax and its cap, but a more complete repair is available if Congress would add to the enabling legislation a provision that it might have included from the start if the rapid increases in life expectancy had been foreseen. It is hard to believe that an ever-lengthening period of benefit collection was either desired or expected by Social Security's drafters, and it is harder still to justify that feature now. Scientists tell me that we should see life expectancy continue to rise over time, then eventually flatten out as expected life spans approach one hundred. Although the human body wasn't meant for eternal life even in the absence of viral invaders, cancer, and other discrete illnesses, the taming of those killers can extend it well beyond today's span.

Raising the retirement age is not the favorite solution of either major political party, but it would be unfair to suggest that they are oblivious to the need for action. Some policymakers, mostly Republicans, have championed privatization of retirement investments as a solution to the broader issues of senior income. Democrats usually look instead to raising the cap that limits the payroll tax contributions of wealthy taxpayers. There is a colorable enough argument for each of these approaches that they deserve attention. The economics of the privatization argument rest mainly on the difference between returns on Treasury debt securities and returns available in equity markets. Equities can be anticipated to outperform Treasury debt over any substantial time period by a wide margin. The expected gap looking forward today might be as much as five percentage points annually. Just to see how powerful the effect of this size gap can be, consider that an investment at 8 percent compounds to something approaching five times the initial stake in twenty years, while an investment at 3 percent will not yet have doubled in that same period.

Investments in corporate equities will always carry a higher expected return than corporate debt in economic equilibrium, and corporate bonds will carry a higher expected return than supersafe Treasuries. The privatization proponents can thus correctly assert that, had the Social Security trust assets been kept in a diversified common stock portfolio from the start, there would be little or no funding problem to solve. On the other hand, they generally acknowledge that the architects of Social Security were wise not to let our government pick favorite stocks and thus distort market capital allocation signals, or to let federally controlled trust funds own voting stakes in private-sector corporations. Their solution is to let individuals control the investment of their own portions of the Social Security fund, much as future retirees can do with their 401(k) plans. In the aggregate, it is just about certain that the equity or balanced portfolios of participants would beat the trust fund's Treasury returns over time. The proposed solution is better characterized as targeting the overall retirement income situation for elders than the solvency of the Social Security accounts, since the program itself would not receive any of the anticipated higher returns.

There are problems, though, with privatization. At the household level lie additional complexities for any serious privatization proposal to resolve, especially in an era when divorce and remarriage are common. The largest issues, though, arise from the unpredictability of broad market volatility and individual variances from the market averages. While a broadly diversified stock portfolio should always outperform debt holdings over a long enough period, this cannot be said with confidence about the overall market in any particular year or, in rare instances, any decade. The generalization is even less reliable with respect to any particular undiversified portfolio. And investment skill and sense are by no means distributed uniformly throughout the participant population. Some folks, if not severely limited by rules of the plan, would make foolish or highly risky investments. If in response the investments were constrained to blue chips or index funds, which could solve the skill problem, a new problem would arise. Government would then be favoring large companies over the smaller entrepreneurial businesses that disproportionately power our economy and grant us the gifts of innovation.

Individual decision making, with wide variations in outcome, implies that a fraction of the participants would inevitably reach retirement age with a need for Social Security income but having dissipated the kitty. This country is not so heartless that it would leave penniless seniors to starve. So another government program would have to pick up their living costs as the benefactor of last resort, meaning that other, wiser or luckier taxpayers would be double-charged: once for their own Social Security savings and once for the poor souls who lost theirs. The mere existence of such a secondary backup would raise the temptation to try go-for-broke strategies on the part of risk-prone participants. The foolish and the greedy would find themselves subsidized along with those who were just plain unfortunate with respect to their investments or the timing of their life events.

There is yet another difficulty in privatization. Although its economics might be sound enough over the population as a whole once the new format reached steady state, there is no way to avoid transitional costs during a shift of formats. In our pay-as-you-go system, the withdrawal of substantial funds from the common trust fund into individual accounts would leave the system short of cash to pay the benefits already accrued. Opponents of privatization tend to offer high estimates of these transitional costs, which would presumably have to be met by payroll tax increases, while supporters see them as bearable. Economist Martin Feldstein, a leading proponent of privatization, concludes that the "net extra costs incurred by older employees during the transition would be very small and would generally be more than offset by the positive net benefits that their own children would receive."[57] I am not sure how many elders would be eager to take this bargain.

One palliative for capital market distortion, for paying twice to cover those who lose their stakes, and for transitional tax increases would be to allow private control over only a relatively small fraction of each participant's Social Security savings account. Although some of my friends may view this as treason, a modest enough step in the direction of privatization has never seemed to me objectionable—and certainly not so if it were established as a mandatory supplement to, rather than a substitute for, the current program. A large leap toward privatization would, however, be reckless, and, more important, it would call to the fore a core issue of Social Security that few in politics want to address directly. There has never been clarity with respect to the intended balance in Social Security between its insurance nature, implying premiums set in accordance with risk and payouts proportional to prior contributions, and its wealth transfer nature, featuring premiums set in accordance with ability to pay and benefits uniform across the spectrum or tilted toward those who need them most. Many proponents of full privatization favor that route precisely because Social Security privatization would yield authority to the insurance interpretation and render transfers impossible.

Yet Social Security, as we know it now, is at its core a chimerical mix of insurance elements and transfer elements. Its redistributive aspects cause lower-paid workers to be able to withdraw over time more than an actuarially based annuity would pay them, while high-income taxpayers pay in more than what is required to cover their eventual withdrawals. With maximum benefits fixed, a principal determinant of the degree of redistribution is the cap on the payroll tax. The current $118,500 cap is set more politically than mathematically, raising more than enough to fund a high-earning individual's benefits but allowing less redistribution than any higher cap would permit. The usual Democratic partiality to a higher cap is a preference for tilting the balance of the program to its redistributive, ability-to-pay nature, just as privatization would shift its core toward its actuarial nature. This is the true nature of the debate.

Currently, a taxpayer must contribute 6.2 percent of earnings annually to the Social Security Trust Fund, but only up to the income cap. The maximum annual contribution payment from an employed individual is, therefore, less than $7,500. The case for lifting this ceiling on payroll tax payments should not be lightly dismissed. High earners can certainly afford to pay an increased fraction of Social Security funding, and this would be a modest vector in contravention of the huge recent shift of incomes toward the top of the pyramid. The change, moreover, would adversely affect fewer than 6 percent of all households filing individual tax returns.[58]

The payroll tax, though, is an imperfect instrument for effective progressivity in its essence. The huge bulk of ability to pay resides with those who enjoy dividends and capital gains, forms of wealth accretion entirely omitted from the Social Security tax base. Another troublesome problem with raising the cap dramatically is that at some tipping point, it would weaken support for the very existence of Social Security. The belief that Social Security is an insurance regime and not just welfare is useful—and not entirely a myth. Its popularity as a program is fortified by the highly visible insurance features a high enough ceiling would negate. Just as important, increased taxes are hard to achieve, and this may not be the best use for the expenditure of that chip. To fully fund future deficits in this manner, it appears that the caps would have to be removed in their entirety.[59]

Boosting the payroll tax cap is hardly unreasonable, but only if implemented in moderation. Linking the retirement eligibility age to retirement life expectancies, though, remains the soundest way to keep from quietly expanding the actuarial value of lifetime benefits every year while kicking down the road the cost consequences of doing so. If the threshold that Social Security experts call the normal retirement age had moved upward all along with life expectancy and actual retirement ages, the long-term financial health of the system would have been assured. One argument against increasing the retirement age is that some careers must come to an end early, because they are too dangerous or too strenuous for elders to perform, or because years in those jobs age a person quickly. Coal mining might be an example. When these jobs are also low-paying, as is often the case, the worker is likely to be retired well before seventy and not have much in savings. Those are cases, if there are not too many, for which there should be no objection to creating narrow exceptions from the increased eligibility age. Combining some element of means testing and a hazardous occupations list could provide a societally equitable answer.

A variant of this brief against raising the eligibility age is based on statistics showing that some ethnicity and gender combinations characteristically predict shorter lives than are enjoyed by the population as a whole. Some have argued against raising the retirement age on the basis that Native American and African American males have shorter life expectancies than whites. This is a less persuasive argument than the case for an exception by income and job type. It suggests that we should distribute large amounts of tax money to 95 percent of the population in response to a need felt by 5 percent of the population — if indeed the expectation of some fixed number of years in paid retirement can be called a need. This point is worth reinforcing. It comes up often in public policy choices. When a small percentage of the public needs help and a large fraction of the whole can be made to provide it at reasonable cost to each, overall welfare may be increased. If a large segment needs help and a small but highly affluent segment can provide it, there can be an overall gain. But it is seldom wise to take enough from a wealthy few to cover a distribution to everyone else just so some sympathetic few can enjoy a tiny fraction of that general redistribution.

Life expectancy differences among various subsets of the population, moreover, would persist wherever the retirement age is set, and life expectancy differentials are substantially smaller in the elder years than at birth, facts that those who advance this argument tend to blur.[60] But the overriding point is that the notion of taxing the few and distributing to the many in order to help only a small, differentiated subset of the many is just plain poor government. So, just as fundamentally, is shaping policies for the American population by examining slices of it cut by gender and race where this is other than absolutely necessary. If all programs and situations with differentials in outcome measured by gender or race were handled by universal benefit increases, the Treasury would be bare.

Social Security is a hybrid program that should be kept that way. I can comfortably call increases in the payroll tax cap, or privatization of a small or incremental portion of individual accounts, or progressive indexing, second-best solutions. All of these could provide supplementary power to a retirement age change. But neither tax nor benefit changes bear the irrefutable logic of pinning the retirement age to reality. To lock the retirement age in concrete as life expectancies rise makes no more sense than annual reductions in the eligibility age each year would have made had retirement life expectancies stayed constant over time.

The essence of the matter is not hard to grasp. Advocates for the elderly understandably want to keep the income replacement rate, the ratio of retirement income to earlier working income, from falling. This is a logical goal. The challenge is in the long-term demographics. Most of the proposals for mending Social Security shortfalls deal with the baby-boomer bulge adequately, but they can only guess at how great a problem longer life expectancies will create. A recent issue of *Time* magazine features as a cover story the possibility that a baby born today can live to be 140.[61] That number was mainly an attention grabber, based on a recent experiment with laboratory mice, but life expectancies running into the nineties seem to me realistic rather soon. If the replacement rate is held constant, and retirement eligibility ages remain unchanged, every increase in life expectancies will raise the number of payments a beneficiary receives and thus raise the program cost. This is beyond dispute. How much life expectancies will rise is eminently disputable, though, since that depends on predicting scientific breakthroughs on cancer, heart disease, and other causes of death — not exactly the sweet spot for economists and actuaries. If and when the average retiree lives to be ninety-five, the number of monthly payments that will call for funding will have increased by almost 50 percent.

A focus on replacement rate necessarily leads to different policy recommendations from a focus on lifetime program cost per participant. The former is an admirable social objective; the latter is the key to Social Security's solvency. At the moment, the eventual repair of Social Security's finances is in doubt with respect to both method and timing. With trust in our political process at a low point, it is no wonder that people feel insecure about the reliability of the Social Security safety net. This is why an automatic nonpolitical indexing of retirement ages to expected years of life may be about the only way to assure the public that the program is secure. This chapter and others in this book point to numerous ways that the federal government can save money or enhance revenues in other arenas. If, *after* Social Security's solvency is assured and confidence in it restored, Congress wishes to commit the funds to secure the replacement rate as well, that would be a welcome debate. I am not proposing to settle the argument between those who want to keep middle-class retirement streams constant relative to the beneficiaries' earlier incomes and those who want to reduce annual benefits as lives lengthen. My argument has more to do with assuring our next generation that the retirement incomes they are paying for now are secure and beyond politics.

The 2014 report of the Social Security trustees lays out a gradual path to accomplish indexing to longevity as one of a dozen alternatives. That path would increase the normal retirement age three months each year, starting in 2017, until it reaches seventy in 2032. Simultaneously, it would increase the earliest retirement age to sixty-four for those reaching that age by 2021. Thereafter, it would index the retirement age to maintain a constant ratio of expected retirement years to work years. The trustees estimate this change alone would eliminate 60 percent of the balance shortfall in the out years.[62] Combine this with small adjustments from the list of second-best solutions, as needed, and concern about the future solvency of Social Security will disappear from your list of legitimate worries. The disability portion of the Social Security program has dire issues of its own and will require a restructuring in the very near term. Disability eligibility and benefits should certainly be reconsidered if the retirement age is increased in any significant way, but that is not my subject here.

Medicare and federal pensions also require attention and modifications, but the cures to their problems are less obvious and more complex than those needed to place Social Security on secure footing.

Two other long-term budget busters are Medicare and pensions. Pensions are not on my list of easy theses, and Medicare is a topic that will reappear in another chapter, but both merit some attention. It was ten years after the enactment of Social Security that President Harry S. Truman floated the idea of a national health insurance program for the elderly. Social Security would pay their rent and buy their food, but few seniors had health insurance of any kind. Truman failed to get a program passed, and it took the political genius of Lyndon Johnson, decades later, to get it done. Johnson said at the signing ceremony that "the need for this action is . . . so clear indeed that we marvel . . . that it took so many years to pass it."[63] Johnson had both the merits and politics right. The once-invincible opposition melted as the program went into effect, and Medicare has nearly universal public acceptance today. The press loved the recent story of the South Carolina conservative who warned his congressman to "keep your government hands off my Medicare."[64]

Medicare, unlike Social Security, makes no pretense of being a fully funded insurance program. There is a trust fund for one part of the program, but Medicare spending is essentially financed from general tax revenues, payroll taxes, and beneficiary premiums, and it constitutes about 20 percent of the Treasury budget.[65] Among the elements it has in common with Social Security is a predictable future imbalance. In 1966, the House Ways and Means Committee projected that by 1990 Medicare would cost the nation about $12 billion. The actual cost in 1990 was $107 billion, and the same demographics that plague Social Security make the future look far less rosy.[66] Medicare costs will rise with better and more expensive treatment, with longer lives, and with the baby boomers upending the worker-to-benefit-recipient ratio.

In the beginning, the Medicare payroll tax was a combined 0.7 percent,[67] averaging about $60 a year. The premium participants paid during retirement was $35 a year.[68] Looking at these figures some fifty years later, you might think they are typographical errors. Today, the average annual payroll tax, at 2.9 percent, amounts to an average take of about $1,000, and the annual average premium in retirement is also more than $1,000.[69] On a per-capita basis, Medicare expenses have risen by an average of 7.7 percent annually over the past forty years — well faster than inflation.[70] Although some experts are predicting based on highly welcome recent information that the increases are slowing, I fear that they are mistaking waves for the tide. Nothing is likely to change the demographics or the trend in enhancements of care. Relatively conservative projections show the total annual cost of Medicare is destined to rise from slightly over $500 billion now to at least $850 billion in ten years.[71]

I would never suggest repealing Medicare or rolling back eligibility for the elderly poor, but sometimes and for some people Medicare is unnecessarily generous. Let me use a very personal example. My late father was a walker. Like me, he could stride for miles effortlessly, and he favored walking over use of cars, taxis, or buses. This continued until late in life when sciatica caused his left leg to hurt when he walked. So he went to a doctor, and a specialist . . . and another specialist and another. When I offered to pay, he assured me that the visits were all free. By free, he meant that they were covered by Medicare, and he had already exceeded his annual deductible and could easily cover any applicable copayments.

Over the years since then, I have heard literally dozens of

such stories. If something is free or nearly so, its users simply won't apply the normal degree of prudence or frugality. Even small fractional payments can make people think. Medicare today has both copays and deductibles, but the levels have not been set for a maximum of fairness or effectiveness. While nothing that has societally serious financial costs ought to be taken for granted by users, and there are plenty of people who can afford to contribute more than they are currently asked, it is also the case that hardly any service merits equality of access and quality more than health care.

A package of changes in health care for the elderly is warranted, and these are addressed in another chapter. A good starting point, though, would be larger and progressively scaled copays and deductibles. While other countries with universal coverage don't need these disciplines, our country is in need of a cultural change with respect to health care, and these payments would be a good start. The scaling would be designed to have relatively little cost impact on the neediest, but it would reduce coverage for the wealthy to something akin to catastrophe coverage. A person at the lower end of the income scale should be asked to put down a single-digit fraction of medical costs, and only up to a reasonable annual limit. Someone in my bracket can be asked to pay as much as 80 percent, with real protection only at the highest layers of annual expenditure.

The benefits to this approach are, on the revenue side, that the program would collect more cash from copayments and deductibles and, on the cost side, that utilization would be more mindful. As with the savings from eliminating corporate interest deductions, it is hard to estimate how much would be collected because some people's behavior would change. It wouldn't be all bad for a few more Americans to realize that not every health problem merits nearly free attention.

Pensions are the oft-forgotten stepchild of the federal budget debate. I offer no detailed thesis here, just a few suggestions for consideration. There are at least two pension regimes for civilian federal workers. The older, smaller one is a traditional defined benefit plan, and the newer and larger one is somewhere between a defined benefit plan and a defined contribution plan. Together, these pensions cost the federal government about $75 billion annually.[72] Military pensions are entirely in defined benefit format. These have cost the government about $50 billion each year.[73] Everyone agrees that the future costs, after two serious wars, will make this payment level look small. As one Democratic representative put it, "We have a disconnect between these sacred promises we've made and how they are not backed up by anything."[74]

Private-sector employers are required to set up reserves to fully fund their pension programs. Although most state and local governments fail to fund their pension programs even close to adequately, they are required to set aside at least partial funding. The federal government sets aside no funding, and there's no dedicated tax for this expenditure. The accruing liability must be paid as due and wholly from tax revenues. There is no lawful or moral way to save money on the existing unfunded pension obligations. The future growth of the liabilities, however, is manageable. The 401(k) defined contribution format used overwhelmingly now by private employers is largely free of technical underfunding risk—although the amounts put aside by employer and employee are lower than many of us think they should be. Whether a 401(k) will provide enough for any individual's retirement depends on the individual's propensity to save in the plan, and on the extent of employer matching—which is done in cash by the time of vesting. We have used a typical 401(k) format for pensions since the start of Plymouth Rock over thirty years ago, and, while there is—and should be—concern over the adequacy of the retirement income any of today's 401(k) plans will produce, I have never heard a complaint about the plan's basic format. Defined benefit plans ought to be abandoned altogether, including for federal employees.

Logically, the local, state, and federal pension systems should all be identical, and identical as well to the private sector's pension format. The 401(k) approach is sound enough to use as a model for new government employees, as long as incentives for increased employee contribution levels are present and employer matches are sufficient — which means mandatory and larger than today's. Much could be done to improve the retirement performance of 401(k)s by legislating mandatory minimums for employees and higher minimums for employers. At the very least, there should be automatic savings at higher levels of contribution at the start of each employee's participation in the plans to set higher expectations than are typical today. People tend to contribute more if they have to explicitly opt out of participating at a desirable level than if they have to contradict an apparent norm to opt in. The 401(k) structure is a good idea, but carried nowhere near far enough to provide retirement security. Its magnitude renders it subject to fair criticism today, but it can be remedied. The use of a standard format for all public and private pensions has another huge advantage, which doubtless influences my positive feelings about uniformity. Standardization can expedite the real nirvana of pensions — automatic and full portability. That, however, is a story for another time.

The current federal deficit can be vanquished simply by repealing some counterproductive tax expenditures. Long-term fiscal balance is also achievable, and a first step should be conforming Social Security to demographic realities.

The easy thesis in this chapter is that fiscal balance can be restored to both the present-day federal budget and its more troublesome future picture. Common sense, as well as self-interest, argues that you should no longer subsidize the use of debt by either individuals or corporations. The savings that could be realized by eliminating just these two interest deductions would be sufficient to balance the current budget. And there are plenty of other tax expenditures worth reexamining. The longer-term budget can be balanced only by bringing Social Security outflows and revenues into concordance. This requires little more than restoring the original relationship between working years and retirement years. Fiscal soundness is readily within our grasp.

Other suggestions or unanswered questions raised in this chapter do not qualify as easy theses. While we could improve the Medicare balance by imposing universal deductibles scaled to the users' means, its costs will remain a problem until we deal with some larger issues in our health-care system. Adopting the private sector's 401(k) format for future federal pensions is worthy of serious examination and would ultimately favor a transition to full portability of pensions, but pension reform is beyond the bounds of an easy call. And, if the wasteful tax expenditures on interest subsidies are eliminated and the budget thus balanced, there will remain the felicitous chore of determining a disposition of the new bounty. There will always be tough questions as well as easy ones. The easy theses are sufficient to tell us that with bipartisan courage and leadership, it wouldn't be hard to put the fiscal house in better order. And, if we do, the next generation will look back on these better laws and wonder why it took so many years to pass them.

TWO

Inequality

This country, in contradiction of its admirable values, is among the least equal in the developed world in its distribution of wealth and income. These disparities are growing. Disparities in wealth are more extreme than the more widely studied income differentials and have longer-lasting impacts. This drift of assets toward the rich carries us away from meritocracy, productivity, empathy, and mobility. It can ultimately deprive us of our democracy and social cohesion. It has many causes, some of which are aspects of our technological era and will be nearly impossible to counteract. Some, though, result from poor policy choices. Extreme inequality can be moderated by effective estate taxation, but a reversal of the trend would require taxation of unrealized capital gains and a revocation of the tax advantages of trusts.

THAT INCOME AND WEALTH inequality was a worsening problem for the United States didn't fully sink in until I was the Insurance Commissioner of Massachusetts in the 1970s. I had grown up believing that America was already pushing the edges of what was possible for mankind and headed steadfastly further in the direction of an inherent and universally admired fairness. We were lucky not to have to live with the inequities of a Latin American banana republic, a European hereditary aristocracy, or an ancient oriental empire to weigh on our consciences. Our country, I was taught, had both a higher level of distributional equity and more social mobility than just about any nation-state in all of history. Quite a few of us believed then that if we could only overcome race and gender bias, our society would be on the way to near perfection. Looking back, it seems apparent that the perfection many of us had in mind was ill defined, with some seeking a pure, unbridled meritocracy and others preferring the far edge of an egalitarian flat plane — neither of which is in reality a sound destination. Whatever definition of perfection with respect to distributional equity is used, more importantly, it has by now become clear that this country isn't going to get there, and in fact, if we were ever on the road at all, we missed our turn and we are now headed in the wrong direction.

At the Massachusetts Division of Insurance, the issue that opened my eyes revolved around setting premiums for car insurance on the basis of a policyholder's socioeconomic status, a technique used in most of the country. Income is not a terribly bad predictor of claims cost and is statistically better than most — and it is easy to find proxies for it that sound like palatable pricing factors. The problem with this approach is twofold. It lacks incentives for responsible driving behavior that could improve outcomes and lower costs for the population as a whole, and it frequently results in charging clean drivers from disadvantaged neighborhoods unaffordable rates while giving bargain prices to drivers with poor records in wealthier areas — thus worsening the disparities. The deeper I delved into the issue, and the more I learned about our income and wealth distribution generally, the faster my rosy, distorted view of economic equality in the United States fell away. The topic of inequality has stayed high on my list of interests since the Massachusetts government job ended long ago. But it was a source of no small disappointment to discover how small an audience, including among academics, the emerging picture drew until quite recently.

Attention to inequality has recently increased, now that the concentration of wealth has become too pronounced to ignore. Defined properly, mobility among socioeconomic classes has declined as well. This combination is a threat to pluralist democracy. It has many causes, some irreversible.

Recent events have made it harder to ignore the issue of distributional equity. If you wonder where the Occupy Wall Street movement that arose after the 2008 crash got its steam, despite its singular lack of leadership or focus, consider that the three-year recovery from the recession that followed was absorbed almost in its entirety by the top 1 percent of the income distribution.[1] The same reality, ironically, may also be lending additional power to the Tea Party movement. Since 2000, income for 70 percent or more of Americans has actually been flat or declined a little, thanks in part to the financial crisis.[2] Meanwhile, for the top decile in this millennium, income is up by double digits, despite the crisis.[3] The average net worth of households in the upper 7 percent rose by 28 percent in the initial recovery years of 2009 through 2011 while the wealth of the other 93 percent fell by 4 percent.[4] It should not be surprising that so many people think the recession isn't over yet, and some are pretty angry. The only silver lining is that political and scholarly attention is finally being paid to the increasing economic inequality and the fading of our long-admired mobility.

The view over a longer timeline provides no more comfort. The median income in this country hasn't risen at all in real terms for forty years.[5] The United States since most of us were born has regularly harvested more wealth than any other nation in the history of the world, but the fruits have been increasingly carried toward the tip of the pyramid. While income in the middle brackets stagnated over the past four decades, income for the upper 1 percent tripled.[6] As recently as the middle of the twentieth century, the share of the United States' national income taken by the top 10 percent of income earners was about one-third. Now it is more like 50 percent.[7] The fortunate pinnacle, the top 1 percent of all households, received 10 percent of the nation's total income in the middle of the twentieth century. Now the upper 1 percent takes about one-quarter of the grand total.[8] If you are in this segment, I hope you can be grateful without believing that this is the way things ought to be.

Meanwhile, the Congressional Budget Office estimates that the share of total income held by the bottom 20 percent of American households, which was never out of the single digits, has fallen by two points.[9] That means that the middle classes have absorbed the loss of fifteen of the national income points that shifted to the possession of the top decile. Another widely quoted measure of growing disparity, affecting mainly the middle class, is the ratio of CEO pay to the average American worker's pay. This ratio, which stood at about twenty to one when I was young, is now close to three hundred to one.[10] These trends are just not healthy for the nation.

I have always used a kind of shorthand to describe our socioeconomic classes. In this categorization, the all-important middle class consists of those people who can live reasonably comfortably if they are willing and able to work and improve their comfort level by harder or better work. The upper class is composed of those folks who can live well without work if they so choose. The lower class consists of those who can't scratch together enough money to live decently even if they are willing to work hard. The economics of our society just isn't working for the middle class, the majority of its citizenry, when those who are willing and able to work cannot better their financial position. This is increasingly becoming the case in the twenty-first century. The American dream, moreover, has embodied an assumption that able and hard-working citizens can move upward freely from one of these classes to the next, including exits from the lowest classes and access to the top spots, and that sloth or incompetence will lead to a downward class shift. This is less true than it used to be, and it will be less so still as concentration at the pinnacle vacuums the opportunities from the spaces below.

One could go on here with pages of numbers reinforcing the same point, but it's probably not necessary to recite them. They are readily available now that this issue has begun to receive a full share of the academic spotlight. The French economist Thomas Piketty has recently written a best-selling text, *Capital in the Twenty-First Century,* which establishes rigorously that wealth and income disparities in the West are both large and growing. The book's prodigious sales came as a surprise in the publishing industry because his is a dense and lengthy tome. But it is extraordinarily good, and worth reading if you want the facts in detail. The trend toward decreasing equality is not some statistical anomaly, fluke, or brief wave interrupting a favorable tide. It is a genuine shift in an ugly direction.

Legitimate worry, moreover, should extend well beyond individual income and wealth imbalances. The growing concentration of corporate power is equally threatening to the values most Americans share. You are not being an alarmist if you fear that lobbyists and superrich contributors have excessive influence nowadays in every aspect of politics. Corporate power in the halls of Congress has waxed and waned over the history of our republic. It is probably greater now than at any time since Boss Tweed and Mark Hanna reigned from behind the scenes. Statistics show that the great majority of elections are won by whoever raises the largest war chest, and a friend of mine who served in the Senate told me that U.S. senators now typically spend about one-third of their time raising money. For House members, with a two-year election cycle, the situation must be worse.

Democracy itself is endangered by this trend. Our treasured form of government is not something to take for granted. The more you learn about governments around the world, the more grateful you should be for our democracy, and the more clearly you should discern what a delicate flower it is. Not only is democracy far from inevitable for all places and all times, it is historically rare and fragile. Look how seldom democracies have occurred and thrived, in both time and place. The United States and Switzerland, after all, have the oldest two functioning democratic republics on the planet. Contrary to what some in our government thought as they tried to transplant our system elsewhere, democracy requires more than selection of leaders by popular elections. A true democracy is characterized by due process, minority rights, an independent press, reservations of various liberties, and effective separation of church and state. Without those essential corollaries, majority voting can become little more than what a wise humorist suggested: a dozen wolves and a sheep voting on what to have for lunch.[11]

At its fundamental core, democracy requires as a precondition a healthy measure of pluralism — an underlying society with a wide distribution of money and power. Although they are nicely symbiotic, democracy and a market economy are not the same, and democracy is certainly not identical to prosperity. America's attachment to a market economy is relatively robust and its prosperity secure . . . as long as we can maintain our culture of challenge and innovation. The threat is that we may find ourselves living in a market economy where a tiny fraction of the people and a small number of institutions reap virtually all of the rewards and make all of the social and economic policy decisions, presumably with a bias toward serving their own interests. This would be a democracy in name only. True democracy is surely not the most natural form of government for human beings, and perhaps it is only barely compatible with human nature, but it may well be mankind's greatest invention. And the growing degree of concentration of wealth and power in our country today threatens its continuation. If our pluralism erodes, with it will vanish America's brightest gem.

The numbers I have quoted were mostly income or earnings statistics. These are more widely available for study than wealth statistics because the tax authorities tend to have them on hand and can publish the data once personal identifiers are removed. Wealth, however, is more important. The data on wealth is less available to the public and harder to interpret, but inequalities of wealth are materially greater than those in income. The top 1 percent of earners make roughly fourteen times the median income.[12] The top 1 percent of Americans by wealth have at least seventy times the median household wealth.[13] Those at the summit (the top one-hundredth of 1 percent of U.S. taxpayers) had a combined net worth of at least $6 trillion in 2012, about the same as the bottom two-thirds of the household population.[14] This is the case because the poorest deciles have, on the whole, accumulated no wealth at all, while the wealth of the middle class is largely confined to retirement savings and home equity. Yet wealth, more than income, determines socioeconomic class, and wealth is more directly portable to the next generation than income. Its differentials are far more durable. The wealth of the most privileged subset, moreover, didn't stop growing in 2012; it may be reasonably estimated as $8 to $9 trillion today.

Some political economists will tell you that wealth and income disparities don't matter because large distinctions in a mobile society spur ambition to succeed. But America is rapidly becoming less mobile as the distinctions grow. More wealth held tightly in the hands of fewer families implies a diminishing reward for hard, honest work on the part of everyone else. The chart in Figure 2.1 is based on a Boston Federal Reserve Bank study.[15] One can argue reasonably about where to strike the balance between a pure meritocracy, which can be unduly harsh on those with low endowments of various sorts, and a leveled society, which risks trading prosperity for equality if redistribution is taken too far. That is a fair debate, but it is rare to hear

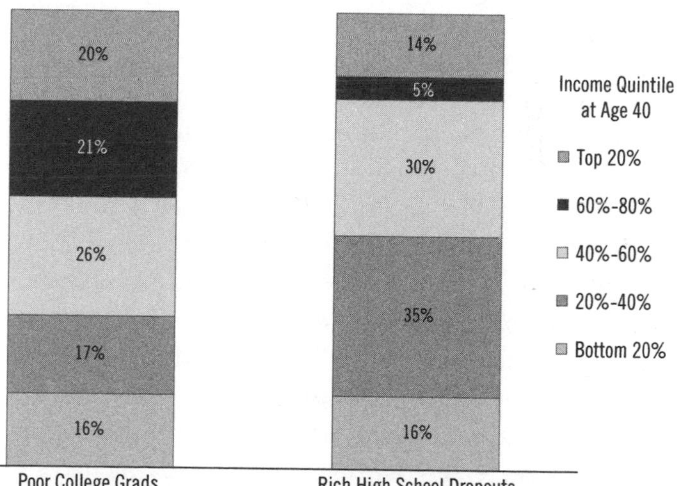

Figure 2.1

anyone defend hereditary aristocracy in principle. Aristocracies by bloodline tend not to be efficient, fair, or creative.

The chart compares the outcomes at age forty of two very different groups. On the left are the outcomes at that age for college graduates who were born to families in the lowest 20 percent of the income distribution (and thus the shorthand "Poor"). These are folks who, by some combination of talent, grit, and struggle, have managed to work all the way to a college degree. On the right are the outcomes at forty for high school dropouts lucky enough to have been born into the highest income quintile (and thus "Rich"). The right-hand population lacked the ability, discipline, or some other quality required to finish high school. What this chart shows is that the odds of ending up in the lowest income quintile at age forty are the same for the two groups. The educated have a bit of an advantage elsewhere on the ladder, but not nearly as much as you would probably have expected. The odds of reaching one of the top two quintiles as a well-born high school dropout are nearly identical to the odds of being in the top quintile for a hard-striving college grad who starts at the bottom. Thus, the likelihood of a college grad being in one of the three middle quintiles at forty is essentially the same as the likelihood of being in the larger two of those quintiles for the dropouts. If the outcomes for the very highest few percentiles had been tracked rather than those of the much broader top quintile, the intergenerational stickiness of outcome would presumably be all the more pronounced. This is far indeed from the profile of a meritocracy, and it casts a cloud of doubt over the widely held belief that educational attainment is a magical key, or sufficient to assure a positive outcome. Yes, a strong education can help elevate you to a higher position on the income ladder, but hardly more than having had a prosperous parent and a badly truncated education.

The set of outcomes you can see on the chart, unfortunately, looks dangerously like the pattern of a hereditary aristocracy. Even historical aristocracies, after all, have left some room for merit. Ours in America is not the pattern of either a pure meritocracy or a well-tempered social democracy. And this result is based on income rather than wealth quintiles. The disturbing result would presumably be all the more extreme if the study had been performed with wealth data.

That American income and wealth are distributed less equally than in the past and that this trend has been accelerating rather than abating are incontrovertible facts. There is enough academic debate, however, about whether mobility has decreased that the question is worth addressing. Economists who study mobility employ two standard types of indices. One examines absolute mobility. An intergenerational comparison in real dollars of a whole group's average income with the average income of the same sample's parents would be an example of an absolute mobility index. So would an intragenerational comparison of a whole group's income today to the same group's income twenty years earlier. The other type of measure looks at relative mobility. The idea here is to compare where individual members of a sample set fell in the income hierarchy at a starting date with their hierarchical placement at the end. Mobility would be indicated if the sorting of the individuals into deciles or quartiles at the end differed markedly from the sorting at the start. The more the results at the end defy individual outcome prediction by an observer looking only at initial placement, the better the mobility can be said to be. Perfect mobility would imply no correlation between starting position and ending position. If, at the opposite extreme, everyone (or every family) stayed in the same bracket over the period, that would suggest no mobility at all. Both kinds of measurement are commonly cited. By absolute measure, the United States doesn't look so bad. It appears substantially less successful — as Figure 2.1 shows — by relative measures. The problem is that both of these measuring devices can easily miss an incredibly important variable and thus provide false comfort.

Imagine a dystopian society structured like this: At the start of a measurement period, the bottom 20 percent of the population has an annual average income of $10,000. The next 20 percent has an $11,000 average income. The third quintile's is $12,000. The second to the top averages $13,000 per member. The top quintile, though, averages $100,000. The societal mean income is about $30,000, though the median is less than half that. Time passes and another measurement is taken. The mean is now $70,000. The lower four quintiles have come to average $10,500, $11,500, $12,500, and $13,500, respectively. The top quintile has tripled its average income to $300,000. The absolute measure of mobility shows upward direction in all income slices, so an economist who wanted to defend this nasty society could accurately claim upward mobility on that basis. This assertion holds without the need to examine changes in the composition of the various quintiles. Another economist, who preferred to use relative measures, would explore the mix. Imagine that this second economist discovered that 75 percent of the membership in each of the lower four quintiles moved out of the original quintile and were distributed randomly over the other three of those lower slices . . . but the top category was composed of exactly the same people from start to finish. In the hands of a defender of the status quo, this test, too, could be cited to show that the society had reasonable mobility. Obviously it does not.

The problem is that this imaginary society has walled off real success from most of its population. At the end of the period in the example, 86 percent of the society's wealth is sequestered beyond reach from anyone but those born to it. And the walled-off percentage in this example is expanding. The society pictured here is similar to a Dark Ages feudal aristocracy, where mobility among the serfs is fluid but depressingly inconsequential while the nobles keep virtually everything for themselves. Mobility measures, in the end, can be instructive or deceptive. They are most meaningful when they concentrate on measurements of movement from the bottom ranks and into the top, or when they look at shifts weighted for purchasing power and don't just tally numbers of participants. It is all too easy for a statistician with an ax to grind on behalf of maintaining extreme distinctions to avoid telling the story that really matters. When you hear that our society still has admirable mobility, be careful to check out the methodology and not to be fooled by accurate but disingenuous statistics. The greater the share of the nation's wealth and income is impounded within a durable elite, the lower will be the mobility that matters to everyone else. And that, unfortunately, is the direction in which our country has been heading.

There is an active debate today over whether the minimum wage should be increased. This is an important topic, to be sure, but not my focus here. The study of inequality in this country can be rather neatly divided into three parts. One involves the special problems of those at the foot of the economic ladder. Another field of study is the distribution of income and wealth in the vast center, defined for this purpose to encompass all but the tails of the economic distribution. Among the vectors influencing outcomes here are wage policies, the role of labor unions, and a variety of educational issues to be taken up in the next chapter. Finally, there is what I have called the sequestering of wealth in the rarefied top percentiles. All three fields are important, so I ask you not to take my concentration on the last as suggesting that the others are of little consequence. My focus derives in part from an observation that this is the subpart of the equality debate that has received the least serious attention over the years and in part from my lack of optimism that antipoverty programs and modest adjustments to the wage distribution can free up a meaningful portion of the increasing sequester. Unless that is done, and the impoundment of wealth reversed, slight shifts in shares within painfully squeezed middle and lower ranks may be all that can be accomplished.

Supporters of minimum wage increases in the present debate urge us to focus on breadwinning low-wage workers who struggle valiantly to support their families on a pittance. Opponents point to small, often marginal, businesses that may be jeopardized by the imposed raises, and to the undertrained and unemployed potential workers who can't find jobs that employers believe will justify their pay at legislated minimum levels. My fear is that all of the above will be losers if the incremental wealth our nation's great economic engine produces continues to flow to a smaller and smaller fraction of the public. It is for that reason, and not a lack of compassion, that I focus here on the policies to reverse that imbalance in the flow of wealth.

As one starts to explore why the shift toward financial overweight in the top percentiles is occurring, it is useful to keep in mind that we are not the only country with this type of distributional challenge. Some less developed nations have almost unbelievable disparities. Some of those countries we used to criticize for lack of equity are on the cusp of prosperity but have not improved in this regard. Parts of the Middle East have never put a value on equitable distribution of wealth. Russia and China, until recently revolutionary egalitarian regimes, have reinvented wealth and income gaps. Russia already has its new breed of oligarch, and as China transforms itself into a freer modern economy, it may be at risk of re-creating — under a different name and with different players — the aristocracy it had for thousands of years as an empire. The United States bears the dubious distinction, though, of developed-world leadership by a length in the growth of inequality, not just statistically but also owing to our special place as the economic front-runner and role model for the rest of the world. The United Kingdom, Australia, and Canada are racing rapidly along the same track behind us. The other European powers, including Germany and France, are a lap behind but headed the same way.[16]

There are multiple reasons for this, some of which are signs of our times and especially hard to counteract. One of these is the inadvertent segregation of our elite into an increasingly cohesive and permanent upper class. As communications and transportation improved, the most prestigious colleges got better at attracting the best students from all over to their campuses — where these students have inevitably interacted with, and often mated with, people intellectually like themselves. This magnet effect, rooted in an admirable search for excellence, has necessarily promoted the exaggeration of hereditary class distinctions. And, as a former academic, I have witnessed the trend among the most talented students to fields of concentration that will join them together again after college in careers on Wall Street or in Big Data.

Another causal factor is the expansion of the knowledge-based economy, which tends to exclude much of the population from the best-paid jobs. In some sense, what is happening now continues a trend in cultural evolution as old as the species itself. In hunter-gatherer societies, food tended to be shared sufficiently that the best hunter or gatherer was only a bit better fed than the average member of the party. Much later, as technique and organization became endemic to agricultural life, the best farmer could be several times as productive and prosperous as a less skillful, less informed, or less patient neighbor. A preeminent industrialist, with the birth of industrial technology, could be dozens of times, maybe later a hundredfold, more productive than a laborer. But today, with nearly unlimited financial leverage compounding a trader's gains and losses, and with vast corporations run by tiny numbers of leaders, a top dog can bring in thousands or millions of times what the lesser hounds produce.

Technology is inevitably a driver of such shifts of income and wealth. Other than Luddite zealots, there are few doubters of the assertion that technology helps create wealth. No one seriously argues that we should use less of it. Technological advances prove a double-edged sword, though, when distributional impacts are considered. Everyone can gain from the larger pie created in a technologically sophisticated society. There is more to share. On the other hand, the use of more capital relative to labor may tilt the returns toward the owners of the helpful technologies — or to the owners of valuable high-tech outputs such as Big Data. And, as technology increasingly favors knowledge workers, it shifts a growing share of its economic benefits to the holders of the relevant training and knowledge. This shift is greater today than ever before, but it is hard to see how it can fail to be greater still tomorrow.

Piketty focuses on another powerful line of argument. He observes that most of the population, with little by way of investments, sees its financial posture improve only at the general growth rate of the economy. The wealthier see gains more closely in proportion to the rate at which their investment assets appreciate, almost always faster than the overall growth rate — except when disrupted by major world crises. These trends are all real, and they make modern distributional issues extraordinarily difficult to solve. Solve them, though, we must — because the stakes are of historic proportions. The place to start is where public policy, rather than forces in the economic or technological background, has exacerbated inequalities. Our tax system in the United States has become especially perverted in this regard, overtly favoring the accumulation of great wealth and its passage intact through the generations.

Concentration of corporate power is as threatening to pluralist democracy as individual wealth concentration. And it, too, is increasing. Solutions to this problem, though, will be much harder to come by than solutions to inequities on the individual level.

The forces concentrating corporate power are different from those shifting the distribution of individual wealth and income, but they are no less important. Power, more than wealth, is undergoing concentration in the corporate sector. It is not clear from the data that the business sector as a whole is more concentrated than it used to be. This is a debated point among economists. On one hand, in a few industries increasing concentration is obvious even to lay observers. When most of us were young, there were no mega-banks. Banking was distributed over a great many small depository and lending institutions. Now, after more than ten thousand mergers since 1980, the top ten banks have the majority of all deposits, which you can compare with the one-fifth of deposits they held at the start of the period.[17] Similarly, it would be hard for a shopper to have missed the consolidation in food distribution. The market share of the twenty largest food retailers has risen by twenty-four points since 1993.[18] On the other hand, America is blessed with a great many entrepreneurial companies, which tend to decrease concentration by taking market share from more established competitors. Giant businesses rise and fall, with new competitors constantly nipping at their heels. Only about 10 percent of the largest companies ranked by sales when I was a kid were still listed in the top five hundred under the same identifier when my kids were the same age.[19] That is all to the good. Entrepreneurship is the best of all possible remedies for concentration.

Concentration and corporate influence can increase indirectly when firms are under common control. The rise of private-equity firms is a development that boosts concentration of power in a manner that may not show up in economists' indices. The relatively small but well-endowed population of these firms, known informally as "buyout" firms, now dominates a great many companies but tends to operate them as separate entities. Over $2 trillion in corporate assets today are managed by private-equity firms.[20] There are thousands of private-equity deals every year, many of them transferring ownership and control from widely dispersed public shareholders to private partnerships. To the extent that the purchased businesses are still treated in the collected data as separate entities, studies of concentration will understate effective concentration.

It is a reasoned guess that effective concentration in American business has risen in the past fifty years, but it is certain that corporate lobbying is up. Professional and reported lobbying is a multibillion-dollar industry.[21] Lobbying lawfully excluded from reporting requirements, because it is conducted by operating executives and their lawyers, may be even more expansive. Bigger money still is in campaign contributions, an increasingly protected form of corporate free speech. In the wake of the Supreme Court's Citizens United decision, we should expect not only more spending by corporations seeking advantages from government, but less visibility with respect to the amounts spent on doing this. It is hard to read the Court's decision as other than a blessing for a stronger corporate hand in politics. In legal terms, the decision is a reinforcement of the misguided notion that corporations are people and entitled to the constitutional protections of the Bill of Rights. The Supreme Court in its 1886 Southern Pacific Railroad case took a seminal step down that dangerous path, and perhaps its line of thinking was predictable as the Robber Baron Era was taking hold. But it is a shame that later Supreme Courts failed to correct this fateful error during the Progressive Era or the decades of liberal judiciary that followed. Now it will be much harder. The Bill of Rights was designed to protect fragile, vulnerable mortals from the inherent power and potential brutality of the state. It is downright inconceivable that our Founding Fathers would have extended those rights to leviathans that are nearly immortal, born without consciences, too amorphous to jail, and able to control assets many orders of magnitude greater than those of most voters.

I am certainly not asserting here that corporate executives as individuals have insufficiently developed consciences. In fact, the standard of ethics observed by the corporate CEOs I know probably exceeds the population norms, and it is plainly higher than in some other strenuously competitive fields. It is the corporations themselves that have no consciences or public policy idealism, and even their best leaders find it hard to impose an individual conscience on an institutional space where everything other than profit maximization is optional at best. Collective decision making in corporations, especially over long periods of time, tends toward the common denominator goal of value-neutral profit maximization. Corporations, after all, are formed to make money, and not for any other primary purpose. But, by the same token, any rights they possess derive from permissive statute rather than nature, human decency, or any moral obligation the rest of us owe to them. They neither need the constitutional shields we fragile mortals require nor hold moral title to them. They surely ought not to be major forces in electoral politics, where they will act, if permitted, with disproportionate power and with motives lacking an altruism you can't reasonably expect them to possess. No one should want to modify our paradigm of democracy to read "One man, one vote; one colossus, one colossal vote."

There has been an attitudinal shift in this country over recent decades toward more favorable treatment of large and powerful companies generally. Scholars and policymakers used to ask whether "bigness was badness." Now thought leaders are more likely to ask how they can help keep our largest corporate players dominant on the world stage. In early 1992, one of the candidates for President of the United States told me that among his missions would be to restore American banks to primacy. Japanese banks had passed ours in scale, he said, and this disadvantage threatened to render us a second-tier nation if uncorrected. The candidate was simultaneously wrong and prescient. It turned out to be Japan that paid the price for the outsize scale of its banks, but the drift of American politics went his way nonetheless. Looking back, it seems that Richard Nixon was the last president to pursue an antitrust philosophy Theodore Roosevelt would have admired. It used to be that exercises of corporate power in this country were never beyond question, and proposed mergers that enhanced market power or political influence were looked at with suspicion. The informal burden of proof lay with the businesses to show that any such expansion of power was justified by commensurate consumer benefits. The informal burden has now shifted so completely to the government that the younger generation today scarcely knows what the word *antitrust* refers to.

One familiar argument against all attempts to restrain excessive corporate size and power is that the sizes of our businesses are driven by useful market forces, pulling relentlessly toward maximum efficiency. Any use of the brakes under these circumstances will harm efficiency—and thus be an overall drag on the economy. This argument assumes that industries grow concentrated mainly because of scale economies that reflect efficiency in operations. This is an overstatement of the role of operational efficiency in rewarding size. The economy would not, in fact, become more efficient with increased scale if branding advantages were the principal benefit of increasing size. Similarly, to the extent that a larger company performs better due to favors it receives from the government upon the application of political power or in response to fundraising help, bigger is not better. Financial success can, and often does, expand with scale without commensurate efficiency or consumer benefit.

One undeniable advantage of large scale is that larger companies can buy up smaller rivals, whereas small fish can seldom swallow whales. This can be done to increase some efficiency advantage, but it can also be done to squelch a smarter, more creative method of doing business. If access to capital, branding, and political muscle helps large companies overcome or acquire their smaller and more creative rivals, scale can be a source of actual harm. And, even in those cases where scale efficiencies do represent a natural vector in the direction of greater size, I would consider giving up at least a modicum of this efficiency advantage for the benefit of a more pluralistic democracy, which is of incomparably greater value.

Globalization is also a factor in the rise of corporate power. The declining importance of national borders has tilted the overall balance of power from the public, which enforces its will mainly through host governments, toward corporations, which can transcend the political boundaries. Modern corporations are all too able to shift assets and questioned operations to more compliant jurisdictions when pushed hard at home. A refrain commonly heard whenever limits on corporate power are proposed is that restraints will simply cause businesses to relocate. Globalization has indeed made it hard to prevent shopping for the least restrictive, lowest-taxing domicile. Attempts by sovereign states to impose worker and environmental protections within their borders are already being defeated by shifts of operations to less responsible nations—or ones that simply feel the economic gains are worth turning the blind eye. The same argument can be applied to calls for antitrust enforcement. If our businesses stay small while other nations' businesses grow, under current rules, their businesses could eventually buy up and control more of our economy than we should want.

Corporations, it is worth repeating, have the property rights society gives them, and no sacred rights at all. In the language of the Declaration of Independence, their rights are neither "self-evident" nor "inalienable." The corporate sector is every bit as important to prosperity as is generally assumed, but its boundaries must be set to serve the best interests of natural persons and not vice versa. There is surely no moral or economic principle that forces us to acquiesce to demands that corporations doing business in the United States, whether foreign or domestically incorporated, be free to produce their products with whatever low standards of care for their employees they select or any manner of disregard for the environment. The duty of government to impose conditions of this sort is well recognized everywhere. It is the courage to supervise effectively that is sometimes missing.

The task of constraining extraterritorial behavior is tough enough when the corporations involved are domestically organized here in the United States. It is proving exponentially harder when the corporations are foreign based and want to enjoy our markets or acquire control of our companies. Our own corporations relentlessly lobby for access to foreign markets and the freedom to own interests in foreign firms, readily conceding that reciprocal rights should be granted to their counterparts from other nations. Yet, if we permit unbridled acquisition of American firms by foreign competitors — allowing, as a corollary, takeover bids from companies unfairly enriched by rapacious labor practices, shortcutting of critical environmental responsibilities, or bolstered by large subsidies from their own governments — we will find ourselves increasingly working for unworthy bosses over time.

The playing field for international commerce should be reasonably level and well groomed for the maximization of trade between nations, but it should not be leveled at the lowest common denominator of decency. Both carrots and sticks are presumably available to help us on this issue if we muster the political will to use them. This is among a few rare topics of controversy around which I welcome acrimonious debate between factions in Washington. Trade treaty negotiations have many degrees of freedom. They are often originated at the behest of our international corporations, which then act as their manager-cheerleaders during the negotiation and ratification processes. In order that treaties find a healthy, balanced equilibrium between free trade and protection of both workers and the environment, they must also have opponents. Only out of vigorous debate is balance likely to be found. It would seldom, if ever, serve our country's interests (either economic or political) to stifle opportunities for more trade, but it would be an equal disservice to nurture foreign-based marketplace bullies, oppressive employers, or environmental abusers. Reasonable restrictions on both market access and acquisition of control by bad actors are not renunciations of the principle of comparative advantage that underpins the permanent case for trade. They are, instead, necessary antidotes to the adverse side effects of hasty, unbridled globalization.

Limiting the power of multinational corporations is a formidable task by any standard. It is made tougher by the fact that corporations are so much harder than individual wealth holders to discipline. Many companies accept that aggressive strategies will result in penalties and see it as part of the game. They have become accustomed to an occasional slap on the wrist or a fine that reduces short-term earnings, and they carry on. An individual's career, or self-esteem and ambition, can be ruined by disciplinary action. It is rare to see a corporation so affected. In any sufficiently large organization of human beings, where the leaders themselves feel protected by a collective shield, defiance of outside authority and institutional megalomania tend to displace the best of internal cultures and fear of admonishment over time. But, with nearly one-third of the world's gross national product (GNP), the United States should certainly be unafraid to lead. If our trade representatives demand unconditional corporate globalism elsewhere, and offer unrestricted access here at home, we will have failed as a world leader. Free trade and bridge building are all to the good, but, as with free markets (and organized sports), they need rules and referees to work properly. When the arguments are advanced that we can't do anything that powerful companies don't welcome because they might take their marbles elsewhere, or that we can't introduce standards of responsible behavior into trade negotiations, I strongly urge you to reject them.

In a more perfect world, one might set as a goal that all fields of business endeavor would be plentifully populated with competitors, each with a minimum of market power and political clout. Even a start in this direction in the United States would require an antitrust policy more forceful than any in the past, a turn of philosophy not easy to define and certainly not to be counted on to take hold anytime soon. It would similarly oblige the Supreme Court to reverse course and bless the necessary limits on corporate political activity. I am not swayed, at least as yet, by the siren's call for a constitutional convention to short-circuit this uncertain process by trying to amend the Constitution. Not only is there insufficient chance that a convention in today's political climate would put forth a welcome amendment, there is scant assurance that a convention would refrain from proposing damaging changes elsewhere in the Constitution.

The picture is far from ideal, and we must accept that the balance between corporate power and popular sway will almost certainly remain out of equilibrium for some time. There are two fronts, however, on which advances can be gained even now. One opportunity lies with intellectual progress. The more light is shed, in both factual and theoretical terms, on the political role of corporations, the more likely is an eventual shift in course. Great sea-change enlightenments and massive shifts in public opinion may defy prediction, but they are a part of our species' history and will equally be a part of its future. I am not without hope that the error of mistaking fictional persons for real ones will eventually be recognized and corrected. In the meanwhile, the best we can do is to seize upon the latitude for better campaign financing disclosure offered under current court guidance and make the most of it. There isn't a reason in the world why you shouldn't want your Congress to do so.

Some observers still don't see individual wealth and income concentration trends as a threat. The truth is that an overly concentrated economy will not only hurt democracy, it will also undermine prosperity.

Because natural persons are more geographically rooted, have consciences and loyalties, and are sensitive to punishment, the accretion of individual wealth and influence can be tempered more easily than globally flexible corporate power can be curbed. The recent stagnation of middle-class incomes is acknowledged by liberals and conservatives alike. More contentious is whether any imposed remedy would be worse than the malady. In deciding where you stand, you might look first introspectively, at your own notions of fairness. If you believe a country can be judged by how decently it treats its least fortunate, or even by how it treats its average hard-working citizens, then shifting all of the gains of economic growth to the wealthy would seem an unpropitious step toward a fair society. By John Rawls's notion that a just society is one in which virtually all would sign off on the economic distribution pattern in advance of knowing which decile they would find themselves in, ours would surely not qualify.

I doubt most of you are proud that high school dropouts from wealthy families do almost as well at forty as college grads from poor backgrounds. When hard-working middle-class families gain little even from boom years, and find their children increasingly squeezed out of top colleges because they aren't poor enough for meaningful scholarships or rich enough to pay themselves, I hope you would call that unfair. My wife and I travel a great deal overseas. Many of you have likely shared the discomfort we feel in countries where the rich share next to nothing with the bulk of the population. I can't imagine feeling any more comfortable at home in a future where conspicuous consumption by the few forms an ever sharper contrast with the lifestyles of the many. We do not have to worry that our disparities will soon reach the dystopian proportions portrayed in H. G. Wells's fine short story "The Time Machine," but even the whiff of similarity in the wind today is unnerving.

The motto above the doorway to the Supreme Court, EQUAL JUSTICE UNDER LAW, is a statement of monumental historical ambition with respect to fairness. No nation before us has fully achieved this straightforward moral mandate, and ours has never quite gotten there either. "A defendant who is guilty and rich stands a better chance in our courts today than one who is poor and innocent," one judicial observer has claimed. Whether or not this colorful criticism is accurate, our nation has come closer to the ideal than virtually any in our entire species' history but is now moving rather unexpectedly away from it. Inordinate disparities in means, already a threat to the goal, will only make the gap between reality and the ideal greater. An old *New Yorker* cartoon hints at the situation we should be loath to exacerbate. A lawyer sitting behind his desk queries his client: "You have a terrific case, Mr. Jones. Now, how much justice can you afford?"

If there were no other reason for concern about the widening wealth and income gaps, their multifaceted adverse impact on our democracy would be sufficient. One threat lies in outright destabilization, and another is in alienation from civic participation. Extreme unfairness has, in fact, undone governments in the past. Full-scale revolutions are rare historical reactions, but that possibility is what President Obama rhetorically alluded to when he warned a group of financial executives in 2009, "My administration is the only thing between you and the pitchforks."[22] The rich are not likely to be hung from lampposts anytime soon, and the President knows that, but there was nonetheless a message in his exaggerated prose. Lesser, and less violent, forms of destabilization than revolution occur with much greater historical frequency. People can lose their faith in the major parties. Or they may turn to candidates with extravagant, heroic promises, the "men on horseback" who have heralded so much of history's pain. The already disappointing rate of voter participation can fall still lower, enhancing the power of single-issue voters. You can't like their impact, unless you are one of them. Crime becomes more attractive to those who feel left out. Maybe most important of all, if future economic gains are not shared with the middle class, America will lose the unifying spirit, embodied in its social and political cohesion, that made it a great nation.

Given scant turnout in the poorest neighborhoods and the comparatively minuscule population of the upper classes, an angry middle class has the votes to do whatever it wants. It can remedy the situation, or, alternatively, it can use its voting power to do serious harm — even without pitchforks. If the Tea Party movement on the right and the Occupy movement on the left were in fact born of the same middle-class frustration, who knows what kind of more frightening radical movement might arise next?

The proud and appealing ideal of the United States embodied in the "One man, one vote" motto originally meant something more like "One white propertied male, one vote," but time has greatly improved our republic in that respect. The problem today is that while every vote may be equal on one Tuesday in November, for the rest of the year too many of those elected in November tend to offer their attention in proportion to contributions. No American ought to prefer a motto that reads, "One dollar, one vote." The impact of money is always a blemish on democracies, but it can be argued that it does relatively minor harm when there are enough differing voices among the contributors that truth and decency may arise, or be plucked, from the cacophony. One special interest's gain can be the next one's loss. If enough fat cats try to eat off each other's plates, no one gets to devour too much. This is the case for pluralism, and it has merit most of the time — even if not every good cause has a contributor base and not every malefactor has a well-heeled adversary.

Pluralism finds its antipodal adversary in concentration. Every narrowing in the sharing of prosperity, every increase in the market shares of large corporations, reduces the benefits of pluralism. As contributors become fewer but more generous, and lobbying budgets for the behemoths of business grow fatter, pluralism fades as a remedy to the undue influence of money and power over democratic government. We are seeing a fast fade today.

There is also a threat to prosperity from excessive concentrations of wealth and power — your prosperity. Part of that argument is a tautology. For those who don't get to share in any gains, the enjoyment of economic growth is minimal. That's the harsh truth, and increasingly a middle-class story once reserved for the bottom. Just as harsh a truth is that the whole pie is smaller in superconcentrated economies than in those with more evenly distributed wealth. Nobel laureate Joseph Stiglitz has made that point effectively in a recent book, *The Price of Inequality.*[23] Oligarchies and aristocracies tend to be inefficient economic engines. Adam Smith taught the world that monopolists will gain extra profits from constricting output. And when prosperity is not shared, education and opportunity don't tend to be shared well either — and much of an economy's potential talent is wasted. Top-heavy systems are prone to stalling out.

When the concentration of wealth in the upper reaches of the economy becomes generationally sticky, economic power and resources will no longer flow as readily to those who will use them to the benefit of the whole economy. This is the heart of the mobility issue. Warren Buffett made this point about declining mobility cleverly, noting that no one would be foolish enough to pick an Olympic team by heredity. It is beyond realistic imagination that any hereditary aristocracy can be a friend of maximum drive or innovation. Our country's historical leaders have always understood this. Thomas Jefferson wasn't prescient about the future of our capitalist economy, but he understood the dangers of concentrated economic power. Teddy Roosevelt had it right and acted on it as a Republican president. So did his cousin Franklin Roosevelt in office as a Democrat.

There should be a nonpartisan factual understanding that the whole economy will tend to stultify over time if concentration is allowed to go unchecked.

Solutions to individual wealth and income concentration are available. The changes needed to curb individual concentration may sound radical, but so did the income tax in its day.

I hope you are convinced of the case for some kind of action to prevent our pluralistic democracy from migrating toward individual and corporate aristocracy, but perhaps you are puzzled about whether any solution consistent with Western free-market values can be found to change our unfortunate course. The roots of the inequality issues run deep; there is a host of really bad solutions available; and there are no obvious recent examples of nations that have experienced severe inequality problems and banished them. If that is not discouraging enough, there are easily identified obstacles on the road to any serviceable resolution. In fact, I freely admit that the program for combating America's accelerating inequality and economic concentration may be the toughest of my five theses. It couldn't be omitted, though, because it is also the most fundamentally important of the five to the shape of the society we will leave to the next generation.

The accumulation of more wealth by a small fraction of the public and easier generational passage of fortunes within families than is healthy for everyone else are by no means impossible to limit. Lifetime accumulation is overwhelmingly achieved through untaxed or low-taxed accretions of capital, which becomes wealth; it is seldom built through fully taxed ordinary income. Piketty suggests that a universal, internationally coordinated annual wealth tax would be the best way to impose reasonable limits on this accumulation, but he acknowledges that this is an unlikely course.[24] I agree with him that an internationally uniform wealth tax would be a theoretically constructive solution, and I also concur that it falls for now in the realm of the utopian. In any event, an international wealth tax doesn't qualify for inclusion as a thesis here, because it can't — even under the boldest and most persuasive leadership — be effectuated by the American public.

Several tools, however, at the disposal of our nation come to mind right away. The least controversial of these has been used for many years and only needs to be tweaked. We tax short-term investment gains at a higher rate than long-term investment gains, and justifiably so. This distinction can be greatly widened. Speculative and other short-term gains should always be taxed at a higher rate than ordinary income. Short-term gains do the economy remarkably little good, and they are earned almost exclusively by the already prosperous. A laddered tax, with tax rates falling in proportion to the length of the taxed investment's holding period, and no capital gains break to be earned for the first five years, would be major steps forward. Dividends, too, should be taxed in proportion to the number of years the investor has held the underlying stock. Also among the low-hanging fruits, and already under fire, are the tax breaks for carried interest rewards earned by hedge fund and private-equity managers. Other than to reward the campaign generosity of the fund managers, there would seem to be no purpose to treating these as other than ordinary earned income.

Closer to the wealth tax in concept and impact, and within theoretical reach for a single nation, lies a more powerful potential change in tax policy. Currently, the IRS levies taxes only on income and realized gains; consumption and unrealized gains are not taxed at all. I would favor taxing all four — and with a tax structure so simple the tax advisory industry would have little to contribute. A consumption tax, an efficient revenue source but regressive in nature if applied too uniformly, can be made progressive by setting lower rates for necessities than for luxury goods, and scaling the rate with size for the most expensive purchases. Many nations have value-added taxes, and they are straightforward, at least by comparison to our income tax. The existence of a VAT tax would allow a diminished dependence on the income tax, which could then be reduced and simplified to the bone. It would also reduce noncompliance and perhaps temper the irrational zeal of the most extreme tax haters.

The taxation of unrealized gains at a few percentage points a year is the real opportunity, though, to affect national wealth shares. It is here that the vast bulk of the upper-echelon wealth is stored. To use a hypothetical example, if a well-to-do investor had purchased and held a million dollars' worth of a zero-dividend stock in 1974, the value would—if performance equaled the actual Standard & Poor's 500 market appreciation—now be $90 million, but the tax paid so far would be nil. For most of those in the economic stratosphere, unrealized gains are where the wealth comes from and where it sits.[25]

Yes, this would be a sweeping, even historic, change. If it is ever seriously proposed, you will hear loudly and often that it is unmanageable. But all of the most significant social policy changes have tended to look unmanageable at first. Only well after programs like the income tax, child labor laws, and Social Security have been implemented do their impossibilities prove to have been exaggerated. The appreciation of relatively liquid assets, such as securities and bank deposits, would be uncomplicated to track and tax. Opponents of this approach will whine that taxes on unrealized gains would destroy the value of illiquid assets, such as art, family farms, and stock in private companies. To this, I would counter that your most important illiquid asset by far, the family home, is almost certainly valued and taxed locally already. Genuine family farms, if you believe them to have special moral value, can be carved out below some threshold with little harm, as long as the carve-out could not be enjoyed by corporate owners and mega-farmers. A modest threshold would harmlessly exempt most people's holdings of art, and truly valuable art could be appraised regularly and taxed.

That leaves taxation of stock in private companies to consider, where the bulk of my own assets rest in the form of unrealized capital gains. The late Benno Schmidt Sr., a venture capitalist and corporate statesman I admired greatly, once told me about the wife of an entrepreneurial executive who teasingly called her husband "Old Unrealized" because so much of their wealth stayed tied up in the business he built, and she had so little of it to spend. In my own situation, I confess it would have been complicated to sell fractions of my Plymouth Rock holdings in order to get the cash to pay an annual appreciation tax. There is no public market for our shares, and no organized auction is available to help get the best price. The share value has appreciated over time on paper, reflecting the increasing scale and worth of the company, but it doesn't come home in cash unless the company pays dividends. And dividends are not necessarily possible for many young companies or wise for established companies with above-market expansion opportunities. So how would entrepreneurs pay the unrealized gains tax proposed here?

This is just the kind of problem the free market is particularly good at solving. The demand would be a drum call, to which the financial markets would respond with new products. There is a whole array of possible loan formats whereby lenders would front cash needed for taxes. These would presumably be offered in exchange for promises to pay upon liquidity events and would be backed by the collateral of the private companies' shares. Those of us who couldn't sleep with this form of debt would put pressure on our companies for earlier dividends. Would I have liked this? Not much. But overall the pain felt by a few of us would have been small compared to the gains available to all from a more prosperous and harmonious society. Had the nation adopted a policy of taxing unrealized appreciation during Plymouth Rock's early years, the company would have enjoyed a nearly identical trajectory, and my colleagues and I would have quickly gotten used to paying the tax. We would quite soon have forgotten the good old days of tax-free accumulation.

A much-simplified tax structure with its base broadened to include unrealized gains and consumption would be a huge improvement for most Americans, and a serious step toward remedying the flight of money to the top. Just as important, though, is the need to repair the inheritance and gift taxes, which are only barely serving their original purposes as employed today. The unpopularity of the "death tax" is a rare violation of the notion that the electoral public is usually wiser than those it elects. Yet voters of little means seem to believe on the whole that people like me should pay less tax, in life and at death, than we now pay. If you are among them, your preferences don't match your interests.

I have spent a good bit of time puzzling over this phenomenon. Here are a few theories for the dissonance. One commonly heard explanation is that voters without means may fondly hope that they, too, will be financially well endowed someday — whether by a business home run, day trading, or winning the lottery. They don't want taxes to get in the way of their unlikely fantasies, so they pay dearly for the dream's excitement by letting the wealthy ride on the cheap. It cannot be in your rational interest to humor that poor exercise of logic. A second contributor to the mismatch may be that the wealthiest among us have disproportionate influence over shaping public opinion and have sold a bill of goods to the public about how taxing the upper classes will destroy freedom and capitalism. Yet another explanation might be that the middle class does not begrudge those above them, and in fact is downright grateful as long as everyone is making progress. It's no problem, you might say, for some to have yachts as long as you can buy a new bass boat. If this is the underlying psychology of the tax conundrum, it may soon run its course as the middle class realizes how completely its progress has ground to a halt.

A more durable explanation would be that middle-class taxpayers fear that taxes taken from the business elite will largely be wasted on transfer payments to unworthy recipients, who will use their government largess to support less-than-commendable lifestyles. People who see the world in this way don't visualize any likely benefit to be gained of available tax proceeds from my bracket flowing to them, so they would rather see the money stay put, in the hands of those of us who create jobs. This argument can be defeated only by responsible use of tax proceeds.

Taxes on inheritance should be much more effectively imposed. This would imply removing the tax advantages now enjoyed by trusts.

The first tax the public ought to rally behind is the Estate and Gift Tax, a levy that is under brutal attack today. It would be hard to argue that this form of taxation was abhorrent to the Founding Fathers. Its pedigree dates back to 1797, when a temporary stamp tax was imposed in proportion to bequests. It reappeared, as needed, for a while before the Civil War and again at the time of the Spanish-American War. The modern version was passed in 1916. Its logic is as solid as its roots, pushing the society away from hereditary aristocracy and toward rewards in proportion to hard work and talent. Among the most rhetorically forceful of political arguments against it has been that it would disrupt family farming and small business ownership. Yet these are altogether too well taken care of already by the tax's minimum threshold. Nobody with an estate below $5.4 million in 2015 has to pay anything in federal gift or estate taxes. The exemption is twice that for married couples, so, yes, there's an exemption of over $10 million for the majority of wealthy families. Even knowing this, I was quite surprised that only about ten thousand federal estate returns are filed each year, a precipitous drop from the past. Only about five thousand of these filers pay any tax at all.[26] Data shows that a grand total of a couple of dozen farm and small business estates paid taxes in one recent year.[27]

The total revenue collected by the federal Estate and Gift Tax (less formally called our inheritance taxes) is about $20 billion.[28] If you are thinking that doesn't sound like much in a multitrillion-dollar economy, you are right. This amount was just over one-half of 1 percent of total federal tax revenues in 2014. So, another argument of inheritance tax opponents is that their revenue is so paltry as to not be worth the collection effort. But that is only because the tax is shot through with loopholes. The wealthiest one-hundredth of 1 percent of Americans, about sixteen thousand families, you may recall, can be roughly estimated to have had a combined net worth of $6 trillion several years back.[29] The wealth of the Forbes 400 alone now stands at over $2.25 trillion, with a mean wealth of $5.7 billion for the list.[30] The average age of a Forbes 400 billionaire is sixty-six, and between five and ten of these might be expected to die each year. There should accordingly be a $25 billion to $50 billion annual tax base supplied just by this tiny group. It is widely quoted that nearly $60 trillion in assets will pass from one generation in the next fifty-five years. So where are the revenues? They were given away by flawed tax laws.

Among the least justifiable of loopholes is the "step-up" of unrealized gains at death. All of those unrealized gains mentioned earlier can be passed to a holder's heirs without payment of any income taxes on the gains accrued during the original holder's lifetime. The income tax liability is simply erased. Take that earlier example of someone with the combination of assets, luck, and skill to have bought stock for $1 million and held it for many decades as it appreciated to $90 million. When the holder dies, let's assume the stock passes to the children, and federal and state estate taxes are paid. The heirs in this case get to treat the stock for tax purposes, when it is eventually sold, as though it had been bought for $90 million. What happens to the tens of millions in income tax that would have been due on the $89 million gain had the stock been sold by the original owner or sold with the true purchase cost as a basis? It's gone, a gift from the rest of the taxpayers to enhance family wealth maintenance. This weird treatment is categorized by some as an income tax loophole rather than an estate tax flaw, since it forgives a tax that would have been paid only when gains were realized. I prefer to think of it as an estate tax giveaway, because death provides the best of all opportunities to tax unrealized gains and because the existence of the loophole has such a powerful effect on estate planning and investment decisions. The step-up serves no purpose other than perpetuation of inherited wealth, and the sooner it is repealed, the better.

Trusts provide another huge leakage in the estate tax pipes. This is not to assert that trusts themselves are without legitimate purpose. Let's suppose that you have a brain-damaged dependent, perhaps a wounded war veteran, and want to make sure that individual's future is secure when you are gone. You can establish a trust with assets to take care of the dependent, managed by wise, empathetic trustees who can allow you to rest easily in your grave. There's surely no abuse in this; it's virtually a requirement of a decent society. This use, however, is trivial in scale compared to the use of trusts to pass on weighty assets to perfectly functional offspring. And, for reasons that underscore the power of the wealthy in Congress, the government in its wisdom has conveyed to these trusts massive tax breaks to fortify conveyances of wealth. Most of you won't have trusts. They are generally useful only for those of us with estates above the tax threshold, the very people for whom a tax gift from you is least necessary — unless a society of hereditary fortunes has somehow become your goal.

The types of trusts are many. There are GRATs (Grantor Retained Annuity Trusts), CLATs (Charitable Lead Annuity Trusts), IDIOTs (Intentionally Defective Income Trusts), "I-Dig-It's" (Intentionally Defective Grantor Trusts), and other cutely named animals in this zoo. These are not nature's animals. They are Frankenstein's monsters, serving only to increase the concentration of assets in wealthy families over the generations. I might, if pushed, label the Charitable Lead Annuity Trust only a bride of Frankenstein, since at least it assures sizable, regular payments to charities as it matures. The other formats in general can't even make this partial claim to a public purpose. Each trust format is different in its theory and its detail; the complexity of the field forbids an explication here of how each works. The sleights of hand behind some of them, though, can be pretty readily explained.

Understand first that grantors would not be setting up most of these trusts if they didn't save taxes for their families — and, as an extra bonus, shelter assets from unwelcome claimants and spouses. They effectively raise income taxes for you, so take that as a given. Supporting this assertion anecdotally, I don't know anyone with a financial situation similar to my own who doesn't have one or more trusts. The tax code offers big bucks to be taken safely and legally. Herein is the essence of some of the most common trusts. Wealthy persons very often want to pass on fortunes to their heirs, so they create trusts for them. They place in the trust some package of appreciating assets, for which they pay a full gift tax at the inception (if any is, in fact, due after the generous exemptions and other wrinkles). The assets then grow in value, largely still under the control of the grantor or a skillfully chosen designee. The longer the trust's life, the greater is the potential expansion of value. When the beneficiary later receives the corpus of the trust, he or she has no further tax to pay because the grantor has already paid it.

There are several kickers here that convert what sounds like it might be rational policy into expensive folly. The first, and most important, is incrementally favorable treatment upon the grantor's death beyond the fact that tax has already been paid. In cases where the trust amount is below the available exemption, there is simply no tax even when the eventual bequest is huge. More than that, though, wealthier families can use another device to help with the nonexempt excess amount. Certain trusts can "buy" the assets for a promissory note, at a distinctly favorable rate of interest. The word *buy* is placed in quotation marks because these are anything but arm's-length sales. The investment gains of the trust, after the note has been paid (commonly at an interest rate set equal to the rate paid by the Treasury on its own debt), belong to the trust and are not taxed at death. In many cases, the grantor can pay the regular taxes on behalf of the trust on any interim income or realized appreciation of the assets. This supplementary payment in such cases is free of gift or inheritance levies, despite the incontrovertible fact that it is a conveyance of additional wealth, potentially of substantial magnitude, to the beneficiaries. Only when inheritance taxes on amounts passed to a next generation, in trust or otherwise, are fully levied on the actual value at passage are taxes logically paid in the correct amount. Hardly any savvy person of real means pays a tax that meets or approaches this standard. No halfway decent trust lawyer would permit it.

An example can help, so look once more at the outlier example used previously and in the discussion of unrealized gains, now modified to illustrate the use of a trust. The grantor in this situation was wealthy enough at age forty-five to have placed shares of stock worth $1 million in a trust in exchange for a note. Imagine that the grantor used a trust and a note because the children had already received gifts in excess of the exemption amounts, so without the trust vehicle all future gifts and bequests would have been taxable. The stock appreciated in lockstep with the long-term average performance of the S&P 500 until the grantor's death forty years later. Now posit that the interest on the purchase note was 4.5 percent at the time, which is in fact several times the required interest a trust would have to pay for such a note created in today's low-interest-rate environment. No gift was considered to have been conveyed because the trust paid the legally defined full value for the stock with its note. The interest on the original note paid over the years to the grantor would have been sufficient to reduce the total value of the trust at the grantor's death from $90 million to about $50 million, but that $50 million could then be passed tax free from the trust to the grantor's designated beneficiary. This is even better for dynastic perpetuation than the stepped-up basis. Recall, too, that no capital gains tax is due until the stock is sold, if ever, by the beneficiary. If you thought that such a huge bequest, under laws that embody a maximum estate tax rate of 40 percent, would incur a tax of tens of millions of dollars, think again. Zero is a more likely total.

For the simply wealthy, the $5-million-per-person and $10-million-per-couple exemptions from estate and gift taxes are usually sufficient to elude any tax payment and provide a handsome bequest. The richer-still learn to give their gifts earlier in life. An outright gift of $10 million, appreciating at 5 percent over thirty years and assuming no currently taxable income stream, becomes $43 million tax free at the end of the period thanks solely to the threshold. At 10 percent, more like the stock market's true historical return, that's $174 million. For those among the mega-rich who feel the need to pass on more than that, a trust and a note can complete the trick. Einstein is often quoted (though it may be an urban legend) to the effect that compound interest is the most powerful force in the universe. That's half the engine at work here, but the other half is the mystery of Congress's kindness to influential, well-heeled constituents and to its political contributors. The favorable arithmetic of trusts works best when the trust asset, perhaps a venture capital position, hedge fund interest, or private-equity investment, appreciates faster than the market as a whole. But the bogey here can be set at a much lower threshold, a risk-free Treasury interest rate. Assets generally appreciate over time in an economic equilibrium, and it seldom requires investment talent to outperform the Treasury interest rate with equity investments over long periods.

Trust arithmetic works least well in cases where the money is lost. That case is not only less common, but since there is no limit to the number of trusts that can be established, the impact and likelihood of loss can be minimized by multiple redundant trusts with differing assets. One famously wealthy family is said to have, quite legally, employed around thirty separate trusts to assure minimal taxation. The lawfully allowable treatment of trusts is essentially a gift from you and others like you to the families that benefit from the trusts, and especially those with more than $10 million in bequests they wish to pass on to their offspring. This is one of many gifts in the tax arena that you may not have understood you were providing.

Another kicker is that in some trust formats, the grantors get excused from the bulk of the potential taxes without necessarily giving up all measure of control over the trust assets during the life of the trust. If the corpus is stock in a closely held corporation, they or their selected trustees, often chosen from among their best friends or loyal attorneys, may be able to vote it. At a minimum, it will be effectively shielded from ownership by strangers who might have voted it adversely to their interests. If the trust contains fine art, it can hang in their living rooms as long as the trust receives a proper rent. Paying an above-market rental amount allows yet another tax-free transfer of cash to the trusts and eventually to the beneficiaries. Paying below-market rent simply allows the asset to remain in the grantor's possession at a bargain while it is treated for inheritance tax purposes as having been conveyed. If the trust asset is a mansion, the grantor can still remain securely in place for a fixed term as its master under an "arm's-length" rental arrangement with a so-called independent trustee — selected, of course, by the grantor. A trust structure called a Qualified Personal Residence Trust can be used for this exact purpose. The kids, meanwhile, won't be able to squander the family's precious assets (at least until the trust distributes to them) on loud music, recreational drugs, support of strange cults, or egalitarian politics. The grantors in the end get the tax benefit of paying an artificially early tax on the eventual bequest without fully giving up whatever was gifted. Thanks to our tax laws, the grantor of a trust really can have a cake and eat it, too.

Recently, the advantages of what are aptly called "dynasty trusts" have grown even larger. The federal government allows individual states to determine the maximum duration of trusts established in that state. Under a traditionally imposed rule against perpetuities, most states insisted that trusts terminate twenty-one years after the death of the last beneficiary who was alive and known to the person creating the trust at the time it was created. Over twenty states have now abolished these limits on perpetuation. It is now possible for a grantor to establish a trust that lasts for hundreds of years — or indefinitely. And the new rules typically do not require that the grantor live within the state offering this boon. The only wrinkle for the dynasty is the existence of a federal generation-skipping tax, which would fall due on transfers to the grandchildren, great-grandchildren, and beyond. The federal generation-skipping tax, of course, is a political target these days for estate tax opponents, but, as of now, it is still on the books. The last few years have seen the establishment of a plethora of true dynasty trusts.

Now, put together the various tax advantages these recent pages have covered. What you will see is a picture of a lock-tight guarantee that the assets of the wealthy in America never meet a tax collector. First, unrealized gains are exempted from tax as accrued — presumably because some of the asset types are considered hard to divide for purposes of a periodic cash payment and especially so when they lack a liquid market. Then, if held until death and passed on, most of these assets are given a new tax basis (an imaginary purchase price), and the taxes on the accumulated gains are forever forgiven — although there could still be federal and state estate taxes to pay. To avoid paying this tax, the holder can gift the assets to a trust and pay the inheritance taxes in advance before the assets have accumulated gains — or sell them to a trust and let the trust keep any excess of gains over an artificially low and logically inapplicable interest rate. No tax is truly fairer or more useful in a meritocracy than an inheritance levy, but the greatest well of capital in the country — accumulated capital gains passed down within families — is seldom plumbed. The greatest source of wealth disparity is accordingly left undisturbed as it moves from generation to generation.

Unrealized capital gains should be taxed annually. Short of that, the provisions of the tax code that permit stepping up the purchase basis at death should be repealed. Now consider the elimination of bargain-basement taxation of inheritances, and especially a termination of the inexcusably favorable treatment of trusts. Each recommendation stands as sound policy on its own merits, and each loophole should be closed even if others survive. If Congress acts with clarity of thought in the public interest, all sources of the leakage can be plugged simultaneously. Capital gains are the reward for sound investing in the future and aiding the nation's capital allocation process. Trusts that don't depend on gimmickry are compassionate and necessary in some family situations. The tax breaks currently associated with capital gains, however, are devastating to the equitable distribution of wealth. And the laws governing the taxation of trusts have become mainly the product of mischief, the handiwork of lobbyists seeking to maximize the maintenance of great wealth within bloodlines.

Even if all the reforms proposed here were to become law, there would be ample (or more-than-ample) passage of wealth from generation to generation within families. The full estate levy at current levels, without its leakages, does not prevent the majority of a successful individual's accumulated earnings from being passed to heirs. These proposals are better viewed as restoring sanity than as radical leveling. If you favor permitting handsome inheritances, you can still support revoking some of the extraordinary and unnecessary subsidies provided today for building massive fortunes and passing them down to one's heirs. Their elimination will advance the causes of democracy, meritocracy, and tax equity, as well as the economic prospects of your descendants.

The easy thesis is that a tax system that looks to capture a fair share of appreciating wealth is both necessary and within reach. Accumulating assets must be more effectively taxed both during an individual's lifetime and at death.

This country, with most of the Western free-market democracies on our tail, is drifting toward a degree of hereditary economic aristocracy inconsistent with our fundamental values. Concentration of wealth and power in the hands of too few families is all negative. It is an economic killer for everyone else, and destructive to the pluralistic democracy that has been our finest historical accomplishment. The root of the thesis here is that tools are available to stop or slow its trend. International cooperation on a rational, coordinated tax system could work wonders but isn't likely to occur — and, fortunately, it isn't necessary. A great improvement can be made by reforming our own inequitable and overly complex income tax regime. Taxes should be spread over a variety of new forms, none too onerous and none complicated. There should be a progressive consumption charge in the form of a value-added tax on every transaction. Capital gains breaks for short-term speculation and fund managers' carried interest should be eliminated.

Most important, and at the core of the solution, is that unrealized gains on investments must be added to the tax base, and inheritance taxes fortified by wiping out entirely the tax benefits of trusts. Yes, these changes would run counter to the prevailing political winds of the moment. But if you take nothing else from this chapter, please try to remember that they represent an essential step on the path to restoring the country in which you were proud to have grown up or chose to make your own.

As much as I wish it were otherwise, cures for corporate concentration do not fall within the easy theses rubric. But that doesn't mean we should ignore the importance of unbridled corporate power as an adversary of democracy. Corporations must be kept less powerful than the public they were created by law to serve. One useful step would be to re-impose a serious antitrust policy, at least at the modest level of times past and preferably at a higher standard. To do so, we would need to modify the current runaway approach to globalization. Business corporations are, in the end, not people at all but artificial legislative creations — useful only to the extent that they enhance the common good as embodied in our laws and the best of our traditions.

To fully restore the American dream of an equitable and mobile society may be beyond reach anytime soon, but the core proposals offered here would help protect our pluralistic society from further erosion and prevent the formation of a new hereditary aristocracy. They are task enough.

THREE
Education

Education should be the pride and joy of the world's wealthiest nation. Instead, we are failing our next generation through serious errors in our approach to their education. High schools offer false promises and an insufficiently relevant curriculum to a majority of students. Colleges are becoming unaffordable for many of the rest. Cultural and institutional barriers stand squarely in the way of direct solutions to these issues. The most viable path to a solution is to create a universal national service program that will provide career and vocational training to those headed to work rather than college and help finance the costs for those who do go to college.

SOME YEARS AGO, my wife and I attended a small supper where Charles Vest, then president of MIT, led a dinner table discussion on the state of education in America. He asked us to think of an imaginary congress of teachers from all over the world, assembled to vote on which nation had the best educational system on the planet. When the voting was complete, he said, the tellers would report that the United States had won *all* the votes for the top graduate school education, *half* the votes for the leading college education, and *none* of the votes for best kindergarten through twelfth-grade education. This, he concluded, could be America's greatest weakness going forward. It is indeed a weakness, but it doesn't have to be.

We have a nasty problem today in the United States, not just with the academic quality of education, but with its efficacy for both society and too many of the individuals it exists to serve. And it is not just at the K–12 level. It is true that our country never ranks among the top dozen nations for overall high school educational outcomes. Those kids who are not likely to be college bound are badly underserved, in part due to well-intentioned attempts to assure a uniformity of treatment across the population. It also, however, underserves those who do go on to college. For them, the failure is not in quality but in cost. All too many families find university training prohibitively expensive — which can lead students to drop out halfway or take on a crippling debt burden that hangs over their next stage of life.

> While best-practice remedies wouldn't cure all of the problems of American education, improving overall grade school quality and our international ranking would be simple, absent the politics. Educators already know a lot about what best practices look like.

Shown below are the results of a popularly cited survey of nations ranked by the Organisation for Economic Co-operation and Development (OECD).[1] The data, some say, is a bit skewed by the test having excluded elite private schools (a charge denied by the data curators), and skewed again by having included in the United States' data numerous rural residents and recent immigrants, who might not be educated at all in a few of these nations. Still, I haven't heard anyone say that removal of these biases would move us far up the list.

1. Singapore
2. Korea
3. Japan
4. Liechtenstein
5. Switzerland
6. Netherlands
7. Estonia
8. Finland
9. Canada
10. Poland
11. Belgium
12. Germany
13. Vietnam
14. Austria
15. Australia
16. Ireland
17. Slovenia
18. Denmark
19. New Zealand
20. Czech Republic
21. France
22. United Kingdom
23. Iceland
24. Latvia
25. Luxembourg
26. Norway
27. Portugal
28. Italy
29. Spain
30. Russian Federation
31. Slovak Republic
32. **United States**
33. Lithuania
34. Sweden
35. Hungary
36. Croatia

The United States ranked thirty-second in this compilation (thirty-third if a single entry for China, which would rank at or near the pinnacle, were included), behind dozens of nations with economies that don't compare to our own. There are many reasons for this, but parsing the elements of social causality has not usually led to curing the problems. It may be more useful to directly compare policies that have worked and those that have not. Applying sensible best-practice standards to all of our schools would not take the United States to first place, but it would surely move us up in the list.

Both my wife and I spend time on high school education in Boston. I serve as the chairman of a panel that awards a $100,000 cash prize every year to the most-improved public school. We call it the School on the Move Prize. The panel offers pleasant duty, since the members get to see half a dozen success stories in the public schools every year, instead of just reading about the usual procession of disappointing outcomes. The prize panel narrows a large field of applicants down to three and then visits those schools. The winner is the school that best meets these criteria: objective success in having raised standardized test scores in the four most recent years, a clear strategy and a persuasive narrative about the tools used to achieve those results, and a lesson that may be replicable in other schools. I've been a member of that selection panel for nine years now, so I've seen nearly fifty Boston public schools on paper and two dozen for visits. Cathy has remained actively involved with the private high school one of our twins attended.

We are also involved with two contrasting high schools in Boston, picked as learning tools for the two of us because of their extreme contrast. Cathy serves on the board of directors of a local charter high school. That school takes its kids by lottery, as required by law, and draws a population that looks socioeconomically and racially similar to that of the Boston district schools. That school has managed year after year to elevate its kids, the majority living in single-parent households, from poor eighth-grade testing performance on statewide exams to near the top of the statewide compilation—on a par with students from the Boston suburbs' most privileged communities. My work has been as an informal adviser to a district high school that cannot seem to break out of the cellar in the Boston school rankings. It is usually in or near last place according to standardized testing results. I have followed that school through the tenures of three principals, all talented but none able so far to solve its problems.

I cannot say that the student populations of the two contrasting high schools are identical, although they are superficially similar in family income and ethnicity. A parent or guardian had to take the initiative to apply to the charter school, so it can be presumed that its students come from a subpopulation that has someone caring and informed looking out for them at home. While the charter school application requires no screening questionnaire, essay, payment, or interview, the requirement of an application in itself introduces an element of non-randomness. At the opposite end of that spectrum, the school I follow has historically gotten many of its students by central administrative assignment—because no one in their families indicated any school choice preference at all to the district's assignment office. We can guess that this provides an opposite bias. Some of the students come from especially dysfunctional households. Having said that, I still believe that the charter school does its work better than the district school, and that much of the difference lies in practices that are easy to discover.

Let me make one conclusion plain from the start. The introduction of the charter school concept to Boston has made a powerful contribution. This is not a generalized endorsement of all Boston charter schools; some are, unsurprisingly, much better than others. It is even less an endorsement of schools elsewhere in the country with records I have never seen and reputations varying across the entire quality spectrum. I admire the top Boston charters, not because they are an adversary of, or potential replacement for, traditional public schooling but because they can help the district-run public school system. With freedom from some of the constraints under which district schools operate, some externally imposed and some internal, they can experiment with better methods and light a path for the rest of the schools — just as the experiences of the School on the Move Prize winners within the traditional district system point the way. I am confident that the quality of America's grade schools can be improved greatly just by adopting many of the best-practice lessons of the successful charter and district schools we have seen firsthand.

In the impressive charter school Cathy serves, a few distinguishing characteristics jump out at a visitor right away. The students wear what are effectively uniforms, a white or blue shirt with a collar and dark slacks or skirts. They arrive on time in the morning and are greeted one by one at the door by the school's principal as they enter. Late students, and disciplinary violators, are admitted only when accompanied by a parent or guardian. The teachers tend to be young and manifestly enthusiastic. Almost every teacher seems to know almost every student, not just the ones in their classes. Perhaps most noticeably, the school day does not come to an end in early afternoon, when the district school day ends. The students in the charter school are generally there for about ten hours, with their homework done before they depart. The feature that permits this is the school's corps of live-in tutors, mostly gap-year students from good colleges who agree to accept room, board, and a small stipend in exchange for a year of tutoring work. Applications for these tutoring jobs every year far exceed available places. Critics have noted that the charter school's ninth grade in the past was considerably larger than its twelfth grade, with too many students moving back to district schools rather than enduring the long hours. Apparently, the completion data looks better now, but given that those choices were largely voluntary on the part of the students in any case, I never found them abnormal or unacceptable. Individuals differ, and schools are not prisons.

The winners of the School on the Move Prize often have longer days as well, and some have tutoring programs. District-run schools don't have all of the same freedoms and can't fully mimic the charter schools. There are, however, some commonalties in the use of readily available tools among the ranks of the winners from which others can learn. All have had strong and collaborative leadership, beginning with their principals. The principals, on the whole, have worked collaboratively with their teachers on curriculum, student supports, and standards of accountability. They have been collegial and, at the same time, demanding with respect to progress. Their measurements of progress have generally been objective and unambiguous. Each of the winning schools collected student data in excess of district requirements, and most of the schools employed assessment tools well beyond the required standardized tests to identify gaps in learning. The expectations of the students, with respect to behavior as well as achievement, were clearly communicated to the kids and their families, fostering a culture of respect for education and for teachers. To the extent their funds allowed, the schools also provided high levels of support beyond the classroom to address students' academic, health, social, and emotional needs.

The following eight-point program would boost the United States out of thirty-second place and probably into the single digits for educational outcomes. All of these best practices have proven themselves many times in many places.

1. **Increased Early Childhood Schooling.** Experts of all political persuasions seem largely to agree that kindergarten and pre-K programs help in many ways. One Nobel economics laureate, a conservative, told me he would readily give up twelfth grade for mandatory universal kindergarten, a no-cost trade. I think he'd agree with me that we can actually afford both. The point, though, is that the brain is most flexible in the very young. Instilling respect for learning, and pleasure in learning, can hardly be done too early. Whatever is to be done later, an early start will at least be an aid, and it may be essential. Other prosperous countries in the world enroll almost twice as high a percentage of three-year-olds in learning programs as we do.[2]

2. **Longer Hours.** It serves us ill to send students home in the early afternoon. They learn less and get into more trouble. An optimal school day at the high school level should be about eight hours long. School day extension can be designed so that most every student would gain from the extra time. Those who have no homework deficiency would gain from the many benefits of extracurricular activities, including arts, music, and sports. Those whose homework performance is substandard could spend more of the extra time on the school grounds doing supervised homework before leaving.

3. **Personal Attention.** Kids whose home environment emphasizes learning and disciplined effort can thrive under almost any schooling format. If that positive reinforcement and close oversight are not found at home, though, the schools must try to provide as much as possible. This may require smaller schools in some places and plentiful tutors, both paid and volunteer, in others. Capable, caring, and empathetic teachers, of course, count as well. Without

close attention and a nurturing interpersonal reward for good academic results, we can't expect students to value learning.

4. **Data-Driven Administration.** Standardized tests are controversial, but they are a necessary ingredient of improved results. They are not, however, sufficient. There are multiple evaluation tools available to school leaders to monitor each child's progress. These should be applied and used extensively in teacher conferences to evaluate each child's needs and most promising routes to constant improvement. Absent common core standards and considerable grade school uniformity of curriculum, moreover, the task of systemwide improvement will be out of reach. Standardized programs and tests can always be improved, but we are not going to find the path to betterment through thick woods without the compass they provide.

5. **Leadership Training.** Schools *always* do better with strong, inspirational leaders. Principals and superintendents should be chosen with great care and ambitious objectives in mind. Training programs for school leaders are as important as graduate schools of education. Their training should assure that once on the job, leaders have the tools and the incentives to maximize buy-in and collaboration from their key constituencies: teachers, students, and parents.

6. **Hiring Flexibility.** Teacher quality counts, possibly more than any other factor, and the search for the best teachers requires changes in criteria. School districts should not be looking only for full-career teachers. A mix of energetic idealists with three- to five-year horizons and veteran teachers with full career commitments is likely to

outperform homogeneity of either sort. While tenure at the university level is essential on free speech grounds, that is not its purpose at the grade school level. Contractual buyout provisions could provide a more useful form of financial protection for teachers without sacrificing the principal's ability to seek constant improvement in teaching staff quality. On the other hand, we underpay rather than overpay for teaching talent, so any change in tenure rules should be designed not to cut overall compensation. Reward programs for teachers who demonstrate exceptional effort and results can provide a constructive form of extra pay.

7. **Increased Discipline.** Young people, especially from dysfunctional home environments, too often need to be taught respect for education and their teachers. It doesn't come automatically. A disciplined school environment need not seem harsh. Most kids find a sense of order more reassuring and pleasing than oppressive. Treating teachers and other school personnel with respect cannot be optional. School uniforms (even if only loosely defined), school patriotism, and other symbolic tools can also be helpful in providing a sense of order, security, and belonging. Parent and community involvement in defining and maintaining disciplinary standards is a must if proper respect for education and educators is to survive beyond the school doors.

8. **Use of Modern Technology.** Teaching is going to be different in the next generation. Lectures, books, and tests will be available on the Internet and in packages designed for hand-held tablets. I look forward to flexible self-modifying textbooks that alter the curriculum as the student proceeds and demonstrate through quizzes a student's

individual proficiencies and needs. Lectures might look more like movies, with optional tangential features along the way. Tests may look more like games that students actually enjoy, or at least not despise. All of this is to be welcomed, and certainly not feared. The information age is offering us wonderful new tools, and we must make certain they are available to all schools and not just those whose communities can most easily pay for them.

Just adopting best practices is not enough, however, even to serve their limited goals. District responsibility for school standards and budgets is taken too far in this country.

One of the obvious differences between the United States and most of the nations that score above us in results is that we have a great deal more diversity than other countries, not only in the composition of student bodies but also in budgets and curriculum. Each of the nation's fourteen thousand school districts sets most of its own standards, and most localities determine their own school budgets. Not until the 1990s did many state legislators and education officials, concerned about widely divergent student performance, even begin to develop uniform statewide sets of reading and math standards. Only as recently as 2009 did the nation's governors agree to the principle of shared standards, which led to the Common Core.[3] This is valuable progress, as is what I hope to be a developing consensus that standardized testing, however imperfect, is here to stay.

Nonetheless, differential spending may remain among the thorniest of barriers to improving our nation's academic performance. The explanation does not lie solely in different educational philosophies or varying inclinations to invest in public education. There is an unsurprising correlation between spending on schools and a school district's ability to pay. Community income drives a good part of the differential, and there should be no need to repeat the case here that income and wealth vary sharply across neighborhoods and regions in the United States. The fifty states and their localities vary in spending on education from close to 8 percent of gross state product all the way down to a little above 2 percent.[4] Per capita, there appears to be more than a two-to-one span from the highest-spending state to the lowest. Connecticut, Vermont, Alaska, the District of Columbia, and New York are at the high end. At the rear are Utah, Idaho, and Oklahoma.[5]

According to one recent study, Vermont districts are the highest spenders, at close to $20,000 per pupil, while Arizona districts, at the low tail, spend $7,000 per pupil.[6] Census Department surveys of district spending nationally confirm the degree of spread.[7] Fourteen states had arithmetically regressive distributions by income level, and only fifteen of the other states have built in any progressivity.[8]

These funding problems are not about to get better on their own. In an absolute sense, they are getting worse. The states' contributions to grade school education spending have been falling since the 2008 financial crash.[9] Thirty-five states have reduced their pupil spending since then, fourteen of these having cut by more than 10 percent.[10] In the lead for slashing is Oklahoma, where per-pupil spending has fallen by 23 percent.[11] Sadly, the states with the biggest cuts are disproportionately among those already underperforming the national averages in educational proficiency. As contrary as this may be to American educational tradition, there may be no viable alternative to having the federal government play a role in tempering these disparities.

The inescapable depressing fact is that we rank lower by international standards than we have any excuse for. And that, too, like the state spending trend, seems to be a worsening condition. Only 20 percent of young American men have more education than their parents, and 29 percent have less education.[12]

The problems of American education run deeper than relative test scores. Affordability issues at the college level represent an even less tractable problem than average high school proficiency. The middle class bears a disproportionate share of the pain.

Our disappointing national results, though, present the most readily manageable of challenges in American education. Diminishing affordability of college and lack of career preparation for those who are not college bound call for a greater stretch of imagination and, ultimately, more fundamental solutions. The majority of high school students today start a college of some sort.[13] That only half of matriculating students will go all the way to a four-year degree, however, is another failing of our system.[14] The most commonly cited reason for the attrition is cost. Many students can't pay what is demanded and drop their lofty educational goals after a year or two of college. And even those who appear to be winners in the graduation statistics all too often come through the process with a debt load so crushing that no available job will likely allow them to amortize it. This is not particularly painful for those with prosperous parents, but for many middle-class kids the matter is serious.

The whole college experience, from application to graduation, has gotten harder for a great many people in recent years. It is an open secret that some colleges are favoring low-income and high-income applicants over middle-income applicants. This is an inadvertent result of colleges stretching their finances to provide aid to those at the lower end of the socioeconomic scale. That stretch in turn results from their principled commitment to enhance diversity, and to at least approach enrollments that mirror the population in ethnicity and socioeconomic status. The direct beneficiaries are mainly low-income students. Indirectly, though, this trend is also a win for the wealthiest applicants, those whose parents can be expected to pay more than their own children's tuitions. This barbell approach allows the wealthy to subsidize aid to the poorest students and permits the colleges to finance their diversity expenditures. The losers are in the middle class, who used to own — by their numbers and resources — a greater majority of the admissions places. They are now squeezed from both directions, by an increasing reservation of seats for those below them in income and by favoritism for those who will pay more than their own share of college costs. If this is an open secret, it is no secret at all that rapidly rising college costs are in themselves a growing burden on the middle class.

That college tuitions have grown at a rate well above general inflation is much discussed. The statistics require only brief repetition. In the thirty-year span from 1978 to 2008, the overall cost of living roughly tripled.[15] The medical cost component of the Consumer Price Index outpaced it and rose nearly sixfold in that time interval.[16] College tuitions at four-year private colleges, however, beat this formidable increase handily, rising by a factor of almost ten.[17] In 2014–15, the average cost of annual tuition for private four-year institutions was $31,000.[18] Add another $10,000 or more for living expenses, and the costs exceed 75 percent of the median family income in this country.[19] The highest costs were, not surprisingly, at the most academically elite schools and in the most expensive locations. Columbia University's estimate of its tuition, fees, and living expenses in New York City now runs to just about $70,000 for an entering freshman.[20] The equivalent estimate for Harvard, where our son is an undergraduate, is about $65,000.[21] At Brown, his twin sister's school, it's about the same amount.[22] These top schools, of course, have endowments that permit them to subsidize many of their needier students generously. At Harvard, more than 70 percent of students receive significant financial aid.[23] At Brown, with a much smaller endowment, about 50 percent do.[24]

Only a few other colleges, though, can afford to match the Ivies in this regard. Most would not claim that their admissions are need-blind, and you can assume that hardly any private universities are *wealth*-blind. This is an important distinction. State schools are less costly. Their all-in costs tend to run about half those of the private universities.[25] This, however, may not keep. In an era of tax cuts, state schools have been compelled to raise their tuitions and fees at a rate even faster than the private colleges. The real-dollar increase in tuitions and fees at private nonprofit four-year institutions was 10 percent from the 2009–10 academic year to 2015.[26] Public four-year colleges on average raised in-state tuition and fees by 17 percent in the same period.[27]

When middle-class students arrive at college, having overcome whatever degree of admissions bias was working to their disfavor, the stress is far from over. Numerous students at the less richly endowed private colleges have discovered the harsh reality that the scholarship aid they received in their freshman year was not renewable in subsequent years. I was saddened to hear recently that only about half of the students who graduate from the most elite public exam school in our city will finish a four-year college in the normal time. The lack of aid in the later college years is among the most commonly cited reasons for these well-prepared students failing to complete their degrees. Work is often available, but too much work can hollow out the college experience, eating into study hours and fully consuming what would otherwise be extracurricular time. The recourse for most middle-class students is likely to be a student loan.

It's hard not to like the student loan concept. It neatly fits the natural cycle of life. A young scholar of insufficient means borrows to invest in a college education and, based on this investment, has higher lifetime earnings—which allow repayment of the loan. This is all to the good, but, as is often the case, too much of a good thing has its drawbacks. The student loan burden has ballooned with the rapidly enlarging costs of college. About 70 percent of the graduates of four-year colleges have debt to accompany their degrees at the end of their undergraduate years.[28] The average debt load for graduates of private nonprofit four-year colleges is more than $30,000, and the same number for graduates of for-profit four-year institutions is about $40,000.[29] The aggregate school-related debt load held by students and graduates in this country has more than doubled since 2006, from about $500 billion to $1.2 trillion.[30] You may be surprised to learn, as was I, that student debt in the United States now exceeds credit card debt or car loans.[31]

This does not imply that student loan excesses will trigger the next crash, and not everyone agrees that the burden on the graduates is unmanageable, but clearly this is a suboptimal situation for a country as wealthy as ours. I would be less worried about the college loan problem were it not for the other economic woes of the strapped middle class—on whom almost all of this burden falls. Those below them on the economic ladder, if lucky enough to go to college at all, are more likely to have received pure scholarship aid, while those above them don't need to take on the loans. The current state of affairs would be a more tolerable outcome for the middle, and the debt burden more easily manageable, if the employment market for young graduates were better. But it is weak and sticky. The youth unemployment rate reported by the U.S. Bureau of Labor Statistics was 14.3 percent in July of 2014, in sharp contrast with the current overall national unemployment rate of 5.3 percent or the lovely 3.8 percent unemployment recorded during my boyhood years.[32]

The interest rate for student loans is another subject of concern these days. Undergraduates borrowing in 2015 under the federal program are paying 4.29 percent on their loans.[33] One influential Democratic senator has repeatedly pointed out that this is a great deal more than what the Federal Reserve charges the banks to borrow public money. She and others have also noted that while mortgages and consumer loans can often be refinanced when rates turn lower, past student borrowers are stuck with their interest rates for the life of the loans. On the other side of the aisle, a Republican senator with an expressed interest in higher office has said that a better approach than adjusting interest rates is to automatically enroll students in "one unified income-based repayment plan."[34] Maybe they can come together on such a plan. But meanwhile, I can say with confidence that the loan burden on middle-class college students is nothing our country should be proud of. At the very least, it is psychologically demoralizing for those carrying its weight, and it represents a credit risk and collection burden for the lenders. It may push young people away from lower-paying service careers such as teaching and nonprofit work—or away from college in the first place. Financing college educations is a fine national investment that benefits the country as much as the individuals, and we should be looking to make the outcomes less burdensome.

The cost of loans and the increasing charges for tuition are two parts of the same whole. Some observers are now wondering whether the incremental value of a college education is falling. In past years, I have always seen seven-digit numbers attached to the value of a four-year college education. *Bloomberg BusinessWeek* has recently estimated, however, that the thirty-year return over cost for the average college graduate is only $353,000, even with what Bloomberg considers generous assumptions.[35] According to this survey, engineering schools produce net returns twice that of liberal arts schools, but only a handful of schools produce the seven-figure lifetime gains that have been loosely estimated in the past.[36] Any such measurement, moreover, is an admixture of understatement and overstatement that should be separated into component parts to be useful. Children from the upper end of the economic spectrum earn more at age forty than children from the lower end, regardless of education. It is a safe wager that education at *any* level is worth less than the luck of having been born to parents with endowments of capital and powerful friends. Educational success stories are always heartwarming, but winning what someone cleverly called "the ovarian lottery" is more valuable.

Bootstrappers will first be faced with a disadvantage in the admissions process. Then, they will be confronted with those ever-higher college charges. Next, if they take on loans, they will have a burden that hangs heavily over them as they start new phases of their lives. Finally, they may discover that the degrees they earned were not as valuable to them as to their more privileged roommates. Social mobility is a key factor in the worth of a degree. As mobility declines, and wealth becomes stickier at the top, the value of higher education declines. At the extreme, a society with zero economic mobility is definitionally one in which a degree, no matter how admirable and hard earned, can offer no upward momentum. The majority of American families are caught in a vise. One jaw is the rising cost of education, tending toward the unaffordable, and the other jaw is the decreasing return to education, powered by income and wealth stratification. I don't foresee the pressure from either jaw relenting anytime soon on its own. Because this situation is a fundamental threat to the country's future, we must accept the need to look for solutions beyond the small fixes. True solutions will require policy directions the country would otherwise not be ready for.

The current educational system is doing a worse job for those who are not college bound. We Americans are embarrassingly far behind the rest of the developed world in vocational and technical training.

When I first visited the troubled high school that I am involved with, I noticed at once the profusion of Ivy League college banners in its halls. While appreciating the inspirational purpose of these pennants, I wondered aloud if they might not do more harm to youthful spirits than good. I asked one of the principals to research what percentage of the students in that school's ninth grade some years back had graduated from *any* four-year college by now. The data was imperfect, but the estimate he and I developed together was less than 1 percent. While the equivalent number for the entire school district is obviously better than that, it barely breaks out of the single digits.[37] Chicago, whose statistics I happened to see recently, has results no better and likely worse.[38]

There's no doubt that one of the purposes of grade school education is to prepare people for college, but that can't be the only purpose. The raw statistics on educational attainment in the United States should make this clear. Almost 60 percent of American students will embark on some college journey. About 20 percent, or one-third of this group, will drop out without any degree; another 10 percent will stop after getting an associate's degree. That means that just over 30 percent of young Americans will complete a bachelor's degree.[39] The number keeps rising, which is encouraging, but the graduate population is only now approaching one-third of the population.

Boston school superintendents used to give a standard stump speech about preparing every student for college. The aspiration was noble but patently unrealistic. Recently, a more meaningful goal has been reflected in the school officials' talks: preparing every child for college *or career.* That has to be the real purpose of a high school education. And to accomplish that objective, we must offer vocational training as well as liberal arts courses. The degree of preparedness for college or a meaningful job is incomparably more important than the commonly measured high school graduation rate. The latter is too often little more than a proxy for attendance.

There was mention earlier of a conservative economist who would trade away twelfth grade entirely for mandatory kindergarten. A former Labor Department Secretary of the other political persuasion has suggested combining the last year of high school with the first year of a serious vocational training program. As he puts it, "Too often in modern America, we equate 'equal opportunity' with an opportunity to get a four-year liberal arts degree. It should mean an opportunity to learn what's necessary to get a good job."[40] The key to sound technical training is teacher involvement with employers in program design, and student involvement with employers in the course of the actual training regimen. The most effective associate's degree programs and nonprofit organizations combine schooling with internships. A couple of the best are here in Boston, working by contract with major employers to simultaneously train kids and start them off in real work.

Making all students aware of their options and granting them access to useful preparation can only have a net benefit. But these steps won't be enough. The scale of voluntary, private programs is nowhere near sufficient, and it can never be. While this will be no contribution to rigorous analytics, you should someday take a cruise through any rough neighborhood, anywhere, and count the number of people you see sitting idly on their doorsteps. It will help to drive home the point on the emotional and intuitive level. We are failing a large portion of society and failing ourselves by wasting all of that potentially skilled manpower and bearing all of the corollary social costs. Unemployment rates, frightening enough in areas where school performance gaps are greatest, exclude people not actively looking for jobs. They don't begin to tell the sad story of chronic *non*-employment in America.

The European Union has long emphasized vocational education. The United Kingdom has offered technical training in trade schools since 1907. Starting in 1994, publicly funded Modern Apprenticeships have been available to provide "quality training on a work-based route," and the government has committed to making apprenticeships a mainstream part of England's education system. Germany is arguably the leader in vocational education. As many as two-thirds of all German students participate in vocational training programs.[41] German law codifies the shared vocational training responsibility of the state, the unions, and associations of trade and industry. Over 51 percent of all young people in Germany under the age of twenty-two have actually completed an apprenticeship.[42] One of every three German companies offers apprenticeships. The vocational education systems in the other German-speaking countries are similar, and qualification from one such nation can generally be carried to the next. In the Netherlands, around 50 percent of students leaving lower secondary school enter one of four vocational programs.

The Scandinavian countries have also made large commitments to vocational and technical training. Nearly all of those leaving Swedish compulsory schooling enter upper secondary schools, divided into thirteen vocationally oriented and four academic streams. The vocational programs include fifteen weeks of workplace training over the three-year period. After the nine-year comprehensive school, almost all Finnish students choose to go either to an academic high school, which prepares students for tertiary education, or to a free vocational school. Half of Norwegian lower-school graduates enter one of nine vocational programs, which generally involve two years of schooling followed by two years of apprenticeship in a company.

Asian countries, including Japan, Korea, India, and China, have relied for years on a massive vocational education structure. Australia offers traineeships for students in tenth, eleventh, and twelfth grades, followed by contractually binding apprenticeships in traditional trades and traineeships in service occupations.

> There are two principal reasons that our country neglects first-rate vocational training. One is that local financing of high school education causes funds for this work to be least available where the need is greatest, especially in an era of tax parsimony; and the other is a fear of injustices that may arise from early tracking.

The United States is in the minor leagues for vocational and technical training. We rely on individual initiative and market forces to educate and place young people. This is not necessarily a bad call for most of the population, but it works miserably for folks at the bottom of the economic pyramid — and especially for those without resources and of color. It is straightforward to see that this passivity has been contributing to the creation of a permanently underemployed and unemployed stratum. The existence of a multigenerational cohort of marginally employed citizens, in turn, imposes all manner of pain on its members and all manner of costs on the rest of society. So, I hope you are wondering why this country doesn't set up vocational and training programs like everyone else. The answer is a strange-bedfellows alliance across the political spectrum. The tax revolt mentality of our era helps keep conservatives from supporting these programs. At least as important, a comprehensive solution will require funding that cuts across neighborhoods, and conservatives see this as undermining the local control they hold dear.

Liberals, and more than a few of their conservative colleagues, find a wholly different reason to balk. Their concern is that many other nations' training regimes depend on tracking students from roughly age fourteen into either the higher-education track or the technical track. This is unacceptable to the Left due to a fear that rigid teenage tracking, even if nominally or substantively voluntary, will cause serious, irreversible injustice to late bloomers or young folks whose talents just don't show up on standardized tests. Another concern, given the performance gaps often noted in high school statistics, is that a destructive, divisive signal would be sent if our technical and higher-education tracks differed in too great a measure by race, color, or ethnicity. This last specter, sometimes referred to as "soft bigotry," is largely absent in more homogeneous societies with which the United States is often compared.

What well-intentioned thinkers fear in terms of signaling may, in fact, represent a danger, but we can all work to avoid invidious signals without placing illusory, utopian goals in front of young people and denying them training that would actually be highly useful later in life. There is a difficult tightrope to walk here, but surely it is important to walk it. The first African American president of this country has joined a number of his predecessors from everywhere on the political spectrum in calling for more vocational education, and he's no bigot.

I grew up in an era when explicit tracking was taken for granted. At the start of seventh grade, my class of about 240 was split into deciles of two dozen each. Those students thought to be most academically promising were placed into Section 7-1, the next most talented in 7-2, and so on to 7-10, which might today be labeled as a special education segment. The material taught in the classes became less academically challenging and the curriculum more vocational as the ranking numbers got higher. All of us knew where everyone else was placed. Today, that scheme would be considered repugnant, and the reasoning is understandable. The rub, however, is that we have allowed a variety of less explicit forms of tracking to continue. The top students can go to public exam schools or to elite private and prep schools for a challenging curriculum. Those with learning issues have special ed. It is only in the middle that distinctions have been lost, mainly to the detriment of the less academically proficient slice of that middle. The loss of distinction has become an obstacle to instituting the vocational training needed to match the rest of the developed world.

If this country wanted to insert meaningful vocational and technical training courses into the high school curriculum, it could do it. Course selection could be emphatically voluntary, and a good bit of flexibility could be built in for switching paths in the later high school years. But this simply isn't happening. A more realistic alternative is to concentrate on the years after high school, when tracking is seen as less objectionable. Tracking at ages beyond eighteen doesn't carry the same degree of unfairness for late bloomers; and as the individual affected gets older, it is easier for that person and for the rest of us to see the adverse consequences of neglect with respect to career training. No one can deny that adult life in a market economy will inevitably create tracks. One strategy for investing in vocational training after the high school years is to build more and better facilities for technical training at the associate's degree level. I would be happy to see that. Unfortunately, budget constraints and residual fears of injustice remain teamed up to marginalize these efforts. High schools could do more, but even attenuated forms of student tracking may be incompatible with our national culture.

> The best cure for what ails education in America is universal national service. It would be good for all strata of society. It could provide technical training to those not headed to college, and financial support for those who are. At the same time, it would reinforce a constructive form of patriotism and, not incidentally, produce highly useful work output for the benefit of the economy.

Universal national service is an attractive idea for a number of reasons. The first is that it is a way everyone can acknowledge the gift we receive simply for being resident in this tolerant, free, and prosperous country. Patriotism is not a bad motive for a program. The second is that there is much constructive work to be done by a corps of young workers, work that would benefit all of us economically. Third, the social mixing that a universal service corps would necessarily provide would be a spiritually healthy tonic for a melting-pot nation that is otherwise becoming too stratified. These three reasons have been cited in the occasional debate by proponents of the national service concept since it was first discussed. All are good enough arguments, but they have been insufficiently convincing over the years to gain traction.

A fourth justification, though, has pulled me on board. If we rule out the explicit tracking of students that other nations employ, universal national service is the best possible complement and supplement for an educational system that is becoming hazardously less functional for all but the well-to-do. You may at first think national service too indirect or sweeping a remedy for educational shortcomings, an overly broad cure for what seems a narrow problem, but it is in fact the only realistic remedy likely to provide us with educational outcomes worthy of this country. When obvious routes to solving a puzzle are blocked, sometimes an oblique attack is not only required but proves to be even more powerful in the end.

During my junior high school days, John F. Kennedy's inaugural speech called out to all of us: "My fellow Americans, ask not what your country can do for you. Ask what you can do for your country." Nobody I knew thought it was corny or utopian at the time. The modern version of universal national service, a particularly responsive answer to Kennedy's call, had been talked about since around the time of JFK's birth. In a much-quoted essay, philosopher William James called for the "conscription of the whole youthful population" so that "injustice would tend to be evened out" and our young would "get the childishness knocked out of them."[43] Franklin Roosevelt's Civilian Conservation Corps was the first large-scale working embodiment of this notion. Although full universality was not a part of the plan, at one time the CCC was arranging for more than 2.5 million corps members to work in its more than four thousand camps. They planted something in excess of three billion trees and developed many hundreds of parks that remain in full use today.[44]

Then, after a hiatus, came Kennedy's Peace Corps. Like the CCC, it was less than universal. By the late 1960s, at its peak, the Peace Corps had around sixteen thousand volunteers.[45] President Lyndon Johnson expanded the menu of service options with the Job Corps, Head Start, Community Action, and Volunteers in Service to America, or VISTA. He called for a program by which "every young American will have the opportunity—and feel the obligation—to give at least a few years of his or her life to the service of others in this nation and the world."[46] In 1976, California governor Jerry Brown founded his own state-level version of the CCC, which (like Governor Brown himself) has survived all these decades and is doing the same job today. These are good programs, but they are much too small to solve the education issues you should be concerned about.

Service to country and to those in need is not a particularly partisan issue. In 1988, then Governor Bill Clinton and others proposed that federal college student aid be conditioned on a period of national service. After President Clinton convinced Congress to establish a new national service program called AmeriCorps, forty-nine governors, amply representing both parties, signed a letter to Congress supporting its strengthening and reauthorization.[47] The program found strong support from the Republican chair of the House Budget Committee. The number of AmeriCorps positions would reach fifty thousand. In 1997, President Clinton and former President George H. W. Bush convened a bipartisan summit, attended by four living presidents and chaired by General Colin Powell, to launch another voluntary national youth service program.[48] The second President Bush advocated a two-year required service program for every American in 2002, and Republican Senators John McCain and Orrin Hatch joined Senator Ted Kennedy as strong supporters of the 2009 Serve America Act, expanding the voluntary AmeriCorps and adding five new service initiatives.[49] But out of all this has still come nothing like a truly universal national service program.

Although the exact details are not as simple to construct as the concept, my notion of universal national service would call for every young person to perform at least one year of service in an approved field, sometime between the ages of seventeen and twenty-two. A second-year reenlistment would be available on a voluntary basis. The work to which the young people would be assigned would be, at the option of the participant, in one of three areas: military, public works and infrastructure, or social services. All of the existing youth service programs of the federal government would be folded into one of these three umbrella categories. There would be compensation in each category, of course, with pay scales designed to provide by incentive the right number of volunteers for each route. On the military side, where compensation would almost surely be highest and a two-year enlistment would likely be required, the need is obvious. The national service program would replace the all-volunteer military recruiting structure in use since the abolition of the draft. While the military, even now, is among the most ethnically diverse of large organizations anywhere in the country, the national service program would diversify it further. Today's military, moreover, if measured by family income, is not particularly diverse. The national service program would make it more so.

Potentially useful work on the maintenance and creation of American infrastructure is not hard to identify. Here is the American Society of Civil Engineers 2013 Report Card on American infrastructure.[50] The society grades on the basis of "capacity, condition, funding, future need, operation and maintenance, public safety and resilience."

AVIATION	D
BRIDGES	C+
DAMS	D
DRINKING WATER	D
ENERGY	D+
HAZARDOUS WASTE	D
INLAND WATERWAYS	D-
LEVEES	D-
PORTS	C
PARKS & RECREATION	C-
RAIL	C+
ROADS	D
SCHOOLS	D
SOLID WASTE	B-
TRANSIT	D
WASTEWATER	D

A grade of C is characterized by the society as mediocre, and a grade of D is poor. The figure offered for estimated infrastructure investment needed by 2020 is a whopping $3.6 trillion.[51] A sage once warned that you should never ask a barber if you need a haircut. Perhaps the nation's civil engineers, as infrastructure barbers, will tend to bias their estimates upward, but not one expert on this subject I can find seems to disagree directionally. Our existing infrastructure is fraying and needs serious attention.

Many young hands could be used to build new types of infrastructure as well, perhaps to help green the economy for independence, efficiency, and sustainability. Infrastructure often represents an investment in future economic prosperity. Our parents' and grandparents' generations understood and acknowledged this better than we do. As President Dwight Eisenhower was later to say of his massive 1950s Interstate Highway initiative, "More than any single action by the government since the end of the war, this one would change the face of America . . . Its impact on the American economy — the jobs it would produce in manufacturing and construction, the rural areas it would open up — was beyond calculation."[52] A corps of young workers would be a solution to a physical deficit that otherwise seems intractable. On the social services side, the opportunities are legion. Volunteers, under the umbrellas of AmeriCorps, Senior Corps, Learn and Serve America, the Peace Corps, Teach for America, and other initiatives, are already doing much of what a universal program would encourage — and there is always more to be done.

As for the psyche of our society, I can't imagine that the mixing of people from many diverse backgrounds, working together for common purpose, would be other than felicitous. The World War I and II drafts, as almost everyone who talks about them attests, helped meld a disparate population of immigrants, industrial workers, and farmers into the nation that became the envy of the world. People will never tend to trust those they know little about. False prejudices and narrow suspicion would surely be reduced if everyone were exposed to, and labored side by side with, others of all stripes and origins. Compassion and the sense of national unity would surely be increased. For the privileged, this mixing would provide a healthy wake-up call and a lesson in our fundamental sameness. For the others, there would not only be these pluses but also the baked-in economic gains from training and work experience.

Among the most commonly asked questions when this suggestion is raised relates to its compulsory nature. Obviously, some young people would have to be excused on the basis of physical or psychological disability. That kind of exemption poses nothing by way of a conceptual problem. But what of the healthy youth who simply refuses, even when offered a broad menu of jobs that should satisfy most any conscience? In our society it is hard to imagine sending anyone to prison for this. I came of age in the Vietnam War era, and I recall struggling with the ethical and policy complexities implicated when a college acquaintance was taken from school and sent to federal prison for burning his draft card. Many of us would have trouble supporting criminal penalties for a young person refusing national service, whether the impediment was on moral or religious grounds or simply a case of juvenile stubbornness. I hope you could, however, support the loss of any of the specific rewards that go with national service — and some additional hold-backs of a noncriminal sort. We could logically, for example, set back the retirement age for Social Security by the time not spent in service by those who simply refused. We could deny the use of various government grants and subsidies that would otherwise be available. We could refuse eligibility for certain government jobs until national service was completed. None of these sanctions involve plucking someone from home and caging the young violator in a penitentiary. And there is no reason why a person with a change of heart, moreover, couldn't perform the refused service requirement at a later stage of life. Not all of the participants would have to be young to be of use.

All of the traditional arguments for universal national service might be marginally insufficient were it not the best answer to problems we must solve within our educational system. But it is. National service can provide a response to the pain of college costs. Part of the compensation for service could come in a sizable reduction of principal or interest on student loans. This approach could transform our student loan programs from a mixed blessing into an unquestioned benefit, and it could rescue the middle class from the emerging nightmare of finding education beyond reasonable reach. If properly designed to emphasize technical and vocational training, national service would be an even greater boon to those who are not college bound. For many of these young people, it could be nothing short of rescue. For those who would stay for the voluntary second year, moreover, the national service corps might even be able to extend an associate's degree. Everyone who might otherwise drift after high school would have a chance to find there the essential skills and discipline to change life's course for the better.

There are other objections to compulsory national service. A 2013 article in the *Atlantic* listed thirteen contrary arguments.[53] A publication of the Brookings Institution in 2002 listed five reasons to describe national service as a "Bad Idea Whose Time Is Past."[54] No lesser intellects than the late Nobel laureate economist Gary Becker and Judge Richard Posner listed their arguments against compulsory service in a 2007 blog.[55] Those national service opponents who list among their verbal assaults that the whole concept violates the Thirteenth Amendment (which prohibits slavery) will presumably not be convincible. Most of the other, and more reasonable, common objections are based on various forms of numerical cost-benefit analysis. Some learned opponents estimate the annual cost of a service program at about $27,000 per person.[56] Since there are roughly four million Americans reaching their eighteenth birthday each year, this leads to an estimate of the costs for a universal program at more than $100 billion annually. Then, the critics say, we should add the lost value to the economy from diverting young people from their private-sector jobs and throw in more for interrupting the work of those already volunteering. To this, they wish to add the costs to individuals of postponing their education for a year or more.

The cost arguments are not frivolous. Care should certainly be taken to be as frugal as possible in the operation of a service program. It doesn't have to cost $27,000 per person, though, or even close to that. An Aspen Institute publication estimates the cost of present national service programs to be more like $16,000 per full-time equivalent.[57] Parsimony requires paying for different types of work at different levels such that the demand for labor and its supply are balanced, and no more. It requires minimizing housing costs by allowing many civilian service corps workers to remain in their own private housing. It calls for use to the fullest extent possible of existing structures and programs consistent with service goals — with a maximum of participant choice. Finally, it means — in the case of many participants — using educational subsidies in partial place of salary. For many participants, reduced interest on, or fractional forgiveness of, student loans could be more attractive than full current salaries. Outright grants might be reserved for those young people meeting a need test or serving extra time at reduced salary.

While a universal national service program needn't carry the gross cost of $100 billion a year that critics imagine, even half that cost would not be a trivial sum to allocate. The real problem with the critics' argument, though, is that it intentionally confuses gross costs with net costs. To go from gross to net in this case, one must subtract the value of the output from the labors of the four million annual recruits. By the simplistic gross cost argument, no one could have believed that the Roosevelt administration's WPA (Works Progress Administration) and

CCC qualified as sound expenditures. If benefits are ignored, Eisenhower's highway program should also be considered an extravagance. And the enormous recent spending in China on fast trains, roads, and new urban housing units could be universally written off as a wasteful undertaking. The real story is much more complicated.

Net is the same as gross only when a program produces nothing at all. It is inconceivable that the useful work product of any serious universal national service program would be zero. Infrastructure spending on this scale would surely engender some yield today through its direct stimulus effects and more tomorrow through enhancement of economic growth. There would be economic savings in some amount from vocational training that puts people in jobs rather than prisons or relief programs. When the full accounting is taken, those of us who support national service see it as actually providing a net benefit rather than a net cost. The Aspen Institute study confidently states that the ratio of economic benefit to cost in publicly sponsored volunteer youth programs is already nearly four to one.[58] It estimates the narrowly defined benefit ratio (taking only direct taxpayer benefits into account) for programs involving seniors today at nearly two to one.[59] The same source sees this ratio as amenable to a dramatic improvement if the programs were larger, perhaps bringing the overall benefits to five times the cost. This is an advocate's view, and maybe the ratios will not in fact prove to be quite so impressive. We should readily grant that the projection of results for a hypothetical program defies objective precision. What we can quite confidently assert is that to ignore economic benefits and talk only of the costs is sophistry. And recall that the revenue enhancements proposed in earlier chapters, including the repeal of unproductive tax expenditures and counterproductive trust and estate giveaways, would pay even the inflated gross cost estimates of the sophists several times over.

The easy thesis on education is that universal national service is not just a sound answer to the issues in American education. It is likely to be the only feasible answer.

American education is not properly serving the country or its largest constituencies. Educational attainment results are disappointing by international standards. Middle-class kids are being prejudicially screened against in college admissions or, if admitted, saddled with more costs than they can be reasonably expected to bear. Although loan programs help, the subsequent debt load can be crushing. Middle-class kids who are not college bound, and all the more so kids from lower economic strata headed for careers after high school, are given few of the skills that will ready them for the careers available to them. Our country offers only a meager fraction of the technical and vocational training opportunities that other economically advanced nations provide their youth.

There are a number of ways to alleviate these problems, starting with improving high school quality generally—which can be accomplished by the adoption of established and proven best practices. While high schools might be able in theory to upgrade vocational training, two potentially insurmountable fiscal and cultural barriers have so far stood in the way. The mismatch between need and available local funding is an intractable feature of our society, and the youthful aptitude tracking used most places in the world is mismatched to deep themes in our culture. High schools, moreover, cannot solve the financial burdens of college.

The nexus between universal national service and education is not obvious at first. Universal national service, however, offers the only workable answer to the major issues in American education compatible with cultural realities. It would be an attractive course for its patriotic and social harmony benefits as well. The right program would trade service for financing in the case of the college contingent and provide the absent vocational training for those ending their academic training after high school. It would give a boon to the rest of us as well, in the form of useful output—for the military, for public works and infrastructure improvement, and for the social service sectors. It would be transformational for the kids and for the country.

FOUR

Health Care

> The United States spends over a trillion dollars a year more than it should by peer standards on health care, and our health outcomes are no better for it. It is far easier to identify where we spend more money than peer countries do than it is to prevent the overspending. A full measure of savings can be gained only by moving away from competition among providers and toward what is generally called a single-payer system—although the single-overseer aspect of such a system is more important than the unification of the payment mechanism.

WHAT COUNTRY SPENDS the highest percentage of its GNP on health care in the developed world? I would be surprised if you don't already know the answer. It's our country, of course, and by a wide margin. It is a safe wager, in fact, that anyone who has shown the interest to read this far already knows the central story about our American system of health care. The depressing truth is that we spend substantially more than other prosperous nations on health care, yet our health outcomes are less favorable than most. The supersize spending comes right from your pocketbooks, through a combination of out-of-pocket costs, health insurance premiums, and taxes. The excess over international peer norms is, by any standard, thousands of dollars per year per person, and it is money you should think hard about whether you really want to be spending. Here is a refresher on the facts, followed by a discussion of why it doesn't have to be this way.

A report from the Institute of Medicine sums up the outcome data this way: "When compared with the average of peer countries, Americans as a group fare worse in at least nine health areas: infant mortality and low birth weight; injuries and homicides; adolescent pregnancy and sexually transmitted infections; HIV and AIDS; drug-related deaths; obesity and diabetes; heart disease; chronic lung disease; [and] disability."[1] The World Health Organization makes the same point with different metrics: average life expectancy at birth, infant and maternal mortality, healthy life expectancy at birth, and life expectancy at age sixty. In every category the United States ranks less favorably than the other wealthiest nations, without regard for continent.[2] The Commonwealth Fund has recently ranked health-care systems in eleven leading economies according to both quality and access. It ranks the United States eleventh.[3]

Yet another useful comparison is with our single most similar peer and using the most salient statistic. At birth, the life expectancy of a Canadian male is eighty years, four years more than that of a U.S. male. Female life expectancy is several years longer in both countries, and the gap between the two nations is about the same. For those who prefer to look a little more subjectively at "healthy life expectancy," the picture is similar. The American newborn, without regard to gender, can expect sixty-nine years of healthy life; the equivalent Canadian, seventy-two.[4] So, whatever the costs may be, we should not be smug about our health system. Despite the familiar boastful rhetoric to the contrary, our health care would certainly not appear from the outcome data to be "the best in the world."

"Hey, wait just a minute," someone may say. "The relative deficiency is not in our health care but in some differential genetic factors, demographics, or lifestyle choices." The genetics are still largely unknown, but it is certainly not obvious that our genes are on the whole worse than those of the citizens of all those other countries. The demographic facts are more accessible. One fallacious argument I hear, based on demographics, is that we must have an older population than the others. If we did, we might be spending more than our peers and seeing higher death rates, but our lifetime results shouldn't be worse. And, more important in rebuttal, we aren't older than most of our wealthy peers. Our country's median age is about thirty-seven, ranking us somewhere in the second quartile of all nations. Japan, at nearly forty-five, has a much grayer population and sits near the top with respect to outcomes. Canada, too, has an older population, and so do almost all of the European countries.[5]

Some of the difference may be attributable to higher levels of poverty in America, although the bottom decile incomes in our peer nations are not so different from our own lowest deciles. Another element could be the now-evaporating pool of uninsured citizens, who may have sought health care more reluctantly during the outcome sample periods than they would have in nations with universal coverage. This almost certainly biased our score on the Commonwealth Fund rankings. On the other hand, several studies suggest that even Americans who enjoy all the demographic advantages—white, insured, and college educated—have less favorable outcomes than similar individuals in other countries.[6] Maybe we overeat more often, or smoke and drink more, or exercise less than the others, but that, too, appears to be less than obvious in the available data. If you travel, you have probably witnessed high rates of smoking and drinking elsewhere, and gym rats seem to predominate here in the States. I don't wish to claim certainty about how much explanatory power some genetic, demographic, or lifestyle difference may have in shaping the results. It can be safely concluded, though, that if we have some adverse distinctions, our health-care system fails to compensate for them.

Now turn to the costs. Americans today spend about $2.9 trillion on health care annually, which is 18 percent of our gross domestic product.[7] No other wealthy nation spends more than about 11 percent of GDP.[8] The European average is less than 10 percent.[9] To make matters worse, the costs here have been rising faster than inflation for many years. In the years from 1990 to 2008, it rose at an intimidating average annual rate of over 7 percent.[10] President Obama took notice of this in 2009 when he said, "By a wide margin, the biggest threat to our nation's balance sheet is the skyrocketing cost of health care. It's not even close."[11] The average cost to the system for one night in a hospital bed in Western Europe is less than $1,000. That bed you'd prefer to avoid costs over $4,200 a night here in the United States.[12]

If this isn't story enough, a study by Deloitte Consulting suggests that we are underestimating the costs by the accepted measurements. The usual measurements exclude what Americans so generously spend on all manner of alternative medicines and practitioners. They similarly exclude weight loss, diet, and fitness programs taken on for health improvement; a good fraction of ambulatory services; nutritional supplements; health periodicals; and, most of all, supervisory care for the infirm and the elderly performed by other than for-pay professionals. The Deloitte team believes that the hidden costs may amount to almost another 20 cents for every dollar reported in the government's National Health Expenditure Accounts.[13] While the numbers that follow ignore the Deloitte findings, thus allowing the use of conveniently available data, I have no reason to doubt Deloitte's estimates.

These nearly incredible costs, inexplicably, seem to be taken for granted now by many health-care policy analysts—as though they have always been a feature of our "best in the world" system. This is simply not the case. Take a look at the chart in Figure 4.1, which looks at the period from 1960 to 1986.[14]

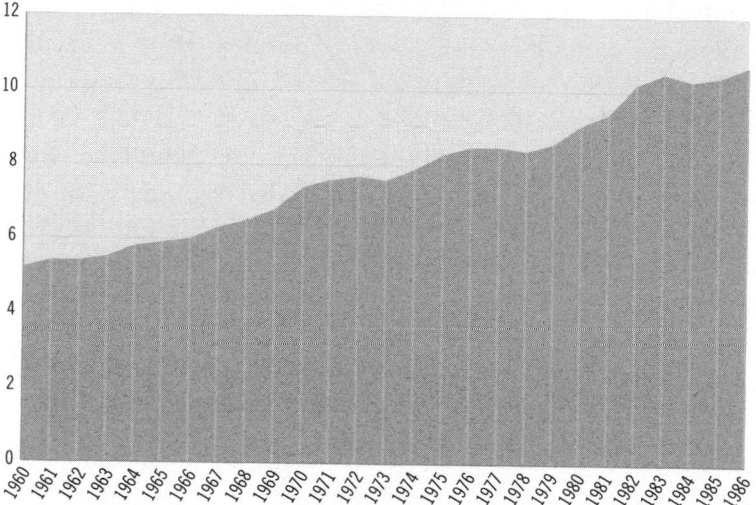

Figure 4.1

As recently as 1985, the United States was spending only 10 percent of GNP on health care, about the international standard today. In 1950, we were spending only 4 percent of GNP. You might want to look at the current spending disparity this way: In our economy, with a $16 trillion gross national product, the aggregate cost of health care is almost $3 trillion, and the extra eight points we spend that others don't spend runs to just about $1.3 trillion. And that's an annual number. Imagine what impact this much money could have if the overspending ceased and the difference became available for other private or public purposes. As a bonus, and not an insubstantial one, American manufactured products would be better able to compete in world markets. Not that I recommend it, but every couple of years of saving at this rate could cover a whole new war. Estimates are that the war in Iraq and the war in Afghanistan have together cost us about $6 trillion from inception.[15] Or, better than that, we could restore the country's infrastructure and rebuild the schools and bridges. Or, since nearly half of health-care costs leave your pocketbook in the form of taxes, we could have the mother of all tax cuts.[16]

A trillion is an incomprehensibly large number. One commonly used device to give it some intuitive meaning is the observation that a trillion dollars laid end to end would reach all the way to the sun and halfway back. A friend suggested another metric. Based on recently published New York City real property market value assessments, a trillion-dollar investor (if such existed) could purchase, without benefit of a mortgage, every single nonexempt building in the Big Apple—and still have more than $10 billion left over for redecorating them to suit.[17] And that's the amount I am suggesting we shouldn't have to spend. And, I repeat, it's an annual amount.

A direct quantification of total health spending, rather than just the excess amount, may also help in absorbing the reality at play here. Ultimately, whether through taxes or premiums, you and I are collectively paying the entirety of the health-care bill. On a per-capita basis, the total cost of American health care is close to $9,000 annually, or almost $23,000 for the average American family.[18] You can multiply that $9,000 number by your own family size for a rough approximation of what you are spending every year. The next-highest number for per-capita spending I could find is Norway's, at $6,000.[19] And Norway, by the way, has the highest per-capita income of any other substantial country in the world, almost half again our own — so the pain there is doubly reduced.[20] Japan's per-capita cost is about half as much as ours.[21] The chart in Figure 4.2 sums up the situation visually.[22]

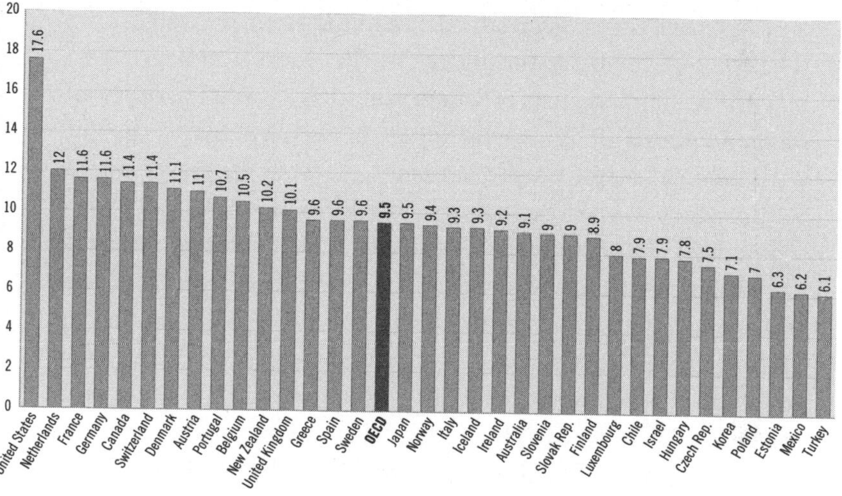

Figure 4.2

We are the only true outlier in the upward direction. We're number 1 — and that's not good. And what you spend each year on health care, directly and indirectly, is likely more than you spend on anything else. The average annual expenditure on housing is about $18,000, but that cost is per family unit, so it is less than the health cost total. Transportation spending is about

$9,000 per year, but again this is per family. Food costs are almost $7,000 per family unit.[23] Nothing else is even in the ballpark of health care. These are, via government and private expenditures, your big outbound dollars.

There is little mystery to the sources of the costs. Five categories of expense explain the total fairly well. The first place many analysts look for excess is in doctors' and nurses' incomes.

The essential drivers of high cost in our system are well known. The apple of outsize spending can be sliced any number of ways, so various scholarly lists of where our costs exceed the other advanced nations' differ. My list looks, in no particular order, like this: medical sector pay, technology and testing, prescriptions, administration and marketing, and end-of-life care.

Medical sector compensation is a touchy topic. I know hardly any doctor or nurse who doesn't feel underpaid. As one who deeply admires the dedication and sacrifices required in this grittier profession than my own, and where most all are paid less than a top business executive, I don't enjoy arguing with medical professionals. The better comparison for this analysis, though, is not with business entrepreneurs, but with doctors in other nations. The facts are easier to ascertain than to interpret. Our doctors are, without a doubt, paid more than their counterparts in other nations, but the comparison is a little short of apples to apples. The most commonly cited distinction is that a higher percentage of doctors in the United States are specialists. This is certainly true, and it is just as indisputable that specialists give up more of their youthful years in training than general practitioners — a reasonable justification for higher pay. Were I a specialist, I would expect a reward for my hard-earned skills, and I might be edgy if anyone challenged my right to pretty darned good pay. This book, though, is not looking to blame anyone for high incomes but rather to raise questions about the system. So, it is fair to ask what our society gains from paying doctors, including specialists and generalists taken together, more than other countries do.

The mean income for a primary care physician in the United States is about $225,000 a year. The average specialist earns more like $400,000, which is the highest average pay in any of the major American professional occupations — which mine (business) is not considered to be.[24] The average physician in Norway, Sweden, Portugal, or Italy brings home less than $100,000 in equivalent purchasing power.[25] In the United Kingdom, Germany, France, and Canada, physicians' compensation averages something closer to $150,000.[26] Our general practitioners earn more than the other countries' generalists, and our specialists earn more than other countries' specialists. The mix in the United States, moreover, favors specialists about three to two over generalists, which raises the combined average; elsewhere the general practitioners tend to outnumber the specialists.[27] Specialists are, understandably, harder to see than family doctors. Maybe that helps explain why the average member country in the OECD has about one and one-half times as many doctors' visits per capita as the United States.[28] Society might be better off with a different mix of physician types, favoring more general practitioners, but I can't say that with any confidence. Certainly, the incentives for an upcoming medical student are all the other way.

Incentives, in general, drive results. When incentives influence high-minded career choices so as to produce a less-than-optimal outcome for society, the appropriate public response would be a dispassionate evaluation of policies that might shift those choices. Where the system's incentives and human nature interact to inspire skullduggery, though, indignation and demand for better enforcement are more suitable reactions. In an influential article in *The New Yorker,* Atul Gawande, a surgeon and Harvard Medical School professor, offered an example of how some doctors are gaining, not by investing in expertise, but by gaming the system.[29] The focus of his piece was McAllen, Texas, a poor town on the Mexican border. The average Medicare expenditure per patient there in 2006 was $15,000, twice the national average. It was also twice as high as in El Paso, another border town with similar demographics. And the expense differentials were of fairly recent vintage, almost all of them arising during the preceding fifteen years.

According to Gawande:

> Between 2001 and 2005, critically ill Medicare patients received almost fifty percent more specialist visits in McAllen than in El Paso, and were two-thirds more likely to see ten or more specialists in a six-month period. In 2005 and 2006, patients in McAllen received twenty percent more abdominal ultrasounds, thirty percent more bone-density studies, sixty percent more stress tests with echocardiography, two hundred percent more nerve-conduction studies to diagnose carpal-tunnel syndrome, and five hundred and fifty percent more urine-flow studies to diagnose prostate troubles. They received one-fifth to two-thirds more gallbladder operations, knee replacements, breast biopsies, and bladder scopes. They also received two to three times as many pacemakers, implantable defibrillators, cardiac-bypass operations, carotid endarterectomies, and coronary-artery stents. And Medicare paid for five times as many home-nurse visits. The primary cause of McAllen's extreme costs was, very simply, the across-the-board overuse of medicine.

The overuse, of course, led to higher take-homes for the participating doctors. What happened in McAllen was surely extreme and atypical, and in a recent update of the article Gawande indicates that much of the excess has now been curbed.[30] Still, we should assume that less visible bits of McAllen behavior arise nearly everywhere. That is just human nature. Doctors, like the rest of us, come in all stripes of morality and talent for self-justification. Where the incentive structure allows enrichment from a tactic like gross overutilization of medical services, a few will abuse that structure wholesale, and many more will take just a little advantage of it. In many cases, the harmful behavior need not even be undertaken consciously. The mind has a marvelous ability to rationalize any course of action that serves maximization of personal rewards, especially when the merits of decisions are as legitimately hazy in ethical terms as choosing the right amount and course of treatment for a sick patient.

You can assume that mini-McAllen behaviors abound, even in a profession with more idealism and generally higher ethics than in the population as a whole. Doctors are relatively free to "upcode" Medicare and Medicaid patients, logging in at the margin the more serious of several possible diagnoses and thus raising their own possible billing ranges. They can use, wherever allowable, expensive out-of-network providers to assist and consult on procedures. They can choose to actively treat a condition another physician would watch and wait on. They can design a follow-up visit schedule liberally or conservatively. Almost every doctor I have talked to about this confirms that end runs around price controls are easy for those who want to employ them. And these end runs have equal opportunity availability to cheaters and sincere believers in activist treatment alike.

The market for health care is especially vulnerable to this pattern, because it is a classic example of a market with few of the prerequisites for competitive efficiency. Health-care consumers almost never have sufficient price and quality information, or the skill and freedom, to select their vendors in a manner typical of simpler markets. We almost never know the details of what we ought to be seeking when we see a doctor; we don't know much about the differing choices available through other suppliers of medical advice and treatment; nor do we know much about outcome data or probabilistic prognoses associated with the choices we make. On top of that, our emotions cloud everything when health is at stake. Few of us are likely to bargain fiercely, or even rationally, with someone on whom our lives may depend. We trust and depend upon our doctors and local hospitals in a manner very distinct from the way we feel about car dealers, or even automobile insurers like my own company. This is as it must be, and it is unlikely ever to change. And, on top of these factors, we are seldom paying out of our own pockets, as would be the case in most other markets for goods and services.

Those who wish to rein in the costs associated with seeing doctors sometimes suggest shifting much of the work to skilled nurses and physicians' assistants. These professionals have had less expensive training than doctors, and their time is therefore charged at lower rates, and they can certainly perform a greater share of the tasks than they do today. I suspect this shift of effort is, in fact, a tide of the future. It seems inevitable that improved and easily portable medical records, along with better use of computerized diagnostic tools, will encourage a greater reliance on the nurses and paraprofessionals. How much that will actually affect aggregate costs isn't worth hazarding a guess, but directionally an expansion of the medical service supply ought to help.

Another answer requires more profound change. The incentives to overtreat, whether through malice or compassion, are largely erased when physicians are paid on salary rather than in proportion to services rendered. Many already are, and the number is growing. Some years ago, an influential U.S. senator said bluntly, "Everyone knows that [salaried doctors] is the right model. The question is: How do you get from here to there?"[31] The Cleveland Clinic, the Mayo Clinic, and Kaiser Permanente, no slouches in quality, all employ salaried doctors.[32] So do a great many health maintenance organizations. If enough of the medical economy operated in this manner, I expect the income differentials between the United States and its peers would moderate—and there would certainly be a reduction in low-hanging fruit for the cheaters as well as the overly eager interventionists.

Before we beat up on the doctors too much for high pay, though, let me remind you that this is only one of the factors pushing our health-care costs to exceed international standards—and it cannot be the largest. So don't look to slashing doctors' pay as a way to recoup all of that excess money you are spending. There are roughly a million doctors in this country, including both holders of an MD degree and other recognized medical certifications.[33] Multiply this number by the most we could consider their pay to exceed foreign peer pay, and we could imagine a comparative overage in cost approaching $100 billion. This is without judgment as to whether the differences are justified by higher-quality professional skills or rational consumer choice. The total represents less than a point of GNP, and closer to half a point. Remember that the United States is spending a dozen times that much in excess of its peers. So, there is work to be done, and possible savings for you from better incentives, but there is no magic savings bullet here.

I haven't mentioned nurses so far. There is a reason for that.

You might ask as a starter, as I did, whether nurses' pay might be a major contributor to the high costs of U.S. health care. This does not seem to be the case. One OECD study shows, in fact, that nurses earn only slightly more in the United States than their overseas counterparts on a purchasing power parity basis. When compared to pay in other professions requiring postgraduate work, a nurse's relative pay in the United States is about average for the countries sampled by OECD.[34] Another source ranks our nurses' pay lower than that by comparison and, incidentally, asserts that Russian nurses are paid only about one-eighth what nurses in the United States receive.[35] I trust, for the sake of those Russian caregivers and their patients, that this last piece of data was in error.

> Overutilization of testing is well known as a source of excessive cost. One driver of the excess is misdirected competition among hospitals that causes each of them to purchase and offer the most sophisticated technology regardless of normal supply-and-demand considerations. Another part of the problem is defensive medicine in response to threat of litigation.

Technology can save lives, and properly used, it can doubtless save money in just about every sector of the economy. There is virtually no limit, though, to what it can cost us all if its application is unrestrained. This is particularly so with respect to medical testing technology. Unlike doctors' incomes, this is a source of expense where expert opinion is nearly unanimous about savings to be found by eliminating excesses. I was unable, to my surprise, to find a reliably sourced estimate of the annual total of spending by Americans on medical tests, but an educated guess would put the aggregate cost at something like half a trillion dollars a year. One trade journal reported in 2009 that diagnostics account for 10 percent of all health-care costs, but other sources suggest a much higher number.[36] A loose estimate used by writers in the field is that one-third of the testing and diagnostic cost total is wasted.[37] What we can say for sure is that America's health-care system incentivizes substantial unnecessary testing costs.

The American Board of Internal Medicine Foundation has compiled reports of twenty-five medical specialty societies and determined that the routine use of 130 different medical screenings, tests, and treatments should be scaled back. The societies jointly released lists of these tests in a campaign they called "Choosing Wisely," which urges patients to question certain testing recommendations.[38] There are now about eight thousand distinct diagnoses.[39] If we tested for all of those that are nonzero possibilities in a patient, we would break the health-care bank. The newest budget buster is genetic testing, which friends at Cold Spring Harbor Laboratory tell me is now just on the verge of yielding clinically useful results. A medical journal estimates that molecular and genetic tests will soon, though, represent as much as one-third of all diagnostic testing costs.[40]

A personal story recently added to my education on misaligned incentives in the medical testing arena. Over the course of my early sixties, I noticed a mild impairment of hearing in the upper frequency ranges. So, I thought I ought to track it and asked for a routine hearing test, the kind where you raise your finger whenever you hear a beep. The test confirmed what I knew and added useful quantification. Then, about a week later, I received a letter from the hospital that had administered the test, suggesting an MRI. The logic was that my two ears had less than identical results, and thus a scan for a rare type of inner-ear tumor would be wise. Most people, presumably, would have gone for the test promptly, but with excesses in health spending on my mind, I decided to do some research.

A key part of my academic training involved the use of a tool called Bayesian statistics, to which I have come to be devoted. I won't explain the statistical science here; it suffices to say that this is an ideal technique for examining the need for that MRI. The statistical technique follows intuitive logic. The rarer a tumor is in the whole population, the lower are the odds that it will be found in any individual, regardless of any test indication. And a test statistic is only as indicative as the deviation it shows from a normal result. My test asymmetry was hardly outside the normal range at all, and the potentially suspected tumor is extraordinarily uncommon (and not particularly dangerous even when it occurs). The Bayesian probability calculation of the odds an MRI would find a tumor yielded 0.00003, likely similar to the odds of my being killed jaywalking on the way to the test—which is the way my wife predicts I will eventually be taken from her. I declined the test.

The hearing loss story provides a number of lesson springboards. One takeaway is that a patient can be easily persuaded to accept a recommendation for an expensive test. Anyone less of a doubter by nature, or any less steeped in statistical training, would have gone for that MRI. Published estimates differ widely, but sources peg the cost of an average MRI in the United States in a range from $1,000 to $2,500, perhaps excluding any accompanying doctors' fees.[41] In my case, you—or at least those of you who share an insurer with me—would have helped pay for this. It is hard to blame people for accepting recommendations from doctors, and it is easy to see the systemic bias on the part of the patient toward overemployment of tests rather than underemployment. The bigger lesson, though, relates to the hospital's incentive to recommend the test. The hospital in question had already paid for its MRI machinery and committed to all of the attendant support costs. The only way it can get its money back is to use the machine, preferably to near capacity. The hospital has no incentive at all to go light on usage. This is a fine hospital, by the way, and Boston should be glad to have it available. But multiply this case by millions, and the country has an overspending problem that you have to finance. It should be obvious that hospital competition in American health care seldom looks anything like the wonderful Adam Smith version of competition that disciplines costs so effectively. Here, it too often means acquiring the most sophisticated technology on the block and, when in doubt, recommending its use for patients — who are generally without the expertise, courage, or financial motivation to question expert advice.

The United States is the undisputed leader in this peculiar race to run the most tests. It is likely at or near the top for usage of all 130 tests and screenings identified by the Board of Internal Medicine Foundation, but MRIs are the ones for which the best data is easily available. In a 2014 study, the United States was shown to provide 105 MRIs per thousand residents per year.[42] Spain's number was 65. France, with more typical first-world statistics, provided 82. Canada recorded only 54. If the United States really runs MRIs at the rate of 30 million per year, and they cost about $2,500 apiece, the cost to you is running something like $75 billion annually.[43] And that's just one of the 130 potentially overused tests. I probably get a PSA test (for prostate cancer) too frequently, an admittedly emotional reaction to having been a pallbearer for a close friend after his untimely passing from that disease. I can't hold others to a higher standard. As *Scientific American* reports one tactful expert as having stated, though: "A lot of these screening tests are fishing expeditions. They're very low-yield."[44]

An extreme and novel version of the case against excessive testing was put to a small group of us at Cold Spring Harbor by a Dartmouth Medical School professor. He argued not only that testing is costly, but that it is often more harmful than helpful to patients.[45] Every medical test is calibrated to have a characteristic balance of false negatives to false positives. The false negatives, where an illness is present but missed by the test, are considered far and away the greater threat to the patient — and to the doctor or hospital. A failure to diagnose a serious condition can lead to a health crisis for the patient, and a lawsuit for the medical professionals. False positives, even though they can lead to unnecessary anxiety or potentially dangerous overtreatment, are considered by the designers and providers of tests to be a much lesser threat. The result is that tests are calibrated to generate more false positives than most people understand.

As testing abounds and false negatives are minimized, medical professionals tend to define illnesses by lower thresholds over time. What was once considered normal blood pressure, for example, is now considered treatably high. Diastolic pressure below 120 used to be recorded as normal; now it's 80. The systolic pressure threshold was 160; now it's 120, according to the American Heart Association.[46] As a consequence, thirteen million more Americans undergo expensive treatment for hypertension, without clear evidence of appreciable benefit in the marginal situations. Cholesterol and diabetes thresholds have been reduced, again with the result that treatment intensity and frequency have been increased but without strong evidence of patient benefit. Growths once ignored or unseen are now classed as cancerous or precancerous. Since many suspicious cases would never have developed into full-fledged illnesses, the medical profession considers that it caught and cured a large number of cancer cases when, in reality, patients were not actually going to suffer from them. The triumphant cure and survival rate data you now read from time to time necessarily reflects an inseparable mixture of undeniably genuine progress and remedies for problems that never were. But it is used to support more and more testing. Even if a net benefit is derived from the tests, it is hard to see where any limits lie.

One defense some doctors offer is that overtesting is just a natural protective reaction to an overly litigious legal system. This point deserves your sympathy. An excess of tort actions will predictably draw an expensive defensive response. When I was the Massachusetts Insurance Commissioner, and one of the state's primary health-care regulators, I questioned the costs of defensive medicine and a tort system in which less than half of the money — after costs of medical and legal defense, plaintiff attorney charges and contingent fees, and insurance — ever got to a patient. I proposed that the state legislature consider a change in the definition of actionable negligence. Negligence was too often found simply because of an unfortunate or tragic outcome that elicited jury sympathy for injured victims or their families. My proposal was to encourage an expansion of first-party insurance to cover most of the adverse outcomes without the necessity of a lawsuit, with malpractice awards limited to carefully defined cases of gross negligence. The sole response my proposal earned was a cartoon in the *Boston Globe* portraying a nattily attired trial lawyer reading my proposition and opining to a colleague, "I think I'm going to be sick."

The change in malpractice laws would still make sense, and for all the same reasons. You are paying a great deal more than you should for defensive medicine and for all the extra testing and treatment it inspires. You are paying again for the malpractice insurance and other direct costs of the tort system. And you are getting, even if you are an unfortunate victim, very little of that cost back in exchange. One published study in the *Journal of the American Medical Association* estimates that 28 percent of all testing and treatment is ordered, at least in part, for defensive reasons, and that 13 percent of the costs arise to satisfy defensive motives.[47]

Prescription drugs are more costly in the United States than elsewhere and more costly than they need to be. A portion of the excess is driven by irrational preferences of many patients, and some by the behavior of large pharmaceutical companies.

Almost 10 percent of the nation's total health-care bill is for prescription drugs.[48] One needn't doubt their importance to question both their quantities and their costs. It is easy to find examples of overuse, especially among the elderly. The dynamics of prescription often contradict the usual balance of influence between doctor and patient. Whereas testing and treatment decisions are dominated by the physician's views, the doctor is all too often guided by the patient with respect to prescriptions—and the patient is seldom well informed. When a patient asks a physician to order major surgery the doctor thinks unnecessary or unwise, the physician's medical ethics, decency, and good sense provide strong barriers to going forward. This is much less true with prescriptions, where the medical risks and costs are so much less that the patient's demands are often given the benefit of the doubt. Some years ago, my wife's aunt, at an advanced age, appeared increasingly confused. The family discovered she was taking at least a dozen prescription medicines every day. After family-inspired consultation with a caring doctor, she reduced the number to two, and she immediately improved. I don't have all the facts, but I knew this aunt well enough to wager she had insisted on all of those drugs, probably using several physicians so that none had a full picture.

The price of drugs is also an issue. As is the case for other medical services, the prescription market ill fits the competitive model due to information asymmetries. On top of this, the patent laws are designed more to protect manufacturers and stimulate research spending than to limit system costs. What many view as excessive patent protection allows drugs to be priced where only third-party payers can afford them. The right balance for patent law is hard to discern, but there are easily found examples of the huge commercial value patent protection offers. The price of Lipitor, the cholesterol reducer I take, dropped by 85 percent when its patent protection expired. Before that, though, Lipitor's economic lifetime sales had totaled over $140 billion, making it the world's biggest-selling drug.[49] It's no wonder that drug companies are fighting and lobbying hard for longer periods of protection and for the right to exclude outside parties from challenging patents before issue. The French nonprofit organization Médecins Sans Frontières (of which Doctors Without Borders is the affiliate in this country) has said that if the drug companies get their way in now-pending international negotiations, their proposals "would make it extremely difficult for generic competitors to enter the market, keeping prices unaffordably high, with devastating public health consequences."[50]

Eleven of the twelve cancer drugs approved by the Food and Drug Administration in 2012 were priced for annual costs of over $100,000.[51] During the past decade, the price of the average cancer drug regimen has doubled.[52] In this last case, a number of oncologists have vocally rebelled, but to no avail. One artifice that the pharmaceutical giants are accused of using is pulling a drug off the market as its patent protection nears expiration and replacing it with a new "improved" version, thus starting the clock all over again. In a victory for the opponents of this tactic, an Indian court recently ruled that a new version of the cancer drug Gleevec was not a true innovation but merely a patent extension tactic.[53] This helped clear the way for mass production of a generic version selling for about 4 percent of the cost of the original branded drug.[54]

As with testing and hospital utilization, there is also occasional outright abuse. One of the uglier questions is whether some doctors' prescriptions are influenced by financial rewards from manufacturers. It is fittingly illegal for a pharmaceutical company to pay a doctor a direct kickback, such as an outright commission on the doctor's scripts for the company's drugs. While it is possible this kind of blatant conflict may still be enabled through elaborate disguises in rare cases, this is unlikely to be a major systemic problem. Fees paid to doctors for publicly promoting their drugs, however, are legal. And the line between appropriate and conflicted promotional behavior is blurry. The nonprofit news outfit ProPublica alleges that crossing the line has resulted in settlements of hundreds of millions and sometimes billions of dollars in cases involving indirect kickbacks and improper marketing.[55] As with expensive testing, this is an arena in which the human mind—even the minds of people in the noble medical profession—can be wonderfully elastic when it comes to self-justification. I am not sure anyone can know, including the doctor involved, whether a physician favors a drug he or she is paid to promote as a result of the payment or based on independent, expert judgment. It is unknowable, even when all the objective facts are on the table, whether a doctor leaned toward prescribing a drug he or she promoted in a speech because of an honorarium or felt comfortable providing the endorsement because of a well-founded and preexisting confidence in the drug's efficacy. The effects on the patient and the medical system can be identical, though, when honoraria and biased prescription behavior are linked subconsciously as when direct commissions are paid.

If a pharmaceutical company tracks how much a doctor prescribes of its products, and then—without a formal contract or fixed percentage arrangement—offers to the most profitable and loyal doctors light-duty consulting contracts, exotic travel, expensive meals, or speaking fees for delivering company-approved speeches, the effect is essentially the same as a commission. This is what ProPublica says is commonplace.[56] Without necessarily accepting that extreme estimate, one can certainly conclude that something is amiss when half a dozen large pharmaceutical companies—with names you know and trust—have entered into settlements with authorities for practices just like these. ProPublica's database details approximately $4 billion in improper payments to doctors by seventeen pharmaceutical companies, mainly revealed in connection with litigation and enforcement actions.[57]

American doctors write about four billion prescriptions a year, or thirteen for every citizen.[58] It is estimated that as many as one-fifth of all Americans are actively using five or more prescription drugs at any time.[59] This does not count, of course, nonprescription drugs, herbal medicines, and diet supplements. Drug companies earned profits of over three-fourths of a trillion dollars in the past decade.[60] They are aided not just by market forces but by actions (and inactions) of your Congress designed to help them out. There are many examples. The legislation establishing the Medicare drug plan specifically forbids the federal government to bargain on drug prices; elsewhere in the world government buyers regularly negotiate for the same discounts any large private buyer would receive.[61] In most of our peer countries, when a patent has expired and cheaper generics can replace the expensive patented drug on the shelves, the original manufacturer is forbidden to pay generic suppliers to withhold product—but not here. The Federal Trade Commission has estimated that such "pay for delay" tactics cost consumers over $3 billion a year.[62] Ours is one of a few countries that fail to limit branded drug advertising directly aimed at physicians when generics of like kind and quality are available. This may be part of why the pharmaceutical companies spend $24 billion on marketing directly to doctors, eight times what they spend on consumer advertising.[63]

You as the ultimate funders of the system face the same two problems with respect to drugs as with physicians' services: dysfunctional incentives and market failure due to lack of meaningful competition. Patients have a great deal less knowledge than fear of their medical conditions, and too many can be unreasonably demanding. Doctors, for understandable reasons, are more inclined to accommodate and please their patients with respect to drugs than procedures. And some doctors lean in their drug recommendations toward the wishes of pharmaceutical companies that reward them for promotion of their products. All of this can happen, moreover, without much sacrifice of individual patients' interests or contradiction of conscience. Add nearly full insurance to the picture, and the market failure is nearly complete. The interest sacrificed is mainly that of the public collectively, who must eventually pay the costs.

Another source of excessive cost is end-of-life care. For reasons of moral complexity as well as hospital financial incentives, far more is spent on marginal postponement of death than makes societal sense. At a minimum, we should elicit and obey the wishes of the patients themselves.

The philosophical issues surrounding end-of-life care make patient protection arguments look simple. Start with these questions: How much would it be worth to you to live a year longer? How would that price be influenced by your quality of life or age at the time or by your balance sheet? How much would it be worth to you to see a loved one live a while longer? Does the answer differ if someone else is paying? Who should decide when to stop spending money on life extension and let nature take its course: The patient? The patient's family? The most extreme member of the patient's family? The patient's doctor? A hospital staff? Or only God? Could you bring yourself to "pull the plug" even if you were rationally convinced that recovery of decent life quality was no longer possible? Suppose you were 90 percent convinced? Do patients you might label as irresponsible, such as continuing alcoholics with ruined livers, deserve the same interventions accorded to model citizens? How about an alcoholic whose drinking has precipitated the condition but has sworn never to touch a drop again?

All of us know stories that give us pause. There was a *60 Minutes* feature about a woman with advanced heart and liver disease who spent the last two months of her life commuting between a nursing home and the local hospital. Although she had signed a living will that forbade extraordinary measures, more than two dozen specialists showed up at her bedside.[64] You presumably paid for that. A *New York Times* piece told of a patient who remained in the hospital for a year following a liver transplant. "He had never, ever been told that he would have to live with a ventilator and dialysis," his doctor said. When the doctor inquired whether the patient might prefer to go home and receive hospice care, the surgeon on the case asked him to leave the hospital and not to come back.[65]

I use a personal trainer to help me stay fit. Her mother was kept alive in a hospital setting for more than a year after she had lost her facility to recognize her family members or to communicate in any way. One of her adult daughters, likely for religious reasons, insisted on maximum care even when the other siblings were ready for a loving farewell. I don't know the cost of her care, but we can estimate from hospital bed costs that even without intensive care supplements, it had to be in the $2 million range. Few serious students of health care doubt that extreme measures taken as a part of end-of-life care are significant contributors to the $3 trillion health-care bill we all share.

Readily accessible hard data establishes that a large portion of the health-care dollar in this country is consumed in end-of-life care. It is widely stated that about one-third of health-care costs for the elderly are attributable to care for patients near death.[66] The National Institutes of Health confirms, more specifically, that one-third of the Medicare portion of health-care expenditures is devoted to treatment and care in the last month of life.[67] I have seen higher estimates of total end-of-life costs, calculated on a more broadly inclusive basis. Even the NIH estimate, though, represents about one-tenth of total medical costs in the United States. Three-fourths of these costs result from ventilator use, resuscitation, and other extreme care techniques at the end of life.[68] That's more than a point and a half of GNP, or about a quarter of a trillion dollars a year.

It seems obvious that this is too much, but the philosophical complexities, when combined with the economic incentives that influence hospitals, have rendered solutions out of reach. The chief executive of a major and well-respected hospital put it concisely and candidly to the *New York Times:* "If you come into this hospital, we're not going to let you die."[69] Hospitals vary all over the lot in average spending on this kind of care. The Mayo Clinic is near the low end, averaging about $50,000 per terminal patient, whereas some hospitals spend about twice that. The most expensive providers offer noticeably more intensive care unit days and specialist consultations than lower-cost hospitals.[70] Debates about how long someone should live in the ICU aside, it is not even clear that the high-cost, most activist hospitals actually prolong life. A report by Dartmouth College researchers determined that in its sample the highest-cost hospitals had just about the same end-of-life outcomes as the less interventionist.[71]

The most emphatic assertion I have to offer about end-of-life care is that it is time to start listening to the patients themselves. Dr. Atul Gawande, whom I quoted before, describes a better model than the national norm, and one already proven by use in this country. He cites the case of La Crosse, Wisconsin, where end-of-life hospital costs are in the range of half the national average, and the life expectancy exceeds the national mean.[72] In 1991, apparently, local medical leaders began a campaign to solicit end-of-life decisions in advance from physicians and their patients. Patients admitted to a hospital, nursing home, or assisted-living facility began routinely to complete a form that asked them, among other questions: (a) Do you want to be resuscitated if your heart stops? (b) Do you want aggressive treatments such as intubation and mechanical ventilation? and (c) Do you want tube or intravenous feeding if you can't eat on your own? By 1996, 85 percent of dying residents in La Crosse had such forms in place, and doctors almost always followed their instructions. The results have been genuinely impressive.

A related improvement in the current state of affairs, also cited by Gawande, would be achieved if more people simply died at home. Again, this should be a choice routinely offered to the patient. My own mother chose that course. She wanted to die with dignity in her own bed, in her own clothes, and surrounded only by the family who loved her. I doubt she would have lived more than a few days longer if we had applied extreme methods. Fearful that a hospital would take over the decision process, she refused ever to enter one—or even allow a doctor visit—as the end approached. Hospice provided her the dignified passing she selected for herself. Gawande even suggests that counter to conventional wisdom, patients might actually live longer in familiar and loving environments than in a hospital ICU bed.[73] He notes with approval that although in the last half of the twentieth century the percentage of Americans who died at home dropped from over 50 to 17, the trend has now reversed. In the past five years, the number of people choosing hospice or home settings has returned to almost 50 percent.[74] This is a cultural shift that can only bring good.

Though welcome change may be in the wind, at the time of this writing Medicare still does not reimburse for advance care planning relating to end of life.[75] Combine this with the low percentage of doctors who receive geriatric training in medical school, and the falling numbers of geriatric specialists (down by one-third since 1994), and it spells wasted opportunity. The venerable National Academy of Sciences' Institute of Medicine has recently recommended that Medicare and private insurers reimburse for planning. The American Medical Association has already set up a billing code for an hour-long conversation between doctor and patient and the filling out of an advance care planning form.[76] I hope most of you would agree that this is not the ghoulish "death panel" so many are afraid of. The NAS's Institute of Medicine has also called for more general restructuring of Medicare and Medicaid to eliminate "perverse financial incentives."[77] President Abraham Lincoln set up the National Academy to advise the President and Congress on matters requiring more than a layman's scientific view. This would be a good time to take the Academy's advice. As the Institute's chief executive put it, "Patients don't die in the manner they prefer . . . The time is now for our nation to develop a modernized end-of-life care system."[78]

Remember that the human brain did not evolve for making complex, long-term decisions, and neither did the Congress. But, on end-of-life care, we and our elected leaders must eventually make some choices. Modern medical science cannot extend people's lives indefinitely, but it can all too easily devise ways to spend without reasonable limit on attempts to do so at the margin. Stalling death is a lot easier than extending a fully conscious life of decent quality—and a lot less useful. I doubt most patients want that outcome, and it is not even clear that life is actually extended when extreme treatments are applied. Even if these techniques do have a marginal extension benefit, moreover, and even if patients and their families favor the most extreme forms of intervention, society simply can't afford to pay for them as they expand indefinitely in cost and sophistication. Ask yourself whether it would really be a better world if everyone got to spend a few days or weeks in an ICU at the end of life—and you were accordingly poorer.

> The easiest excess to identify is in the costs of administration. This source of waste alone would justify a single-payer system, but there is an even better reason for establishing a unified system. Competition among hospitals and other providers can never provide reasonable cost discipline, even side by side with a government program. The full unification of regulation is essential if our country is to resolve the discrepancy between costs and outcomes.

Recall that our country's health-care costs are about eight points of GNP higher than the costs in peer nations. If you are tallying my estimates of what the suspected drivers of extravagance might add to the bill, you are aware that much of the gap still remains to be explained. I have saved the most obviously wasteful contributor to the gap for last: the manner in which we administer our health-care system. The United States has somehow found itself with few or none of the benefits we admire in market solutions—while paying all of the costs inherent in a corporate approach to the marketing and administration of health care. This is a bad deal.

A study conducted at the City University of New York looked at health administration costs in the economically most advanced countries, and its lead author wrote, "We were surprised by just how big the differences have grown. The United States is in another league than every other country."[79] The study estimated that administrative costs accounted for more than 25 percent of U.S. hospital expenditures, a figure not remotely approached elsewhere.[80] The report also found that those countries operating under a single-payer health system had the lowest administrative spending levels.[81] A separate study, published in the *New England Journal of Medicine* some time ago, pegged overall administration costs at between 19 and 24 percent of total spending on health care. An update in 2003 raised the estimate to 30 percent.[82] The share of the total health-care labor force devoted to administration had grown by 50 percent, despite the introduction during that interval of numerous managed care systems and massive increases in the automation of information technology. Today, it appears that at least one in every four health-sector employees works only at an administrative or clerical desk.[83]

The two largest components of what we can group together as administrative costs are marketing and record keeping, including patient billing and reimbursement management. Social Security, while not a medical program, shares many of the same tasks and operates with an overhead cost of less than 1 percent. It has substantially no advertising and relatively uniform record keeping. The Medicare program is more expensive to operate, but not much, spending something under 2 percent of its total budget on administration.[84] There is virtually no advertising in the Medicare budget, and although Medicare's records are more complex than those of Social Security, the requirements across the spectrum of providers and patients are relatively uniform. Critics of Medicare like to say the true cost is more like 6 percent. The difference between the trustees' measure of overhead and the critics' measure arises from the addition in the latter of the administrative expenditures incurred by the insurance companies that participate in Medicare Parts C and D. Whether or not that is a fair inclusion actually matters little. Private insurer administrative costs, including marketing, are generally estimated at 17 percent to 20 percent of premiums. The recent Affordable Care Act carries a provision aimed at limiting private insurer spending on administration to 20 percent of premiums, and 15 percent in some group plans.[85] Even if this can be fully and effectively enforced, which I doubt, it would mainly keep matters from getting worse; it is hardly a cure for the high costs you already bear.

I have long argued in conversation on this topic for a single-payer approach, though not usually to much avail. While organizing thoughts for this book, I recognized some major omissions in my accustomed support case for a single payer. Opponents quickly saw these holes as powerful defenses against any argument for change, and not unfairly so. One flaw was that the phrase *single payer* doesn't fully or properly describe the solution that makes the most sense. The other is that we already have what look like single payers in Medicare and Medicaid, and they haven't effectively held down costs other than in administration. Both points are worthy of address.

Single payer is the phrase in common use today, but it is in fact a poor descriptor of what is needed. The preceding pages have covered a number of the sources of this country's unusually high costs: provider incomes rightly or wrongly exceeding international levels; copious utilization of sophisticated diagnostic testing equipment; failure to constrain either utilization or prices of pharmaceutical products; spending on nonproductive administrative paperwork as well as abundant advertising by insurers, providers, and their suppliers; and uncontrolled entitlement expenditures on end-of-life care. Having a single agency act as the monopoly bill payer for the entire U.S. health-care system would help greatly in curtailing administrative paperwork and reducing some marketing costs, but that transformation alone — as wrenching as it would be — would do little to address the other problem areas.

What we really need is a combination of a single payer, a single negotiator, and a single regulator. This might be best called a unified, or single, health-care administrator. Indeed, creating a single-payer format would by itself generate a bounty of savings in paperwork. The economies arising from freeing providers and their staffs of multiple forms and compliance with diverse and occasionally irrational justification regimens represent the simplest of all health-care savings to visualize. If the single payer was also a single insurer — at least for basic care, responsible for collecting premiums and handling all aspects of claims reimbursement — the savings would be that much greater. Insurer operating expenses, including marketing and advertising, do little or nothing in this imperfect market to improve the quality of care. This, however, is about where the single-payer notion, narrowly defined, reaches the limits of its usefulness.

To realize any savings in the pharmaceuticals area, we also need a single negotiator. The country would be well advised to rid itself of the plethora of laws and procedures meant principally to protect drug companies — and then bargain for the best prices a massive customer can get. The consumers' side of the market can never by its nature be a paradigm of effective competition. The suppliers' side, though, would rise eagerly to the challenge in the right environment. If more innovation and research are needed — an argument to which we should all be open — direct incentives for entrepreneurial and nonprofit activities would be unquestionably more cost-effective than subsidizing overall profit levels that benefit mainly pharmaceutical industry shareholders. Here the model can be borrowed from virtually any one of our first-world peers with minimal danger of unintended adverse consequences. It is a certainty that a single purchaser could bargain for, and obtain, better drug prices than we pay today. And an increased use of generics would save a great deal more if we would just cease to protect powerful patent holders beyond all reason. The Commissioner of the FDA has suggested that even the curtailed use of generics under current rules has generated more than $1.2 trillion in savings over a recent ten-year period.[86] The benefits of applying available market power on behalf of the public are not limited to pharmaceutical purchasing. A single negotiator could be a potent public advocate and bargaining representative in negotiations with other types of health-care providers as well, including medical device manufacturers, physicians' organizations, and hospitals.

Even with a unified purchaser and administrator, however, there would be gaps in the effort to moderate the fraction of our GNP spent on health care. Excessive utilization by the public of prescription medicines, wasteful and duplicative purchasing by hospitals of costly testing equipment, and, most of all, unbounded spending on end-of-life care all need to be addressed. Efficient administration and the use of available bargaining power alone are insufficient tools for these challenges. As out of fashion as the word *regulator* may be in some quarters, a degree of regulatory oversight is indispensable if the systemic savings sought are to be anything like the annual trillion dollars or more that lie within our reach. I am nowhere near wise enough to offer precise detail, or withstand cross-examination, on just how the regulation should be applied, other than to urge that it include support for the general savings propositions described earlier in this chapter. I can be sure of this, though: the hardest task will come as a preamble to any specific form of regulatory intervention. Without a major cultural shift on the part of the public and a profound appreciation for the benefits freeing up a trillion dollars annually could yield the American people, regulation will not have the prerequisite consent of the governed.

The other debate weakness in the accustomed case for a single payer is highlighted when an opponent asks why Medicare and Medicaid don't already provide all the benefits attributed to a single-payer system. It is generally acknowledged that these programs control their own administrative and marketing costs much more effectively than their care outlays. We have all seen attention-grabbing reports, moreover, of Medicare and Medicaid fraud. Among the reasons for the limited cost containment success in these programs is that they were intentionally designed to lack some of the tools necessary for greater impact. They are true single payers within their spheres, but they are shackled as negotiators and all the more constrained as regulators.

A parallel handicap is that Medicare and Medicaid sit side by side with a private system where incentives for the care providers too often favor higher costs. The incentives for the private insurers in this complex web, while more complicated than those of care providers, are not a whole lot better. In self-insured group plans, medical costs are mainly charged back to employers while the private insurer takes an administration fee that rises proportionally with treatment costs. When the insurer's revenues vary on a cost-plus basis with spending on care, there is little incentive for tough cost scrutiny. And insurers fear losing their corporate accounts if they are strict with excesses. Insurers in risk-bearing plans do have short-run incentives to be frugal, but they are at even greater risk for account loss when they try to tighten the reins. Their scale in the long term is determined, moreover, by total health-care market size, which in turn is an upward-sloping function of care utilization.

When the private portion of the market sets the standards for frequency of testing, drug usage and cost, and compensation for every variety of medical services, it is extremely hard for any accompanying single-payer programs to be more parsimonious. Since 1997, Medicare statutes have provided for a "sustainable growth rate" limitation on payouts, tying the expansion of some reimbursements to the growth rate of gross domestic product. Congress, under pressure, has modified these rules almost annually. When, in 2011, the Medicare Payment Advisory Commission of Medicare suggested cutting some physicians' fees, enforcement was postponed until at least 2015 and has now been postponed again. The single payers, moreover, can do nothing to alleviate the need for providers to maintain multiple accounting and billing systems for their private or shared patients, so little or no advantage can be taken of available efficiencies in this category of cost. Administrative spending runs to roughly $650 per patient in the average hospital.[87] Doctors' offices, too, have to maintain costly redundant billing and reporting systems, with staff to go with them. These tend to be fixed costs, reduced only slightly by the simultaneous presence of Medicare and Medicaid, where accounting is standardized. It simply isn't fair to judge the existing single payers by the results of a split system in which more than half the costs are private.

Another problem with today's Medicare and Medicaid is that, like the private system, they allow costs to be largely invisible to the patient. A cost doesn't go away, of course, just because it is spread over large numbers of people in taxes and premiums. It is a better bet that when purchase of a service is removed from the direct consequences of price, both cost and utilization will expand. The think tank the Cato Institute has noted correctly that not only do patients overuse those resources that appear to be almost free, but producers of new equipment can sell their products into an unusually price-insensitive market.[88] Private insurance has a wide variety of copayment requirements, deductibles, and subscriber contribution requirements, but few are particularly effective. Medicare has an annual deductible for hospital stays, but no copay for the first sixty days of care. It has a gently means-tested annual deductible and a percentage copayment for doctor's services. The Medicaid program allows individual states to set all three variables, but limiting federal statutes and the need status of the Medicaid clientele make this a tough arena in which to demand meaningful market incentives. When all is said and done, none of the incentives for careful consumption of health care are strong enough. Part of the problem is deep within our political ethos. Americans seem to resent accurate user charges when the good being purchased is seen as a necessity. Health care is the archetypical example.

Some observers understandably look at our first-world peers and insist that the favorable experience of other nations with full coverage shows that there is little need to hold patients responsible for any substantial portions of their charges. Their observations about the peer systems and their results are correct enough, but the conclusion may not be equally valid. The United States has too long enjoyed the habits of overutilization and overspending to permit their curtailment without the enforced discipline of contributory first-party payments. If someday doctors and patients have learned to care enough about aggregate health-care expenditures to maintain a sensible balance between costs and usage, it might be a celebratory event to restore at that time fully reimbursed health care for all — without substantial patient contributions. In the interim, we will need deductibles and copayments, and all the other forces we can muster, if we wish to bring about a meaningful change in national spending on health care.

Annual subscriber contributions have almost no beneficial effect on utilization behavior at the margin. Their usefulness is simply in spreading the financing cost of health care between out-of-pocket costs and insured costs. Deductibles that are applied on an annual basis have only a mild incentive impact in most cases, and none at the point of purchase after the deductible (patient-paid) amounts are exhausted in any year. It is principally copayments, owed by the patient every time a service is consumed, that can restore the beneficial effects of a free market. An economically powerful copayment schedule is about the only tool available to restore some market efficiency to health-care utilization, and a universal and steeply means-testing copayment schedule would be required to make it either effective or just. The obstacle here is the public, which unwisely seems to prefer to pay by the less visible mechanisms of taxes and insurance premiums — even if the true cost is higher that way. Until this preference changes, the government programs will be politically constrained to accept what failed markets deliver. And as long as our private and public systems operate side by side, we are condemned to overspend.

Demographics are currently unfavorable for health-care spending reductions regardless of systemic changes. In the short run there is no way to prevent further increases in the share of GNP devoted to health care. Other countries, though, have models more likely to moderate costs in the longer run.

If the prior pages have implied that better public policies can radically bring down the absolute costs of health care in any near-term time frame, I should clarify my view. Better use of incentives and administrative efficiencies would be a force in the right direction, and they can curb the expanding fraction of

GNP devoted to health care in the long run, but the trajectory of health-care costs in the next decade or so will be upward no matter what we do. That is because demographics count, too. As the baby boomers age, the ratio of expensive health-care beneficiaries to healthy funders of private and public programs is sure to rise. So, the utilization of health services is bound to grow faster than the economy—and by no small margin. Adding to the upward cost pressure may be the impact of the Affordable Care Act, whose proponents made a stronger case on fairness grounds (and for which reason I was a supporter) than they did for its cost control features. Its illness prevention features are, simply put, unlikely to compensate for adding an additional subpopulation, likely of less-than-average good health, to an existing system in need of serious repair. Some experts defended the law as a first step; universality first, then efficiencies. I will feel a great deal more comfortable if that sequence turns out to be more than wishful thinking.

The Affordable Care Act does contain a few cost buffers, and recent numbers indicate a welcome slowdown in the pace of health-care spending. The good news is that the improvement is not just in the total but in the government programs as well.[89] This suggests that the savings are not just a recessionary effect, since recession should mainly impact the private side. The bad news is that much of the improvement is due to one-time effects that cannot be expected to continue as restraints. And, in any case, the trend still points upward. There are so many factors influencing health-care spending that it would be an error to draw any long-term conclusions from short-term results. The tide should always be distinguished from the waves, and the tide is still shifting toward cost increases. No policy response can prevent this for many years. I will be surprised if the percentage of our GNP consumed by health care does not soon approach 20 percent, even if the public learns to treat the issues more rationally than it does today. The opportunity before you does not, alas, include a quick reversal in the direction of costs. The threat is that without rational policy action, the share of GNP consumed by health care won't stop at 20 percent and won't improve as the demographic pull subsides.

Other countries have done a better job than we have. Some of the features of each are potentially applicable in our culture and some are not. Some are attractive models and some are not. I am not suggesting we copy any one of them wholesale. The summary that follows is mainly to show that there is no standard model. We must pick and choose from the available menu of regimes a set of methods consistent with our culture and history—and that will work for us. England has a national system funded by taxes.[90] Every citizen is covered, and other than a small copayment for dentistry, eyeglasses, and prescriptions, there are no bills. The means-tested market incentives I would like to see are largely missing. On the other hand, while most primary care doctors are private contractors reimbursed on fixed schedules, most specialists are salaried by the state. Many of the hospitals are state owned.

Switzerland has a hybrid universal coverage system, where private insurers are prohibited from making a profit on basic care but permitted to do so with respect to advance care.[91] Taiwan, widely praised for its modest administrative costs, has a national system with copayments and universal coverage.[92] The Japanese utilize health care even more than Americans—there are more doctor visits and more prescriptions—yet they spend half as much as we do per capita. Prices for all medical services are heavily regulated, and there is a 30 percent point-of-purchase copay for those who can afford it, varying downward by income and age.[93] Germany, the home of social insurance, has a system with diverse elements that can be confusing to an outsider. Universal coverage is offered, with means-based premiums and by private insurers—but they are nonprofits. The insurers bargain with doctors on prices, while the government helps impose price discipline through a global budgeting process. There is also a parallel for-profit private system available to a relative few.[94] Looking at all of these approaches simultaneously, about the only conclusion one can draw is that the health systems employed by our peers are all different in design, but all seem to share at least these features: universal coverage, effective cost restraints, and superior outcome statistics. It is hard to believe we don't have something to learn from them.

The most common argument I hear against borrowing anything from the approaches to health care of other wealthy countries is that they have longer waiting periods for services than we do. I have read that in the United Kingdom, Australia, and Canada, the average wait for elective surgery is more than a month, and over a quarter of the nonemergency patients in one survey reported waiting over four months. All three of these countries say they will invest extra resources to address the waits.[95] My assumption is that there is validity to the comparison. Our system probably works faster in these situations. If it saved enough money, though, I would accept a longer waiting period for a hip or knee replacement and couldn't possibly object to a wait for purely elective surgery. Delay is less tolerable for more serious or potentially progressive conditions, and I haven't found reliable disaggregated data to see how the waits in other countries vary by type of surgery. Even if delays occur elsewhere where they ought not to, though, please recall that we do not enjoy better health outcomes. So the impact of any such waits can hardly be devastating. Outcomes are more important than velocity of treatment. And our system is costing us over a trillion dollars each year in costs the others don't bear. The American public is not all that good at understanding or accepting tradeoffs that require giving up a luxurious accustomed entitlement, but sometimes tradeoffs simply need to be made.

> The easy thesis about health care is that our woefully ineffective system of provider competition should be replaced with a universal single-payer, single-regulator approach. In the meanwhile, there are numerous valuable halfway measures that can be taken to improve efficacy in specific areas of the system, with a goal no less ambitious than world-class outcomes at costs similar to those of our peers.

The inescapable fact is that you and I pay far too much for the health care we receive, more than a trillion dollars a year too much. The care is good, but outcomes are less favorable than in peer nations with lower costs, and a cost excess with twelve zeros is simply too large to ignore. It should be a national goal to catch up with our peers in outcomes and, at the same time, cut what you pay every year by one-third. Some of the savings would appear in your taxes, some in your health insurance costs, and some in your out-of-pocket expenditures. It is there for the asking.

We Americans tend to be proud of our ways, and quick to defend them. But as Uwe Reinhardt, an economics professor at Princeton University, asked, "How can it be that 'the best medical care in the world' costs twice as much as the best medical care in the world?"[96] That's the right question. There are multiple drivers of the cost overage. There is no easy thesis to offer with respect to doctors' incomes. Fraud should be fought, of course, but don't look there for massive savings. Only a few physicians are intentionally behaving dishonestly; most are just doing what the system calls for—and remain more altruistic than the rest of us. We might well be better off with a mix of general practitioners and specialists that looks more like the rest of the world's mix, and we might want to let paraprofessionals do more of the work, but neither of these changes would make a serious dent in the overall spending pattern.

There is no easy response to burgeoning technology costs either, as long as hospitals are dysfunctionally competitive and our tort system ensures a surfeit of defensive medicine. Technology will continue to improve, and its costs have no natural upper limit. There will similarly be no ready path to reducing the huge expense for end-of-life care until America is ready to face the realities of the situation and cut back. We can make some real progress, though, by insisting that patients' choices about their last days be stated in advance and binding on the medical profession. There is a somewhat clearer logical path to follow with respect to medications. Even if we continue to want too many drugs, especially in elder years, we can take steps to temper the costs. There is no reason for government programs not to use the normal powers of large purchasers to bring prescription medicine costs into line with other nations' costs. Only the politics of campaign contributions need to be overcome.

Excessive spending on administration is the easiest target. There is no more powerful first step the country could take to cut unnecessary costs than to establish a single-payer system for the distribution of health insurance and the handling of its accounting. A unified system would begin paying dividends immediately by eliminating costs for advertising and the maintenance of multiple, incompatible record-keeping and billing systems. Even more important, it would gradually permit the building of useful efficiency and quality incentives into a health-care system now plagued with perverse incentives.

The money you are unnecessarily paying today for below-par

health-care outcomes is coming from your wallets, but the victims of the misdirected spending include generations unborn. The economics of health care are such, given relative propensities to illness, that spending on health care always transfers wealth from the age cohort currently working to the elderly and leaves less to be spent on the young. Ask yourselves whether, if forced to choose, you would rather live in a society that tilts toward spending the next dollar on the young or the very old. If nothing changes in health care, the next dollar is already spoken for. If we stop spending thoughtlessly, though, we can treat our seniors at least as well as they would be treated elsewhere in the world and still save money. Not all expenditures and not all goods produce the same amount of economic benefit. Spending on the young and on infrastructure represents an investment that will pay later returns. Spending on too many tests, too many drugs, and too much intervention in the last days of life is just spending.

The institution of a single-payer health-care system, accompanied by the appropriate cost disciplines, presents an opportunity with few historical parallels in terms of national financial impact. The average American household can save itself thousands of dollars each year, our products can be more competitive in world markets, and our society can amply fund additional investments in its future—all without a sacrifice in health outcomes. Repairing the health-care system in this country is, measured in dollars, worth more to your family and our country than any other conceivable national policy change.

It's not even close.

FIVE

Financial Sector Reform

GIANT BANKS, opaque hedge funds, and incomprehensibly leveraged trading in derivatives are the dominant features of the financial landscape today. None of these are valuable for the country's growth, its wealth distribution, or its commercial economy — and none of them are in any way necessary. All three sources of excess and instability, in fact, are results of past policy mistakes in Washington whose implications no one saw coming as they took shape. The banks, the hedge funds, and the derivatives business should be contracted to a tiny fraction of their current scale and influence. There would be nothing but benefit to the people of the United States from doing so.

People listened intently when the President of the United States took to the airwaves to talk about the financial crisis. He conveyed a reassuring message. He talked about how he would "clean up thoroughly unwholesome conditions in the field of investment . . . in the banking system, in the sale of securities, in the deliberate encouragement of stock gambling, in the sale of unsound mortgages and in many other ways in which the public lost billions of dollars . . ."[1] He assembled a team of intellectuals, wily former traders, and savvy political hands to design a financial sector reform of unprecedented scale. And although it took longer than he first imagined to set all of the required rules and implementing institutions in place, a new regime was brilliantly constructed around the explicit principles of constrained leverage and enhanced disclosure. Franklin D. Roosevelt and his team got it right. The program of financial regulation that they established helped to assure this country roughly half a century of strong, stable, and trustworthy financial markets, supporting the greatest period of national economic growth in the history of the world.

Supporting growth in tangible forms of commerce and expediting real economic activity is the role of the financial markets. Financial markets do not, in themselves, produce goods or—except in the zero-sum game of capturing profits from other lands—generate much, if any, growth in national income or wealth. They are, however, essential lubricants in a free-market economic system. Without its banks, its financial instrument markets, and well-informed investors, capitalism would grind to a halt. What FDR and his team were dealing with, though, was not an absence or shortage of those institutions' services, but excesses and abuses in their operation. The right amount of oil in a machine allows it to work smoothly. Too much can destroy it. During the 1920s financial markets had gotten out of hand. The moment of truth arrived in October of 1929, with the crash of the stock market and, soon thereafter, the start of the Great Depression. The worst drop in the market indices since then occurred in 2008 and 2009, and for many of the same reasons. The lessons of 1929 were properly learned and absorbed into public policy. This cannot be equally said of the lessons from the crash that came eighty years later—several of which were exactly the same lessons.

This one is personal to me. Financial sector regulation dominated years of my life. At the U.S. Commodity Futures Trading Commission, I tried hard to persuade others in power that overly leveraged derivatives and lack of disclosure represented a threat to our economic stability. My efforts were not successful, and as I look back, that should have come as less of a surprise. Here was a green, unknown regulator armed with more opinion than evidence who was unable to garner grass-roots, academic, or press support. On the opposition side were a mighty river of campaign contributions, a growing aristocracy of influential financiers who resented having their livelihoods questioned, and a transformative national revolution brewing against government regulation of all sorts. This was not the Roosevelt era.

Friends and adversaries alike warned me against tilting at windmills. One has to choose one's battles wisely, they said. The defeats damage your head more than the wall you hit it against. A second argument against my continued effort was that the world had changed and the principles of the New Deal were "songs from an outdated hymnbook." The debate might indeed have been unwinnable back then, but it shouldn't be today. The events of 2008 and the horrendous damage that followed have now provided proof beyond reasonable doubt that an unconstrained financial sector can menace all of us. The world has changed since the New Deal, of course, and some new approaches are needed in response. The central elements of the philosophy applied by the Roosevelt administration, however, are anything but archaic in this era of globalism and supposed financial innovation. The principles adopted in the 1930s would have been useful bulwarks against the Crash of 2008 had they not been abandoned by both political parties in the past few decades. And the return to an environment of low leverage and high disclosure, along with a few other reforms, is necessary to prevent a next — perhaps much worse — crisis. Some hymns, and some truths about markets, are enduring.

The 1930s reformers understood that confidence in the banking system required government deposit guarantees and limits on irresponsible bank behavior. They were greatly concerned as well about swindlers and excessive leverage in the stock market.

The situation facing the nation in the 1930s was dire. Panic had spread from Wall Street to the economy as a whole. The unemployment rate at the trough rose to about 25 percent, and that statistic never includes those who have given up looking for work.[2] By comparison, the unemployment rate just before the 1929 crash had been 3 percent.[3] The gross national product fell by nearly half in just four years.[4] Some nine thousand banks failed, in some cases taking with them depositors' life savings, and another three thousand were merged into other banks.[5] Meanwhile, abroad, Fascist governments ruled Italy and Germany, Imperial Japan readied its army for war, and Stalin was crushing the last flickers of idealism and dissent in Soviet Russia. There was even concern that our own democratic republic couldn't survive. I have often pointed out to friends who bemoan the increasingly formidable domestic and international challenges facing us today that while this is a tough time by the standards of our lives, it is nothing like what my father saw when he graduated from law school in the worst of the Depression. Wall Street was given, and deserved, a share of the blame.

Prior to the New Deal reforms, banks were generally small, and often undercapitalized. There was no deposit insurance. If your bank failed, you could simply lose whatever you had entrusted to it. Larger money-center banks existed, with more capital, but these created another peril. They made a good portion of their income from underwriting stock issues for client corporations. Underwriting involves buying the newly issued securities of a corporate investment banking client and reselling those same securities — usually immediately — to outside investors at a profit. Banks in this era were commonly found to have flogged the new issues to potential buyers, with a generous quota of inflated claims and promises of gains, knowing that if the sales campaign fell short, they could always stuff any shares that remained unsold into trust accounts managed by the same banks. The trust accounts, often representing the wealth of clients who had passed from this world, were easy buyers to persuade. In most cases, the bank either had sole fiduciary decision-making responsibility itself or shared it with a law firm — to which it could throw lucrative legal business as needed whenever inducement was called for.

Hazardous practices were all the more rampant in the stock market. Legions of investors were caught up in a naive fantasy that prices could never fall, and unscrupulous securities hawkers could sell them just about anything. There was no licensing or registration of brokers, and scant discipline for outright fraudsters. Securities firms were often no more than phone banks, called "bucket shops," disseminating false information and insincere advice to their gullible targets. Just as important, there were no limits on margin loans. This meant that investors could buy several, or many, times as much stock as they had means to afford. A dollar down could buy multiple dollars' worth of stock in any traded company. The difference between the full value of a position in a financial instrument and what an individual or institutional investor must put up in cash to secure it is what is called leverage. Leverage plays such a large role in what I will have to say about financial reform that it is worth a bit of a primer before continuing.

If you purchase a hundred shares of a stock for a total of $10,000, and the share price rises in value by 50 percent, your new valuation is $15,000. You have made a paper profit of $5,000 on your initial purchase cost, which represents a 50 percent return on that investment. If, instead of rising at all, the share price had gone down by 50 percent, your initial $10,000 would have become worth only $5,000. That's a 50 percent loss. This is an example of an unleveraged investment.

Next, imagine instead that you made the same purchase but you borrowed $7,500 of the money needed to buy the shares. You had to put up only $2,500 in cash to pay the $10,000 total purchase price. Now, do the math for a 50 percent price rise. The shares become worth the same $15,000 as in the unleveraged case, but you made your $5,000 gain on an investment of only $2,500 — so your return was 200 percent. On the other hand, if the shares went down 50 percent to a total value of $5,000, you would have lost $5,000 on an investment of $2,500 . . . so your loss would be 200 percent. This is what leverage does. It increases the percentage gain or loss on your committed cash, potentially by a lot. There might be a charge for interest on the borrowed portion — or maybe not. In a low-interest-rate environment like today's, that would make little difference.

To complete the example, imagine that you are ready to make the $10,000 unleveraged investment when all of this is explained to you. You are extremely confident you have picked a great stock. So, instead of borrowing the $7,500 and putting up $2,500 in cash, you borrow $30,000 and also put up the whole $10,000 in cash you started with — to buy four times as much stock. You can afford a $40,000 position, you say, because it requires only the same $10,000 check you were originally prepared to write. Now, when the stock goes up 50 percent, you have made $20,000. The percentage return on your cash applies to an amount four times as great. Nice deal, isn't it? The problem, of course, is that if the share price falls by half, your loss of $20,000 eats your whole $10,000 original stake, and you still owe the lender the $30,000 you borrowed. You can sell the stock for its newly reduced value of $20,000 and pay it over to the lender, but you will be left with an outstanding debt of $10,000. You might want to hold the stock to wait for the price to recover. But if you can't come up with cash from another source and promptly so, the lender will be the decision maker on when to sell your position. It will likely be liquidated right after the loss, whether you like it or not. And the forced sale, along with others like it on the part of investors who made the same wrong bet you did, would put more downward market pressure on the stock price—perhaps causing still more investors to have to sell. That's the dark side of leverage.

Sometime in early 1929, my grandfather Josh Stone retired and sold his manufacturing business, committing almost all of his proceeds to the stock market on margin, roughly in the manner just described. I don't know the actual percentage he borrowed or the amounts invested. You can guess, though, how it turned out. My dad, who was twenty-one in February of that year, had received a gift of $1,000 from his parents on his birthday. In November, his father asked for the money back. My grandpop's wealth had been wiped out in the first days of the crash. He took it hard, never working again. Some people jumped from windows.

The reforms of the 1930s included limitations on stock market leverage, the creation of the Securities and Exchange Commission to police securities industry behavior, the institution of deposit insurance for nationally chartered banks, and strict constraints on commercial banking operations.

Among the most fundamental reforms the Roosevelt team put in place was a limit on margins. In 1934, a minimum cash payment of 45 percent was established for the purchase of publicly traded stocks. The required margin has been varied occasionally since that time, but from 1974 to the present the percentage an investor must extend in cash to buy stock has been held constant at 50 percent.[6] The Securities and Exchange Commission was created in 1934 not only to enforce systemic rules such as the margin requirements, but also to police the behavior of brokers. Bucket shops were closed down, testing for competence and knowledge of the rules became a requirement for a broker's license, and an enforcement division was created to expel predators from the industry or refer them for prosecution. Insider trading was prohibited for the first time.

The federal government simultaneously tackled banking sector weaknesses by initiating deposit insurance. Without deposit insurance, bank customers who heard rumors of their bank's vulnerability might logically run to the bank and withdraw all of their deposits before someone else got them. Even a bank that was not actually in trouble would be unable to withstand such a "run," because it couldn't refund all the deposits without calling in all of its loans first. And loans generally have terms that rule out instant demands for full repayment. Deposit insurance eliminates the customer's need to run on rumor. The Federal Deposit Insurance Corporation was created in 1933.

At the same time, Congress prohibited commercial banks from underwriting or distributing corporate securities. This portion of the extensive Banking Act of 1933 long retained the name of its lead sponsors and is still remembered as the Glass-Steagall Act.[7] It effectively ended the stuffing of unsold new issues into bank trust funds and at the same time protected the soon-to-be-insured banks from underwriting risks. The forced split of commercial banking from investment banking would lead to the formation of Morgan Stanley as a separate entity in 1935 and the ultimate growth of Goldman Sachs from a family trading firm to a global giant. These two firms would be among the leaders in the investment banking business for all of my life. It was understood that the investment banks would not be government insured and their businesses might be risky. The commercial banks were expected to operate at a lower level of risk to protect depositors and the new federal insurer alike. This was the philosophical heart of the Glass-Steagall Act.

In 1940, the federal government began systematic regulation of investment advisers and investment companies. The Investment Company Act of 1940 still applies to the mutual fund industry. This act and the earlier reforms formed the durable foundation of a healthy, safe market for investors and bank depositors.

The last major set of Roosevelt administration initiatives to follow from the Crash of 1929 came in 1940 with the passage of the Investment Advisers Act and the Investment Company Act of that year. From these two closely related pieces of legislation, which I will occasionally conflate because they work mainly in tandem, arose the modern mutual fund. The new laws laid out permitted and prohibited practices governing pools of money belonging to investors other than the pool managers. Among the policies prohibited for regulated investment companies under the Investment Company Act of 1940 were short sales, the employment of leverage, and the use of pooled investor moneys to take control of commercial enterprises. Managed funds were required to register with the Securities and Exchange Commission and to report in considerable detail the funds' structures, conditions, portfolio compositions, and investment policies. Managers of pooled funds with money raised publicly were obligated to register under the Investment Advisers Act and comply with its behavioral and disclosure requirements. The new laws also dealt with investment company governance, mandating independent directors and restricting the forms of compensation available to portfolio managers. The Investment Company and Advisers acts remain law today, as do most of the Roosevelt-era reforms, with the notable exception of the Glass-Steagall provisions of the 1934 Banking Act. The history of their erosion has been not so much a story of repeal as one of sidesteps and exceptions.

The reforms enacted from 1933 to 1940 created a new sense of confidence in the financial markets. Wall Street earned, or regained, the trust of the whole world. Bankers who had opposed government intrusion into their business gradually came to appreciate the rewards that came with worldwide public confidence. The 1940s and the decades to follow were strong years for the financial markets and their institutions. By the 1960s, when I had my first Wall Street experiences (beginning as a New York Stock Exchange order clerk), the Securities and Exchange Commission was among the most respected agencies in government. Even my bosses in the brokerage businesses, who complained occasionally about SEC red tape and an overly tough enforcement division, expressed grudging admiration for the intelligence and the integrity of their regulators. If I pressed them, moreover, for examples of unjustified toughness on the part of the enforcement division, they usually came up dry. I concluded that the SEC's feared enforcement division struck just about the right balance for maintenance of the all-important reputation for integrity needed in a financial center full of temptations. Bank failures, meanwhile, receded from the public mind as a threat with the success of the Federal Deposit Insurance Corporation. The history of the Great Depression financial reforms is an unusually positive story in the annals of government action. Or, at least, it was until it began to unravel.

> The securities and banking reforms would stay intact for the better part of fifty years. But the seeds of their undoing were laid as hedge funds came into being in the 1940s, largely unnoticed and inconsequential for many years. Hedge funds were recently required to register with the SEC as advisers but still remain free from the substantive regulation of investment and sales practices that applies to mutual funds. Hedge fund compensation engendered hazardous mimicry in other Wall Street institutions.

The regression of the financial sector in the past few decades from orderly to irresponsible and its transformation from servant of commerce to master of the economy were gradual. No single action taken by government can be blamed for weakening the restraints. No single leader or political party can fairly be accused of intentionally killing the goose that laid the golden eggs. A dozen or more contributing steps, or missteps, led us to the cliff we reached in 2008. They are worth reviewing, not just because of the damage to the middle class the recent crash left in its wake, but because of the danger that the crash will be repeated.

The first misstep was to permit the introduction of hedge funds. The deep history of the hedge fund goes all the way back to the two acts passed in 1940. About the last thing the reformers at the SEC and in Congress intended to do at the time was to permit a huge investment industry to flourish outside of their new investment company regulatory scheme, but they inadvertently planted the seeds for exactly that result. These seeds were contained in seemingly innocuous and well-intentioned exemptions for private advisers and small pools. I have been unable to find a record of exactly who first suggested permitting these exemptions in the original pieces of legislation, but it is easy to reconstruct a logical scenario for their appearance.

The statutes that required registration of advisers and money managers, and the accompanying regulations, were plainly intended to cover the vast bulk of financial assets under management. Innocent, naive investors, sometimes loosely referred to as "widows and orphans," were to be protected from Wall Street sharpies by a plethora of rules governing the managers' conduct and incentives. Included were extensive requirements for disclosure, in keeping with Louis Brandeis's dictum that sunlight is the best disinfectant.

Imagine that you were an architect of the legislation, with one eye on its potential effectiveness and the other on expediting the requisite congressional enactment. You are visited by representatives of a wealthy family, maybe one with a good and familiar name like DuPont or Rockefeller, who ask you for an exemption. They point out that the family's money is managed by a family office that has no poor widows and orphans as clients. They explain that disclosure would safeguard not one soul in need of protection, and it would surely generate unwelcome attention—and even perhaps raise the risk of the family's children becoming kidnap victims. (The poor Lindbergh baby's brutal end had been among the leading press stories of the prior decade.) The wealthy families won't oppose your legislation, they say, if there are suitable exemptions. Looking at the practicalities of the politics, and the reasonableness of the argument, you would probably have granted their wish . . . and I would, too.

But, any good reformer might ask, should there really be an exemption from which only the most privileged American families would benefit? Logic and basic fairness said the case could be generalized without any harm to the widows and orphans. So an exemption from investment company regulation was provided for all pooled vehicles with fewer than one hundred clients, regardless of family ties, as long as they did not solicit new investors in any form of public offering. Investment advisers with a small enough clientele, and who did not hold themselves out to the public as advisers, were similarly exempted from the Investment Advisers Act. The exemptions, as intended, were harmless at first, covering only a minuscule segment of the investment market.

Then, in 1948, a particularly smart young journalist at *Fortune* magazine decided to try his skill at managing other people's money and saw the potential the exemptions provided. By 1952, Alfred Jones had designed a structure for his new business that allowed him to do pretty much everything the Investment Company Act and the Investment Advisers Act were designed to prohibit. He would hedge against general market movements by selling short (making him money when his stocks lost value) as well as holding long positions (where gains come from stock price rises); he would use leverage to magnify the potential upside (and downside) of his returns; and his form of organization would be a limited partnership rather than a mutual fund or a general partnership. His compensation would be in the form of an annual fee plus 20 percent of the profits above a defined threshold.[8] Remarkably, no money manager has substantially improved on Jones's structural innovation since then. This is the outline of virtually every modern hedge fund and private-equity fund format, and the descendants of Jones's fund — protected by a set of exemptions originally intended only for a rarefied few — lie almost entirely beyond regulatory reach. Only since 2012 have hedge fund managers been asked to register with the SEC as advisers at all, and, once registered, they are required to provide only minimal public disclosure. Hedge funds remain unregulated under the Investment Company Act, and their managers are still free of substantive regulation under the Investment Advisers Act.

The word *hedge* today, though, is something of a misnomer.

It implies that the portfolio is sheltered (the literal meaning of *hedged*) against the full brunt of major market movements by including both long and short positions. The notion, actually employed by Jones, is that some positions would rise in value whenever others fell.[9] Hedge funds today are permitted to do this, but in reality managers may or may not choose to be both long and short — so they are not necessarily hedged in the classic sense. More uniformly in keeping with Jones's technique, the vast majority use leverage and employ a limited partnership format with a performance fee. The best definition of a hedge fund to keep in mind when you hear the phrase is this: A hedge fund is any professionally managed money management vehicle for multiple participants outside the substantive regulatory scope of the Investment Company Act. In short, a hedge fund is, for the most part, simply an unregulated fund.

> The scale of hedge funds was skyrocketing by the 1990s and continues to grow, while their practices remain free from scrutiny. The combination of readily available, hungry capital and the opacity of the hedge funds creates an inevitable temptation for behavior contrary to the public interest.

By 1968, over a hundred hedge funds were borrowing Alfred Jones's structure, but most were small. Meaningful growth in their assets did not begin to occur until almost twenty years later, when the performance of Julian Robertson's Tiger Fund became the talk and envy of Wall Street. Since hedge funds still have minimal disclosure requirements, I am wary of estimating the assets they control. But BarclayHedge publishes an approximation. According to their numbers, as late as 1997, the total of investor assets managed by hedge funds worldwide had only approached $120 billion.[10] If that seems a large number, read on. Around that time, just as limiting applicability of an important exemption to members of privileged bloodlines must have bothered the framers of the Investment Company Act, another logical inconsistency or potential injustice came to the fore. Why should the benefits of the apparently above-market returns of hedge funds be available only to the already rich? Universities were investing in hedge funds, alongside the wealthy individuals who were the original participants. Pension funds wanted in as well. After all, they could afford losses better than most well-heeled individuals, and their investment gains would be shared by a wide spectrum of hard-working Americans. CalPERS, the California Public Employees' Retirement System, became an early trailblazer. In 1996, the Investment Company Act was amended to exclude from regulation those funds that limited their clientele to "qualified investors," allowing the number of participants to be expanded widely as long as they were all considered wealthy enough to risk investment losses. The available audience for hedge funds rose dramatically.

By 2004, just seven years after hedge fund assets had hit $120 billion, total assets were more like $1.2 trillion, tenfold the earlier count.[11] Since then, after a dip in 2008, the number has doubled again. In 2014, hedge fund assets reached $2.5 trillion.[12] That's a big enough number that only four or five countries in the world have larger GNPs. And, yes, I have a problem with that. The authors of the 1940 investment acts would surely turn over in their graves if they could hear how things have evolved, and you should be troubled as well.

The pension funds, first of all, bring those vulnerable widows and orphans into hedge fund investing, without the SEC's protection. This renders the whole notion of the exemption from regulation something of a mockery. The SEC deserves a bit of credit for a modest challenge about a decade ago to the notion that a pool of investors in a limited partnership should count as a single client for purposes of the exemptions, but it was too little and much too late. The U.S. Court of Appeals for the D.C. Circuit found that this expansion of regulatory oversight exceeded the SEC's statutory authority.[13] The proverbial widow or orphan can be part of a massive pension fund, and that fund in turn can be one of numerous limited partners in a hedge fund, but the fund manager can claim to have but a single wealthy client. The same manager, moreover, could go on to assemble additional funds under common management, each counting only as a single client.

It is a very safe bet that the massive quantity of assets under hedge fund management today would never have been considered fit for exemption by the 1940 Act's framers. Don't forget, moreover, that the available scale estimates look to assets managed on behalf of clients, not assets *controlled.* The assets controlled by hedge funds are some multiple of the managed total; that's the magic of leverage. Most important, though, the operations of the hedge fund world are conducted without the benefit of sunlight's disinfectant.

An unscrupulous hedge fund manager is much more likely than a mutual fund executive to get away with insider trading, the improper inducement of public officials managing pension funds to participate as limited partners, exaggerating past returns, or tax evasion. My Wall Street friends tell me that some of these abuses are the mainstays of certain hedge funds they have seen close up. Gossip of this sort is hardly evidence; smoke doesn't always signal fire. The problem is that whereas the regulated money management world is open to public view, the hedge fund environment is not. In a few of the most blatant cases, fund managers have been caught paying off junior professionals at law firms or accounting firms to tip them off to pending mergers that will move a stock price. When the manager is caught committing a crime, there will be an indictment and the record will become public. So we can be certain of a few such stories. You can either trust that these examples of outright abuse are rare and generally caught, in which case the record reflects the reality of the problem, or you can guess that the illicit exploitation we can observe in the public record is only the tip of an iceberg.

Beyond dispute is the prevalence of clever strategies that are legal but perhaps ought not to be permitted — strategies that offer advantages to the few at the expense of other market participants. These should matter to you because your own direct investments or traditional mutual fund holdings will pay a reduced return if someone siphons off part of the available investment return by dubious means. Since the hedge funds don't reveal their secrets, and these gimmicks are not the subject of enforcement actions, there is mainly logic and rumor to go on. But I hear these stories too often from Wall Street sources to disbelieve them. Here are a few examples. One old Wall Street hand described a hedge fund that pays an emolument to hotel clerks all over the country to tip off the fund when financial executives of a large company visit the city of a potential acquisition target. Multiple visits might provide enough circumstantial evidence of possible takeover activity to motivate a purchase of stock in the target company. Information from credit card companies would serve this purpose all the more efficiently, and I am told that at least one card provider has considered making it available to favored hedge funds. Numerous funds buy space physically close to exchanges to gain a fraction of a second's advantage over ordinary investors in the placement of their orders when news breaks — or over competitor hedge funds in the ordinary course of business.

One financial executive told me that many hedge funds place thousands of times the number of orders they actually want to execute, so that their orders will be at the front of the line if they get a mathematical buy or sell signal. The bulk of the orders are just canceled, all within the second before a trade would have occurred. Moving money rapidly around the world, and forming obscure overseas investment partnerships, can help some funds evade taxes. All of these behaviors can be glimpsed in the hedge fund world on those few occasions when the curtain is lifted; they are almost unheard of in the SEC-regulated investment company universe. None of the ever-so-clever activity creates a lick of value for the economy.

Modern financial theory tells us that it is hard to beat the market. Investing skillfully enough where others don't can accomplish that. So can laborious fundamental research when performed by an investor with a talent for seeing more clearly than the market. These legitimate strategies help us all by making capital allocation more efficient. Despite the nonsense you may hear from traders, there is no public benefit in the volume the hedge funds add to markets, and arbitrage that allegedly adds efficiency for seconds at a time is just as useless. With respect to blatant criminal activity, which more directly harms the rest of us, you should assume that hedge fund managers exhibit roughly the same spectrum of integrity that characterizes human nature everywhere when no one is looking. The net effect of nonfundamental hedge fund trading is to take potential returns from the rest of us, reducing the attractiveness of investments and thereby diminishing the market's ability to provide growth capital.

Although profit performance is hardly a precise measure of social utility, it is worth noting that hedge funds may fail even this narrowest of tests. It is not clear that hedge fund performance, properly adjusted for leverage, has ever really bettered the market as a whole.[14] A recent chart in *The Economist* suggests that for the past decade and even without adjustment for leverage, hedge funds have done substantially worse.[15] There will always be a bell curve of performance results, so some hedge funds have done remarkably well, and these are balanced by many poor performers. On the other hand, no one can doubt that the hedge fund structure has benefited hedge fund managers. The compensation format limitations intended by the 1940 Act have been nullified in the era of the hedge funds. The result is that hedge fund chieftains are America's new princes. Many of the highest-paid individuals in the country are from this rarefied universe. Examine the upper reaches of a campaign contribution report today—from either party—or the membership lists of the boards of directors of prestigious cultural institutions, and you will find a predominance of hedge fund managers that was absent just a few years back. Several of my favorite nonprofit organizations are the beneficiaries of generous contributions from hedge fund partners. In fact, I suspect that because hedge fund managers tend to be more intellectual than other members of the wealthy classes, I would admire their gift choices on the whole more than those of other philanthropists. That is not a reason, however, to exempt them from sensible regulation at the expense of other investors.

The spillover impacts of bountiful hedge fund compensation, moreover, have exceeded any direct harm. As one Wall Street friend of mine put it, the hedge fund leaders wouldn't have been paid so much had money managers under the restrictions of the 1940 Act not been jealous of highly paid investment bankers; and the compensation of the hedge fund managers who then won the brass ring and out-earned the investment bankers would have mattered less to the world had the commercial bankers in turn not become wildly envious of both investment bankers and the hedge fund managers. My hedge fund friends are quick to remind me that hedge funds weren't the cause of the 2008 crash. The banks were.

Unwieldy banking scale also became apparent in the 1990s. The Too Big to Fail banks today are also too big to manage and are incompatible with pluralist democracy. This is widely acknowledged, but scale provides the power to defeat downsizing. The excuses for maintaining their hazardous bulk are unconvincing on the merits.

The second sea change that arose to wash away the tranquillity of the New Deal regulatory regime was in the banking arena. When the 1930s reforms were written, the principal concern was that too many banks were small, undercapitalized, and unprotected. The reforms of the Great Depression era largely cured that problem. What their drafters could not foresee was that their reforms would eventually contribute to the reverse problem. They overshot their mark. The major banks of today are too large and too well protected by government backstops. When I was young, there were about thirteen thousand independent banks in the United States. The number is less than half that now.[16] The assets of the five largest banks taken together were less than $20 billion in 1950.[17] Now the five largest have around $5 trillion in deposits.[18] Just to pick an individual example, the single largest bank in 1950 was Bank of America, and it had assets of $5.8 billion.[19] The Bank of America today is the second-largest bank, and its deposits are $1.1 trillion.[20] In 1960, the ten largest banks held about one-fifth of the banking industry's assets.[21] Now their share exceeds two-thirds of the total.[22] Most of this change has occurred in response to changes in law, increasingly less congruent with the public interest.

As with the hedge funds, the start of this development was slow. From 1930 to 1970, the largest banks actually grew more slowly than the banking system as a whole.[23] Then, in the next two decades, numerous legal and regulatory constraints on bank size were abandoned, and the banking world vigorously bulked up. Until the mid-1960s, banking was essentially local. The pre-Depression McFadden Act had forbidden interstate branching by federally chartered banks, and the Federal Reserve later extended the prohibition to include all state-chartered banks that are regulated by the Fed. The banking business consisted mainly of taking deposits from near the home office and making equally nearby loans. When large corporations sought more sizable loans, the smaller banks could participate with money-center banks that originated the jumbo loans. Neither the local banks nor the money-center banks, however, could branch across state lines. Some states even forbade banks to have branches within the state. Minor exceptions were made in failing bank situations and to allow non-bank lending subsidiaries of bank holding companies to open cross-border offices, but these were of little significance. By 1956, though, the prohibitions were seen to be eroding, and as a compromise with the expanding banks, the Bank Holding Company Act was amended to permit interstate banking when explicitly approved by participating states.[24] Rather surprisingly, though, it was not until 1978 that the first state, Maine, chose to exercise its option and authorize interstate banking — by allowing out-of-state bank holding companies to operate there and remedy a perceived dearth of services.[25]

Other states soon began removing restrictions on intrastate and interstate banking. The remaining interstate banking restrictions were removed wholesale by the Riegle-Neal Interstate Banking and Branching Efficiency Act of 1994.[26] That law permitted bank holding companies to acquire banks in any state and, beginning in 1997, allowed interstate bank mergers. This was a critical event in the development of today's gargantuan banking institutions. The next step was the repeal of the Glass-

Steagall restrictions by the passage of the Gramm-Leach-Bliley Act of 1999, which allowed banks to engage fully in investment banking and in non-banking financial activities such as insurance.[27] These two pieces of legislation were truly nonpartisan initiatives, supported in Congress by both parties and signed into law by President Clinton. And thus was born Too Big to Fail.

The most obvious problem with Too Big to Fail banks is that you and I, as taxpayers, are required to stand behind profit-making enterprises with our wallets open in case they take too much risk. That provides a temptation to engage in economics that almost guarantee an occasional use of those wallets. Imagine a hypothetical activity in the field of finance that has the following characteristics. Every year the "game" pays you either $1 million or costs you $15 million, and you have estimated the ratio of winning years to losing years as ten to one. For every ten winning years, there is a losing year in which all the winnings and then some are wiped out. This would seem like a pretty unattractive proposition for an individual, and a worse one for a bank. Whoever you are, you'd come out behind. And, if you ran a fiduciary institution that needed to inspire trust, you'd be foolish to appear so prone to hazardous adventure.

But now apply a bit of magic government backup dust to this banking game and see what happens. In the winning years, the bank can apply the gains to shareholder dividends or bonus compensation for its traders and executives. The bonus money and the dividends get taken home somewhere and vanish from the table, much of it doubtless into private investments, family trusts, or luxury spending. In any case, and most important, this money is not retrievable in the inevitable losing year. And that's tolerable for the institution and its depositors, because the government can be called on as a backstop in the tough weather. If you are just an individual trader for a bank, the deal works even better. You may not still be in the employ of the bank when the bad year comes, and if you are, you will almost certainly not be the executive who has to plead for the bailout. In the bad year, maybe your bonus will be eliminated . . . and history suggests that even this is not a certainty. It may just be relabeled a "retention bonus."

This example is, of course, oversimplified. Banks and their traders don't really engage in trades that they know to be long-term losers. And the recent bailouts, in the case of banks specifically, have been largely to cover temporary periods of market panic and are thereafter paid back in full. The example is no less useful for this oversimplification. The incentive for imprudent speculative behavior remains whenever government backup intervention is a serious possibility and whenever there is an imbalance between frequent winning years and rare losing years — even if the losses in those years are potentially massive. Should the risky transactions under consideration look like probabilistic winners in the long run, these features will just cause them to be undertaken all the more eagerly at the margin and with all the more at risk. As long as taxpayer wallets are open, and the market punishments that hang over most businesses in the event of failure are buffered, normal restraints will be eroded in the minds of both the traders and the bank's executives. The modern scale of possible losses from leveraged trading activities has a perverse impact as well. Every banker knows the old aphorism that a small borrower is a debtor but a large enough borrower is the bank's partner. The government is a regulator when potential losses are manageable, but the threat of losses with systemic consequences turns the government into an inevitable, if unhappy, partner.

None of this should be news. The American public understands much of what is wrong with the Too Big to Fail syndrome. It just can't seem to make it go away. At least as concerning are the nasty cousins it comes to the dance with: Too Big to Manage and Too Big for Democracy. The notion of deposit insurance was irresistible to the New Deal reformers. But Washington's coins often have an unintended reverse side as well as the anticipated obverse. Deposit insurance unquestionably made depositors feel safer and runs on banks less likely, but it also gave banks an inherent advantage over other intermediaries and a set of ill-fated incentives to take risks. Deposit insurance, in the end, is a variation on controlled bailout, and the concept cannot escape the charge that it will always create a degree of moral hazard. Over time, and with branching and activity restrictions removed, the banks have used the backstop guarantees to help them gather massive assets. Their balance sheets then allowed them to turn away from the simple deposit and loan business to trading businesses they found more lucrative. With leverage, they have become behemoths.

The kind of scale the banks have achieved raises obvious problems in a democracy. Every political hand knows that reported lobbying expenditures are only a fraction of the effective use of money to exert influence. Public relations efforts, issue advertising during political campaigns, bundled contributions, and other fundraising techniques are a great deal more important. Nonetheless, it is useful to note that banks are among the largest spenders of reported lobbying dollars.[28] The total reported cost of bank lobbyists was over $63 million in 2014.[29] The financial sector as a whole is estimated to have spent $4.7 billion on lobbyists in the past decade.[30] I would be amazed, and so would the lobbyists, if it had no influence.

Inordinate scale also undermines good management. Any firm Too Big to Fail is almost certainly too big and complex and cumbersome to operate well. I know a good many people involved in leviathan bank management and board governance. The ones I know are mostly honorable people, of usual talent and proven work ethic, trying to do their jobs responsibly. Trust me on this, though: no chief executive or board of directors, however knowledgeable, talented, and honest, can oversee such enterprises and assure the avoidance of systemic impairment. Nor can any government oversight body. This is the answer to former Federal Reserve Chairman Alan Greenspan's puzzled musing about why the bank directors were unable to apply "self-interest . . . to protect shareholders' equity."[31] The embarrassing $9 billion loss occasioned by a few rogue traders at JPMorgan Chase in 2012 was not an indictment of the bank's senior executive talent or integrity. It was proof that even Wall Street's most visibly successful commercial bank cannot properly mind its own nest. The banks are too big for anyone's good — other than their own executives'.

This is not just the view of Occupy Wall Street activists. Some of the world's most trusted and experienced public-sector experts on banking have reached similar conclusions about excessive scale. Former Federal Deposit Insurance Corporation Chairman Bill Isaac has said that banks have gotten "too big to manage, and too big to regulate."[32] Thomas Hoenig, Vice Chair of the FDIC, has suggested a straightforward breakup of the largest banks.[33] Daniel Tarullo, an influential current governor of the Federal Reserve Board, suggested limiting bank growth from all sources other than deposits and blocking any future mergers involving the largest banks.[34] Richard Fisher, former President of the Dallas Federal Reserve Bank, was quoted as saying, "We must cap their size or break them up — in one way or another shrink them relative to the size of the industry."[35] Simon Johnson, formerly the Chief Economist for the International Monetary Fund and now a professor at MIT, has declared with admirable optimism, "The debate is over; the decision to cap the size of the largest banks has been made. All that remains is to work out the details."[36]

In England, Sir Mervyn King, former Governor of the Bank of England and now Baron King of Lothbury, was all the more vocal about what he had learned on the job as his tenure came to an end. King, whom no one called a radical for most of his career, stated that the giant international banks were putting "profits before people" to a greater extent than manufacturing industries, and that failure to reform the banking sector would likely result in another financial crisis. "Market discipline," he has said, "can't apply to everyone except banks."[37] King has called for the breakup of the country's biggest banks, adding colorfully that unless the UK regulator, the Bank of England, is given more power to ensure financial stability, it would be like a church: able to "do no more than issue sermons or organize burials."[38]

There is always another side to the argument, of course. In this case, I honestly can't recall hearing it from just about anyone other than people whose livelihoods are related to bank executives or academics with consulting contracts from the same sources, but that doesn't necessarily prove it false. There are two versions of the counterargument, related but differing enough to present separately. One is that sophisticated modern commerce depends on activities in which only the very largest banks on the planet can engage. The other is that any attempt by the United States to regulate banking more than it is regulated today will cause the business to move overseas or disappear into the shadow banking world of hedge funds and other unregulated corporate creations.

The first argument is almost entirely sophistry. Spokespersons for the largest banks will say that their corporate clients need institutions of their size and geographical spread. There is certainly truth to the contention that today's business is more complex and global than business prior to the Great Depression. But, with the benefit of today's communications technology, banks around the world can easily cooperate with one another as needed to deal with global needs for a medium of exchange. Syndicates can form in a matter of hours for jumbo loans. And no corporate client really requires that its bank have trillions of dollars in derivatives positions. Just as important, sophistication in hedging is not proportional to institutional size, as multiple boutique investment banking and trading firms have shown.

It is true enough that the reforms of the 1930s cannot simply be transplanted into the modern world and work as well as they did at the time. The concerns today are different. We surely don't need to worry about too many small banks without deposit insurance. Similarly, the cramming of errors in underwriting public offerings into trust funds is no longer at the top of the worry list. If the Glass-Steagall separations are to be restored, they will have to be redesigned. It is the Glass-Steagall philosophy, more than the original law's precise content, that calls now for revival. The combination that most greatly threatens banking stability today is not investment banking and estate management. It is the admixture of insured deposit collection and highly leveraged trading in derivatives.

The insistence that the banking business will move elsewhere if offended by enhanced oversight or conduct limitations is a variation on a theme that every regulator has heard all too often. Had your elected representatives listened to this kind of threat over the past hundred years, we would probably have no income tax, no Social Security or other safety nets, no child labor laws, no Medicare, and none of the Roosevelt financial reforms. It is easy to argue that all public interest initiatives are futile because businesses can just pick up and race to the bottom into the arms of another host. Jurisdiction shopping can be a problem, but only if we let it. We don't have to let businesses domiciled in tax and regulatory havens buy control of our own financial companies, and in some industries — such as banking — it is not difficult to limit their activities here. I would argue, moreover, that better regulation of financial markets is a net attractor of capital. Look where the financial centers are today: the United States, the United Kingdom, and Singapore, to pick a few examples. These are by no means the countries of the world with the least regulation; all three are serious about oversight. America's place as the world's financial center is largely due to our hosting the most honest and well-supervised markets in the world. We have prospered more as a benefit of competent regulation, market integrity, and relative stability than despite those features.

This is a minority view, it seems, on this issue. Too many Americans feel the need for us to be the biggest in everything. It was only twenty years ago that Wall Street pundits and more than a few politicians warned that Japan would eat our lunch because their banks were bigger than ours. Japan never got to enjoy this predicted feast. Instead, Japan's oversized banks helped to serve up several decades of recession. And Japan is not the only example of a country harmed by following this false piper's call. Iceland, Scotland, and Ireland were all charmed by the same tune. If there must be an international race to determine which country has the largest banks, I'd prefer to see the U.S. team forfeit.

The argument that further regulation of banking practices would cause financial transactions and talent to migrate from the supervised banks to the shadow banking world deserves more credence. This could indeed happen, as long as we allow hedge funds and "non-bank banks" to have many of the powers of banks, permit unregulated investment companies to drain off the money that would otherwise be invested through companies regulated under the 1940 Act, and treat offshore entities as well as our own. I hear that argument, though, as saying that because we naively opened the back door to the barn, we now have to give up on closing the front door. The better answer is to slam that back door closed.

Trading in derivatives expanded at the end of the twentieth century from a relatively small business in agricultural contracts to a vast business centered on financial instruments. What began as legitimate hedging is now out of proportion to any useful commercial purpose and overrides sensible constraints on leverage regulation.

The third wave that overwhelmed prudent Wall Street regulation was powered by the explosive expansion of the derivatives market. This is the sector of finance the Commodity Futures Trading Commission was created to oversee. Before the 2008 meltdown, many of you had probably never heard of derivatives. While they are anything but new, their systemic importance is quite recent. One of the most basic derivatives instruments, the futures contract, came into use in the United States before the Civil War. The usual story of the origin of futures begins with midwestern farmers or grain elevator operators who had corn or wheat to sell in Chicago. They found it useful, for several reasons, to make their initial contact with the buyers before bringing the bulky and perishable grain on the journey. The crop, the "physical" in trading lingo, might be waiting to be transported or still in the ground. The major grain dealers would enter into "futures" contracts with the suppliers to buy the wheat or corn at an appropriate later date and at a price fixed in advance.

The certainty of the future price was presumably helpful for both parties. The futures contract price might differ from the current, or "spot," price due to predictions of future supply and demand, finance and storage charges, and various other uncertainties. When the futures contract negotiation was completed, each of the two parties held a piece of paper that spelled out the party's rights and obligations. That paper was said to be "derivative" of the physical commodity to be delivered. A derivative today is still essentially that, a contract to buy or sell some more tangible (or durable) good or instrument at a certain future date and at a price set at the time of the original contract. The one-step removal from the item itself, the fact that the contract does not convey present ownership of any actual asset, is the root of the "derivative" appellation.

The paper contract, the derivative, over time became a negotiable instrument. You didn't need to deliver a shipment of a crop or accept delivery of one if you could find someone else willing and able to enter into a cash transaction with you to take your place during the life of the contract. You didn't, in fact, need to be in the growing or distribution business at all to buy or sell a futures contract as an intermediary. The market only needed to be sure that when the contract expired, there would be someone on one side of the contract who could hand over the physical commodity and someone else on the other side ready to accept it and pay for it. It didn't matter who held either side of the contract before its settlement date as long as the holders were financially reliable.

When there was enough volume in derivatives contracts, boisterous open-outcry exchanges in Chicago, organized originally for handling spot trades, began to trade them. The markets grew large and more numerous but remained principally agricultural until fairly recently. In 1921, Congress authorized regulation of the exchanges and the trading of their futures contracts by the U.S. Department of Agriculture. The goal was to prevent defaults, corners, and squeezes that could injure the markets — and that scoundrels could bring about to manipulate prices. The markets continued to expand throughout the twentieth century and added more and more commodities for trading. These included, for example, contracts for coffee, cattle, eggs, butter, chickens, and pork bellies (which, incidentally, are nothing more mysterious than uncut bacon). As late as the 1970s, the largest sources of volume in futures markets were still the contracts for delivery of wheat, corn, and soybeans. But a transformational change was in the air.

If you think back to the concept of hedging in securities markets, you should see a parallel. When traders own some shares of stock and have sold short some similar securities, they are said to be hedged. When one element of their total position goes up in value, they expect the other to go down, moderating the net impact. When a farmer has grain in the bin, and a contract to sell a comparable type and quantity of grain later at a fixed price, the farmer is similarly hedged. Someone was bound to see the opportunity to extend the agricultural futures markets to financial instruments, and someone did. The leader of the Chicago Mercantile Exchange (now the CME Group) in the 1970s, a man of unusual foresight named Leo Melamed, was encouraged by the Nobel Prize laureate economist Milton Friedman to boldly expand a relatively small Chicago exchange by adding a contract on currencies.[39] Then came a contract for gold futures, responding to recent legalization of the private ownership of gold by Americans.[40] Next, the CME introduced a contract based on U.S. Treasury securities, effectively a futures contract on interest rates.[41] It wasn't long before Treasury Note contracts became the highest-volume contracts traded anywhere. Today the trading of agricultural futures accounts for a single-digit percentage of global futures trading.[42] The derivatives markets are principally financial futures markets.

Strict regulation of securities markets by the SEC made the introduction of contracts on stocks problematic for the futures exchanges. The SEC had already claimed jurisdiction over trading in options on individual stocks, and it would surely want to extend its philosophy of limited leverage and full disclosure to the trading of any derivatives instruments based on stock market indices. Customary leverage in futures, as measured by the margin or earnest money a trader had to deposit to control a futures contract, was about twenty to one. The SEC career staffers were just not the right folks to convince that this was prudent. Disclosure of open positions was unknown in futures trading, another feature of derivatives markets that the SEC wouldn't countenance happily. And insider trading was not a crime in the trading of futures; it was considered a routine business necessity for the large grain merchants. It was with the knowledge that the SEC would not be a happy regulatory home for the burgeoning derivatives market that the Commodity Futures Trading Commission was established in 1974.[43] With only a very few exceptions, the commissioners appointed to the CFTC were happy to provide an atmosphere for the growth of the derivatives industry that maintained just about none of the SEC's philosophical principles. Derivatives based on stock market indices were approved by the CFTC, over my dissenting vote, early in the Reagan administration. Stock index futures soon rivaled interest rate futures for the honor of being the most active exchange-traded derivatives contracts.[44]

The notion of hedging has broad applicability in commerce. An airline can hedge against expensive increases in jet fuel cost by buying oil futures; an American company holding foreign currency earned in selling its goods abroad can hedge against that currency losing future value against the dollar; a power company can hedge against dips in average temperature during a winter season that might cause it to have to supplement its energy sources at high prices. This versatility, and the obvious benefit to commercial users, is the *raison d'être* for futures markets. But don't jump to the conclusion that nonfinancial hedgers are the principal users of the markets.

Traders will tell you that for the hedgers to have reasonable liquidity and a deep market, there need to be speculators and arbitrageurs in the market as well. In fact, although the borderlines are murky, there is no question that nonfinancial hedgers are now the holders of only a minuscule percentage of the open positions in today's markets. The vast bulk are held by hedge funds and banks, and therein lies the rub.

I have never questioned the value of hedging markets. The oil-in-the-machinery analogy works well here, though. The derivatives markets' legitimacy of purpose is hard to dispute, but the magnitude, opacity, and nature of their trading today make them a net negative for all of us. These markets are an archetypical example of too much of a good thing. It was the emergence of huge banks and the development of derivatives markets with minimal regulation of leverage or disclosure that together created the nearly perfect monster of a storm that struck in 2008. The banks, though, were not just enamored of exchange-traded derivatives. Off-exchange derivatives were even less subject to rules and disclosure than exchange-traded instruments. The particular trading instrument that nearly destroyed some of America's largest banks was the off-exchange mortgage derivative.

The federal government has been involved in mortgage markets since 1938, when the Federal National Mortgage Association (universally known as Fannie Mae) was formed to allow banks to expand their mortgage-writing capacity.[45] The idea was that they could write mortgages and then sell them to a government-sponsored agency, freeing up the cash to write more mortgages. A sister agency, called Ginnie Mae (Government National Mortgage Association), improved on Fannie Mae's technique by creating the first mortgage-backed securities in 1968.[46] These were off-exchange derivatives whose values would rise or fall with the payment performance of packages of mortgages. By selling these instruments to the individual and institutional public, Ginnie Mae correctly assumed that it could increase its effective capital base by the addition of investor capital. Soon, the other government mortgage support agencies were also issuing mortgage derivatives, and they were eagerly followed by the banks. Numerous regulatory changes accommodated and expedited the growth of this market, which, it was presumed, would increase the percentage of Americans who owned homes. By 2008, the mortgage-backed securities market encompassed about $11 trillion in securitized loans.[47]

The spawn of the agricultural hedging markets of the 1960s had become a financial colossus. No longer agricultural at its base and no longer primarily serving commercial hedging, the derivatives business had a life of its own — subject to little or no regulation of its leverage or practices. That life is centered in the big banks, which just a short while back were barely in the derivatives business at all. You might guess that banks in the United States hold derivatives positions many times their capital. You probably won't guess how many times. You may be thinking of the two-to-one leverage permitted by the SEC in the stock market. Or perhaps you recall that derivatives require a margin of about 5 percent, equating to twenty-to-one leverage. If so, you are way off. The ten largest U.S. banks, last time I saw the data, held a notional value of open derivatives positions in excess of $200 trillion.[48] That number, by the way, is almost three times the aggregated GNP of the entire world.[49] In the case of JP Morgan the notional value is more than 230 times the bank's equity. In Citigroup's case, the ratio to the bank's equity is a bit higher still.[50]

But our risk isn't anywhere near what those notional values imply, the bankers will protest, and that's right. The loss suffered would be equal to the trillions in notional value only if the bank were to be wiped out to a zero valuation in every one of its derivatives holdings. That can't happen, of course, because some of the positions are hedges for currencies, mortgages, or other direct ownership instruments they are holding — and many are balanced at least in part by countervailing positions that move in an opposing direction. So how much is the real risk? What is the real leverage?

The problem is that no one, not in the government or the banks or anyone else, knows what the real risk level or leverage is. Bankers will tell you that they have built sophisticated statistical models to tell them how much remaining risk they are exposed to, after positions that move in opposite directions are properly "netted" against each other. The regulators have, in general, accepted these models as useful and reliable. They publish numbers for true Value at Risk (called VaR in regulatory shorthand) based on this kind of modeling. The problem is that the model results aren't reliable. They can't, in fact, ever be. The inaccuracies are not the fault of the banks or the brilliant geeks who build the models. There simply isn't any way to build a particularly robust model of a huge interconnected system based on past data. Models cannot ever catch all of the interactions of seemingly independent variables, forecast the impacts of mass psychology and geopolitical disruptions, or work through "butterfly effects" caused by what chaos-theory physicists call "sensitive dependence on initial conditions."

Just as important, models based on past data can never predict hitherto unknown possibilities. These "black swans" are events that have never occurred before, or at least not to the modelers' knowledge, and are thus omitted from the menu of possible events until they are seen and recorded. The hard fact is that the universe we live in can generate an effectively infinite number of these black swans, some of which can be pretty dramatic. Observed and recorded events are necessarily a tiny fraction of all possible events. You should take little or no comfort from models that appear to prove that derivatives risks in the large banks net to nearly zero. Notional values are not powerful as cardinal measures of risk, but they are not bad as ordinal measures. The larger the notional position, the greater the risk and the leverage.

A complete transformation of the banking business has occurred since financial derivatives were first popularized. Traditional banking depended on deposits and loans. As recently as the 1990s, loans were the destination of close to 100 percent of deposits.[51] Now that fraction is closer to 75 percent.[52] Just as important, nontraditional banking activities, such as trading in leveraged derivatives, accounted for only a tiny share of bank revenues and net income until recently. One study shows that by 2010, nontraditional sources contributed almost 40 percent of the revenues and 80 percent of the net income of the top five banks.[53] The shift away from banking dependence on the deposit and loan business is undeniable.

An anecdote from my business life may help make the point. Plymouth Rock's owners have never felt comfortable carrying long-term debt, and it was never needed. In 2013, though, we had requests to cash out some of our early investors. The cost was affordable, but we didn't want to cut our investment portfolio that year by the full amount of the buyback. So we decided to overcome our reluctance and borrow $45 million. The bank loan we sought was flawlessly collateralized. One of the best-known mega-banks made the loan, quickly and professionally, but to be confident we were getting a fair price we showed the opportunity to another of the giants. That bank put a senior team on the matter and reported back to us that they were not looking for new collateralized loans at the time but could put together a package of derivatives for sale to us that would accomplish all of our objectives better than borrowing the money.

You may be wondering why the derivatives business is so profitable for the banks. The answer is mainly that derivatives are sold to clients at whatever price the bank can get for them. The customer has no way to check what the same bank might have charged the previous customer for an equivalent purchase. This is a highly inefficient market that favors the originators and market makers in the derivatives instruments. And, to make matters worse, the buyers today are prone to consuming more of the product than they need. Derivatives are zero-sum investments by nature. Nobody can win without someone else losing. The profits the banks earn on derivatives trading are so large that there is only one possible source of the money that is lost — the nonfinancial businesses that buy the derivatives products. No one else has that much wealth to lose. Yet these, of course, are exactly the economic entities on which real prosperity depends. No one forces these nonfinancial companies to buy so much hedging protection. Companies today display a purely voluntary tendency to overprotect themselves by overpurchasing hedging instruments. Overly eager buyers, opaque prices, and imbalances in sophistication are an inauspicious combination for those of us who admire efficient markets.

When I began my career as a consultant to an insurance broker in 1972, my first assignment was to visit some of America's largest manufacturing companies and convince them that they were buying too much insurance. They covered their risks too completely for at least two reasons. They didn't seem to understand that the transaction cost, insurer overhead, and expected insurer profit embedded in every purchase implied that the expected loss to the corporation from a peril like fire would be lowest if they absorbed (and thus self-insured) as much as the overall parent corporation's balance sheet could handle. And divisional organizational structures gave individual managers an incentive to minimize risk in their own silos even if this was inefficient for the corporation as a whole. Businesses are smarter insurance buyers today, but exactly the same thought errors make them buy too many hedging derivatives.

Think of a hypothetical company that buys something in Norway and sells something else in Sweden — under two different managers. The manager in Norway may buy a derivative to protect against a rise in that country's Krone, while the Swedish manager may buy another derivative to hedge against a fall in the Krona. Neither knows what the company ought to pay for the derivatives, so both may overpay — while the company as a whole actually needed less of each hedge because it already had the other transaction to get it partway there. If the same bank sells the two instruments to the client, incidentally, its models might tell it that the two positions net well enough against each other historically that the bank doesn't need to record an increase in net risk at all. The two currencies may sound similar, but in reality they need not move in unison. The relationship between the Krona and the Krone may be such that offsetting positions in the two currencies offer some intrinsic hedge for the commercial corporation, which it ignores to its detriment in the example, but nothing like the complete and perfect hedge the bank might claim to have.

Nonfinancial businesses have generally not supported price disclosure that would help cure overcharging for derivatives, but they ought to. The price transparency and the reduced costs that would follow from disclosure would be vastly more valuable to them than the protection of privacy they imagine as indispensable for their hedging strategies. Hedging with derivatives can indeed reduce risk in all kinds of commerce — just as insurance policies can — but hedging instruments are likely to be of benefit to the client and the economy on balance only if (a) they are sold at fair and reasonable prices; (b) they reduce the net risk to an enterprise by enough to justify their purchase costs; (c) they are sold by entities that can actually meet the obligations without taxpayer subsidies when things go wrong; and (d) they don't create more systemic risk for the economy than they remove for the buyers. In recent years, these tests have not been very well met by derivatives.

About ten years before the Crash of 2008, the CFTC sought comments on the impact of certain over-the-counter derivatives, an inquiry that could have preceded the writing of oversight rules. The CFTC chair at the time was asked by the other key financial regulators, some say quite harshly, not to continue her inquiry. She expressed a wish to examine the matter nonetheless — and was blocked from doing so by the same administration that had appointed her. At the request of the Treasury, the Congress soon passed the Commodities Futures Modernization Act of 2000, which effectively ended her exploration and prohibited future CFTC regulation of these derivatives markets. The so-called modernization statute of 2000, along with the Riegle-Neal Act and the Gramm-Leach-Bliley Act, were the misguided terrible triplets of financial deregulation. These three legislative signals announced our government's support, and even encouragement, for what the bills' supporters called "financial innovation." Although the benefits of moderate, careful hedging are not to be denied, and innovations like the ATM and a few modern life insurance and annuity types are doubtless pluses for the public, the alleged innovations the industry has fought for most fervently are enhancements of secrecy, increases in leverage, and the creation of new opportunities for tax gimmickry. I urge you to be suspicious anytime you hear a call for more financial innovation. Warren Buffett was closer to the mark when he called highly leveraged derivatives "financial weapons of mass destruction."[54]

> The Crash of 2008 caused damage not just on Wall Street but throughout the entire world. While another Great Depression was avoided, even now the recovery is incomplete. Real estate derivatives gave the storm its initial ferocity in 2008, but it was the weakness of the financial institutions themselves that turned this storm into a crisis. Storms will recur, but with stronger institutions, crises can be avoided.

This is not a book about the Crash of 2008, or the Great Recession that followed it. There have been plenty of such books. It is not even a book about the congressional reforms that were passed in the wake of the crash. Still, the events of 2008 and thereabouts require some brief summary here, if only as a reminder of how vulnerable we are to financial instability today.

We can start in early 2007, when talk was still of "irrational exuberance" in the financial markets. In February of that year, there were ominous tremors. Mortgage intermediary Freddie Mac (Federal Home Loan Mortgage Corporation) stopped purchasing subprime mortgages and related securities. By the end of July, the private rating services had initiated credit watches on some mortgage-backed securities. Countrywide Financial, among the largest of the subprime mortgage originators, warned that it was facing "difficult conditions," and Wall Street broker Bear Stearns liquidated several hedge funds specializing in risky mortgage derivatives. By January of 2008, Countrywide had essentially failed. It was purchased, with strong government encouragement, by the Bank of America. In March, Bear Stearns went down, and the regulators expedited a cheap sale of its remains to JPMorgan Chase. The Treasury then increased its existing credit lines to Fannie Mae and Freddie Mac and announced that it would buy shares in either one as needed. That offer quickly proved insufficient. Few doubted that the situation had become a full-fledged crisis.[55]

September of 2008 was the most dramatic month, as crisis gave way to panic. The Federal Housing Finance Agency placed Fannie Mae and Freddie Mac under government conservatorship. The Bank of America announced it would purchase the potentially failing Merrill Lynch & Co., for decades the national leader among retail stockbrokerage firms. Lehman Brothers, a top investment banker and securitizer of mortgage derivatives, filed for federal bankruptcy protection. And, to the surprise of almost everyone, the Fed authorized a loan of $85 billion to AIG, a New York–based insurer — not a bank at all — to help it survive losses at its London-based derivatives trading subsidiary.

Investors now began to wonder if even the strongest firms on Wall Street could make it through. Smart hedge fund managers began placing big bets against them. In shades of the 1930s, the SEC responded with a temporary ban on short sales of financial sector companies' shares, and the Treasury asked Congress for the authority to bail out banks as needed by buying troubled assets from them for cash. Goldman Sachs and Morgan Stanley, the Street's most revered investment bankers, were invited to become bank holding companies in a hurry. The government was eager to signal that they, too, would have backstop protection. In another first, the Treasury announced it would secure the assets of money market funds if that became necessary. Toward the end of the month, the government closed the massive Washington Mutual Bank and, like Bear Stearns, what was left of "WaMu" was acquired by JPMorgan Chase.[56]

October saw the passage by Congress of a $700 billion Troubled Asset Relief Program (TARP), which soon came to symbolize the bailout process. The Federal Reserve created a liquidity backstop for commercial paper issuers and committed a great deal more relief money to the ailing AIG. The FDIC substantially increased deposit insurance coverage. Next, the Fed helped to close the nation's fourth-largest bank, approving the merger of failed Wachovia into even larger Wells Fargo. Under the TARP umbrella, the Treasury announced that it would make available $250 billion to purchase stock in systemically important financial institutions. The most dramatic moment of the crash was over, but the damage to the real economy was just beginning.[57]

Human beings, and perhaps especially Americans, tend to have woefully short memories. Too many have already forgotten just how harmful the events of the 2008 period were. There was, first of all, the loss of economic value that most of you probably felt directly. Counting the drop in the value of common stock investments, home equity, and retirement assets, the average American family lost over a third of its net worth.[58] Gross national product declined, and real growth did not resume until 2010.[59] Asset prices have recovered in the past few years, but potential growth from the earlier peaks of GDP and GNP is lost forever and can be measured in the trillions of dollars. This does not include whatever the crisis did to people in other nations. Among banking nations, the United Kingdom was particularly hurt, but the pain didn't end with the financial centers. The International Monetary Fund has estimated that the crash will have prevented some seventy million people in developing countries from escaping poverty by 2020.[60]

Unemployment in the United States rose from 5 percent in early 2008 to around 10 percent by 2009, and to higher levels for the young and minorities.[61] Again there has been recent recovery, in this case still partial, but the interim losses and the suffering endured by so many American families cannot be erased. Some economists have speculated that the tight times caused companies to adjust their employment patterns structurally in order to use less labor, or less full-time salaried labor, on a long-term basis. Spending programs aimed at reinforcing the economy helped push the national debt from 64 percent of GDP pre-crisis to over 103 percent six years later in 2014.[62] Bailouts diverted your scarce tax money, at least temporarily, to making up the deficits of government and private financial institutions. Foreclosures of homes hit historic record levels and have only recently been tamed. History will probably view what happened as an extremely painful near miss. The United States did not experience another decade-long event comparable to the Great Depression, but it might have. You shouldn't allow yourselves to forget either the pain of those years or the proximity to a much greater disaster. You certainly should not want this to happen again.

Before the deregulation era began, the financial system benefited from a certain cyclical robustness, and the rest of the economy was strengthened in turn. This has been undone by increases in leverage. Instead of providing ballast for the economy, the banking sector's currently unbridled leverage generates snowball effects, and the interconnectedness of the giants of finance magnifies contagion when market prices undergo adjustment. Conservative institutions of finance, and in particular the commercial banks, used to help the country get through inevitable economic cycles by retaining profits from good years as capital to cushion the leaner deposit and lending years. As much of their business shifted toward trading activities, their compensation patterns shifted to mimic those of the hedge funds and trading firms. Competition for brainpower with high-paying money managers and investment bankers added to the pressure. The loss of this cushioning has been a blow to security, not just for the banks but for the whole economy.

Our largest banks are now vessels unworthy of stormy seas, but free-market capitalism by its essential nature will always continue to provide an occasional storm. The leverage of the banks, their undercapitalization, the ease with which their assets can flee instantly to the shadow banking system, and their internal cloning of edgy hedge fund cultures have all contributed to reductions in their seaworthiness. The seas, meanwhile, are no calmer. Part of the essential freedom that characterizes successful capitalism is the liberty to risk defiance of established rules of prudence and test the limits in ways that will lead to occasional gales. Free markets won't ever stop generating periodic bubbles, fads, irrational exuberances, manic-depressive markets, pendulum swings, storms, or whatever else you wish to call the excesses to which investors can be subject on occasion. The proximate cause of the Crash of 2008 was a blowup in the home housing market, where public and institutional irrationality and some naive government policies generated a mighty bubble, but next time the storm will probably arise somewhere else. The lack of institutional seaworthiness is all you can fix. Our financial institutions before 1929 were vulnerable. For a while they were quite solid after that, with strong hulls and durable ballast to help them absorb the pounding of storms. But they have become highly vulnerable vessels once again since deregulatory fever took hold, and there are many innocent passengers aboard.

The institutional flaws that turned a crash into a crisis included excessive leverage, unscrupulous practices, and inadequate disclosure as well as oversized banks. The administra-

> tion felt that the threat of a depression constrained it from punishing wrongdoers or concentrating on structural reforms to remedy those weaknesses. Congress took only a modest step toward curing the ills.

All of the dangers the New Deal reforms were meant to minimize came to the fore again in the real estate market of the decades before the crash. There was too much leverage. There was inadequate disclosure. Underwriting and risk analysis by lenders and mortgage insurers was shoddy. There were unscrupulous sales practices by mortgage brokers, not subject to any regulatory oversight paralleling that of stockbrokers, as well as by the banks that enabled them. And there were new dangers. Mortgage derivatives, with names like "credit default swaps" and "collateralized debt obligations" (called CDSs and CDOs by the pros), were too complicated even for their issuers to understand. And musclebound banks were unable to react as nimbly as smaller institutions could have. They just did whatever the others did. The epigram that best sums up the pre-crash period in banking was the unfortunate statement by the CEO of one of the top banks quoted this way: "As long as the music is playing, you've got to get up and dance."[63] The music stopped when real estate prices finally reversed their long uphill climb.

There were both rescue operations and law changes to be undertaken by the government. An instructive book on the rescue was written by Timothy Geithner, who had taken over as Treasury Secretary in the dark days of 2009. Although Geithner may have a different perspective from my own on what needs repair, he comes across as an honest, clear thinker and a reliable reporter. His fear was that we would fall into another Great Depression, and he felt he owed the public whatever it took, including the acceptance of personal attacks, to see that the crisis was stemmed before that could happen. He saw the prospect of depression as so threatening that he was willing to ignore blame and provide relief to all of the systemically important institutions that needed it. If my metaphor is a storm at sea, his was fire. "The obvious objection to government help for troubled firms," he wrote,

> was that it rewarded the arsonists who set the system on fire . . . [but] the goal should be to protect the innocent, even if some of the arsonists escape their full measure of justice . . . The potential benefits of avoiding depression far outweigh the potential cost of saving people who don't deserve to be saved . . . even if it seems to reward incompetence and venality, even if it fuels the impression of an out-of-control, money spewing, bailout-crazed government. That's why we stood behind so many mismanaged firms.[64]

On the order of actions to be taken, he was incontrovertibly correct. The metaphorical fire had to be put out right away. By September of 2008, it was clear that bailouts of essential institutions, however unpopular, really were necessary to minimize the risk of inviting a decade of depression. These could have been linked to reforms to render a future crisis less likely, though, and I suspect this would have made them less unpopular with a bewildered public. Some in the public sphere soon after were calling for criminal investigations, which logically follows from the arson metaphor but similarly misses the importance of required structural change. The problem is more with today's laws than with those who push them to their legal limits. Again, I share a view with the British central banker Mervyn King — that except in those egregious cases which King would doubtless also exempt, "Don't demonize individuals here . . . this was a problem of failure of a system. We collectively allowed the banking system to become too big, we gave them far too much status and standing in society, and we didn't regulate it adequately by ensuring it had enough capital."[65] Sure, there are financial criminals, and doubtless more belong in jail than have gotten there since 2008, but anyone who thinks a few glamorous prosecutions will protect us from a recurrence of crisis is naive. In an ill-conceived financial structure like ours, more harm by leagues is done within the boundaries of the law than outside it.

It was appropriate that attention soon turned to Congress, leading to the Dodd-Frank Wall Street Reform and Consumer Protection Act of 2010. Many of us had higher hopes at the start of the legislative process than we should have. With the administration still focused almost entirely on building confidence in troubled, and troublesome, institutions; with issues complex enough to baffle legislators and press alike; with much of the public angry at the bailouts; with the dysfunctional hyper-partisanship of today's parties; and with intensified efforts on the part of financial sector contributors and lobbyists, Congress never showed much interest in any fundamental structural change writ large. The direction of the reform effort was constructive, but history will surely not compare its output to that of the Roosevelt era.

Responding largely to expressed public opinion, legislators placed their primary emphasis on avoiding future bailouts—a questionable goal and one that you should have little faith has actually been accomplished. A prospectively useful consumer protection agency for financial products was established, mainly in reaction to abuses in mortgage brokerage. Some modest, and potentially valuable, steps were taken to increase mandatory bank capital. A version of former Fed chairman Paul Volcker's proposed rule to curb proprietary trading by banks was included in the legislation. And hedge fund managers were finally required to register with the SEC, a possible baby step toward meaningful regulation of their industry—but not more than that. The legislation did not effectively reduce leverage, the scale of the banks, or the opaque autonomy of the hedge funds. The night that the reform bill passed, I happened to be with a congressman involved in its construction. He said, "Jim, you're only going to give this bill a B-minus. But, remember, that's the best grade Congress has earned in financial regulation for fifty years."

> The current situation is at least as hazardous as before the crash. The benefits of massive banks, highly leveraged derivatives, and hedge fund secrecy are far outweighed by their costs. Just as important, the overall scale of the financial sector is out of proportion to its economic value. It is draining the commercial sector of the profits it needs for job creation and economic growth.

Look at what we are left with and ask yourself: What is wrong with this picture? The answer, unfortunately, is that a lot is wrong. You have been thrown a lot of facts and arguments in this chapter, including a smorgasbord of indigestibly large numbers, but all can be easily summarized. The top banks, post-crash and post-reforms, are larger in absolute terms and market share than before 2008.[66] The hedge fund industry has continued to grow in size and clout, free to act without the benefits of close scrutiny and absent a shred of benefit to the markets or society as a whole. The open derivatives positions, and therefore the risk profiles, of the major banks have hit new highs.[67] And the financial sector as a whole continues to divert too much of the nation's wealth and talent into essentially nonproductive activities.

The financial system today exhibits even fewer of the characteristics of seaworthy stability now than before the Crash of 2008. More assets are packed into a smaller number of already unmanageable corporate entities—as a consequence of competitors having been wiped out or absorbed during the rescue effort. You should take little comfort that not all the ships sank in the recent storm, and the calmer seas of the moment provide no test of seaworthiness. But you can be sure that the seas won't always be placid, and maybe next time the winds and waves will be harsher, the available tools may be constrained, or the response may be less skillful. I am told that the chairman of the country's largest bank said that a crisis was "something that happens every five to seven years."[68] Whatever the frequency, he was right that there will always be storms, but they don't all have to lead to full-fledged crises. The banks don't have to be so large, their world doesn't have to be so concentrated, and their derivatives positions don't need to be so intricately interconnected or so leveraged.

Among the particular financial innovations that nearly brought the economy to its knees this time were the mortgage derivatives. These were heralded as the keys to a new and better America, where a great many more families could own their own homes. The facts are instructive with respect to such hopes. At the end of the Great Depression, the percentage of American families owning homes, then a little over 40 percent, began growing rapidly until it reached 62 percent in 1960.[69] The growth slowed after that, and the percentage of families owning homes in 1980 stood at just under 65 percent.[70] This was after the creation of derivatives but before the boom in securitized mortgage instruments really took hold. The real world of housing failed to take notice. The most recent data I saw pegged the ownership percentage at 65 percent.[71] If we look to identify the good and the bad impacts of mortgage derivatives, we can readily look to their role in the crash to fill the latter category. Don't bother to look for an uptick in the homeownership percentage as an example of the benefits.

An issue any of us might easily confuse with the size of the banks is the bulk of the entire financial sector. This is actually a separate phenomenon, much discussed by other observers, but every bit as worrisome.[72] It would be theoretically possible to have large and growing banks within a stable or attenuating financial sector, or an expanding sector with shrinking individual banks. In fact, both the individual banks and their sector are engorged. The financial sector's share of gross domestic product roughly doubled from the final decades of the nineteenth century to the middle of the twentieth century and then doubled again to its recent peak share of about 8 percent.[73] The expansion of this sector's profits is at least equally significant. Not very long ago (which is how I like to think about the year I was born) the financial sector absorbed only a single-digit percentage of America's corporate profits.[74] In the millennial decade prior to the crash, the share of corporate profits taken by finance exceeded one-third of the economy's total, and that share appears to be headed back toward 30 percent now.[75] Over the past several decades, expansion in the profits of the financial sector vastly outstripped the profit growth of the nation's nonfinancial corporations.[76] This is not coincidence. Remember that profits in finance, where no goods are produced, largely come at the expense of the nonfinancial sector. The commercial profits that economists admire and that benefit all of us come from value added—often stemming from successful manufacturing and technology—or from wisely allocating capital to companies that then prosper—which is how venture capitalists and fundamental investors make their money. Finance, and especially trading, is largely a zero-sum game. One company's gain is another's loss.

It's hard to say whether the size, leverage, and complexity

of the large banks and the opacity of the hedge funds together present the weightier issue, or whether the financial sector's enlarging share of the economic pie deserves the honor. Both should cost you sleep. The first set of problems can, and probably will, lead us to suffer another totally unnecessary crash and accompanying recession. The second causes you harm every day, unrelated to stormy seas. There is nothing good for the economy in putting so much talent and such a large share of total profits into finance. In nonfinancial businesses, profits lead to job creation and investment in future growth. In banking and trading, they go right out the back door, contributing mainly to executive and shareholder incomes. Few if any jobs are created, and there is no contribution to overall productivity. Those of you who fret about America's economic future should pay particular attention to this. The current imbalance in favor of finance puts us at a significant disadvantage to competitor nations. I don't know what share of the Chinese economy or Chinese operating profits is devoted to finance, but it is a safe wager that their financial sector takes a far smaller slice of the pie than ours.

Since the number of people employed in banking has remained roughly steady for decades now, and the hedge fund world has never been a large employer, it is the revenues per financial employee and their accompanying compensation that have grown with the sector.[77] And even those measures can mislead if looked at as averages per employee, given that the enjoyment of the growth has been mainly shared by financial executives, money managers, and traders at the top of the sector's pyramid. This helps feed another of the problems this book has addressed — the growing income and wealth inequality. There is a direct correspondence between the rise to dominance of finance and the fall in the United States' position among nations in distributional equity. When an essential element of our economy is dysfunctional for stability, growth, and equity—all at the same time—it is high time for serious reconsideration.

The required remedies may look extreme, but hazards as hefty as those posed in finance today call for weighty solutions. The easy thesis here is that the giant banks should be downsized, derivatives leverage should be reduced, and hedge funds should be regulated to the same extent as mutual funds. All of the necessary tools are readily available.

Let me remind the reader that this book makes no pretense of providing a near-term political road map. It tries to offer *best* solutions, not constrained solutions. Readers from the world of finance or politics will surely see my suggestions as off the table at this time. I agree, and will perhaps go further. My theory of enduring human nature sees us as an intrinsically hierarchical species. If you were alive in the early Roman Empire, a good era for public policy debate, you could freely toss around ideas for change in just about any aspect of society except the place of the emperor. After Rome fell into the trench of the Dark Ages, questioning the secular and religious powers of the Pope was out of bounds. Popes gave way to kings, whose authority had to be accepted as a matter of divine right. Then for a while, manufacturing barons ruled the roost. Now the unassailable few are at the pinnacle of finance. I offer you no illusions that you can alter the hierarchy until their time, too, has passed. But it is worth understanding what *should* happen, nonetheless.

My thesis for the financial sector has three major elements. We should initiate policies to reduce the scale and risk profile of our banks. We should regulate hedge funds as mutual funds under the Investment Company Act, stressing the ageless principles of transparency through maximum disclosure and tolerable levels of risk for fiduciary pools of client money. And we should reduce decisively and dramatically the leverage of derivatives markets.

There are tools readily available for all of these objectives. The best way to limit the scale of banks is for the Federal Reserve to impose progressively steeper capital requirements and not feel bound by weak international capital standards.[78] The next most promising route would be for the FDIC to modify its insurance charges to reflect systemic risk. If the regulators can leave behind the notion that these charges should reflect artificially modeled risk levels, and can instead be used to shape the risk profile of the financial economy as a whole, the rest will be straightforward. This approach would give shareholders the incentive to downsize the banks in whatever manner their private interests prescribed. A market-driven approach to downsizing would be preferable in my view to restrictions on the activities of insured banking institutions, although activity restrictions are a great deal better than nothing.

The best hedge fund regulatory tool has been available all along. All that needs to be done is to end the availability of the exemptions from mutual fund treatment for any fund management controlling assets over a designated size limit.

The best device for curbing derivatives leverage is a meaningful reserve requirement.[79] Banks are free nowadays to put us all at risk in derivatives trading without creating any offsetting cushion. Every derivatives transaction involves some risk. There is what is called basis risk—that two paired instruments will not actually move with, or in opposition to, one another in unison. There is counterparty risk—that a trade will not, or cannot, be honored by the other party. And there is human error risk—which has no predictable or rational limit. Any serious student of derivatives can tell you that netting massive positions to zero cannot possibly reflect the true exposure.

Whenever a new position is taken, there should be a mandatory accompanying reserve. This would increase protection for the public and the banks, while simultaneously blunting the appeal of oversized trading volumes. If the minimum charge, just to construct an example, were to be 0.1 percent of the notional position value, an open position of $100 trillion in derivatives would require $100 billion to be put aside in reserves, an amount inaccessible enough to render that trading scale a bad memory. The reserves on gross position sizes ought to be mandated by the Federal Reserve. The FDIC should calculate its insurance premiums based on the risks imposed by banks' gross positions rather than unconvincingly netted positions. Charges to match the risk created would bring trading volumes back to sensible size — all with a minimum of new regulations and no need to outlaw useful commercial practices. A gross position reserve requirement would simply acknowledge that all derivatives positions impose some element of risk on the holders and the public.

Nothing I have suggested is in the category of an industrial policy or red tape. It is not bringing Washington into a private arena where it doesn't belong. The government, through existing law and regulation, provision of deposit insurance, and the implied guarantees that a history of bailouts represents, is deep in the field already. It just isn't doing the job as effectively as it should. Whatever you hear from banking and political sources to the contrary, you will know that the goal has not been accomplished until the banks are smaller and less leveraged, the hedge funds have evolved into mutual funds, and the entire financial services sector retreats to its proper role as a lubricant to the real commercial economy — safe, healthy, and enjoying the single-digit share of the nation's profits it has rightfully deserved all along.

A Concluding Remark

THERE IS NO cause for despair. The United States of America is not foundering. Our tolerant democracy, for all of its occasional awkwardness, is a treasure by historical standards. Our military prowess assures our position as the most powerful nation in the world. Our economy has long been, and remains, the most productive in the history of the world, and it will stay at the top of the pyramid as long as we can maintain our fearlessly innovative and creative business culture. We can be an even better country, however. I have recommended to you five public policy changes, five logically easy theses that can help safeguard our greatness as a nation and, just as important, our decency. None of the five are easy from a political viewpoint; they may in fact be beyond our grasp. But they are worth the reach. Here is the short version:

1. The federal government should stop making commitments it has no plans to fund. This problem is most severe with respect to our Social Security promises to the next generation of elders. And Congress should cease to offer expensive tax breaks that serve no useful policy purpose.

The most wastefully extravagant of these tax expenditures is the deduction available to corporations and individuals for payment of interest on their debts. The Social Security system can be secured by ceasing to automatically expand benefits as life expectancies rise. The corporate and personal interest deductions should be flat-out repealed.

2. The greatest threat to traditional American values today is the drift toward an aristocracy of wealth. It is harmful in many ways that the fruits of our recent economic growth have virtually all been taken by those at the wealth and income pinnacle. In order to remedy this, and restore the economic strength of the middle class while maintaining a safety net for those in need, we must take some steps that will sound as radical as the income tax sounded a hundred years ago but are just as necessary. We must begin to tax the unrealized gains resulting from investment asset appreciation, in whatever form those assets are held, and we must stop cold the leakage from inheritance taxes brought about through trust loopholes and excessive exemptions.

3. Our system of grade school education and our private-public balance of higher education opportunities have served us well in the past. Both elements, though, are now in need of major repair. The grade school curriculum is poorly serving those Americans, a majority of the population, who will not be earning a four-year college degree. The costs of college are undermining the benefits of higher education to all but the wealthiest students who do matriculate. And our incredibly prosperous nation manages to rank as no better than mediocre by international measures of educational attainment. While it should be theoretically possible to fix all of these problems within

the educational arena alone, various aspects of our culture, our traditions, and institutional barriers render that goal beyond reach. A universal national service program would offer a powerful set of solutions to the educational shortcomings, while providing other social and economic benefits as an extra dividend.

4. The United States spends about 18 percent of its GNP on health care, while the rest of the developed world averages a little more than half that. Yet, our people experience worse health outcomes than those in other nations. The extra spending exceeds a trillion dollars a year, a vast amount you could put to many better uses. There is no remedy for the excess consistent with our hodgepodge of private and public health-care financing approaches. Only within the framework of a single-payer, single-negotiator, single-regulator system can we provide rationality, sensible incentives, and cost-effective administration. The gain to the public of a trillion dollars a year would be the largest available boost to the economy within reach today, and proper incentives would actually improve America's health outcomes.

5. The New Deal reforms of Wall Street's structure and behavior gave this country a financial sector foundation that enriched us all for fifty years and made America the financial capital of the world — without endangering the commerce and the public that finance exists to serve. The emergence of unmanageably large and complex banks whose failures would bring all of us down, the creation of hedge funds whose security and business practices remain beyond regulatory purview, and the rise of derivatives traded with nearly unlimited leverage all contribute to the financial sector's enrichment at the rest of the economy's

> expense — and without commensurate value to tangible commerce. Banks should be downsized. Hedge funds should cease to exist outside of the successful and safe regulatory structure applied to mutual funds. And derivatives trading should be backed up by reserves that would reduce its volume to a tiny fraction of today's unimaginable numbers.

I don't claim that these reforms will come readily, but I do assert that they would fortify our country's values and enhance its prosperity. They are not, moreover, austerity measures or noble sacrifices you are called upon to make in the spirit of altruism. I could have stated them as calls to duty, or as responsibilities to our community, but it is all the more compelling that these changes are in all of the economic interests of the vast majority of citizens. George Washington was right when he admonished the Continental Congress on behalf of his underpaid troops that the number of people who "act upon the principles of disinterestedness are, comparatively speaking, no more than a drop in the ocean."[1] The five recommendations offered here are all to your financial gain and, all the more so, to the economic benefit of your children. They will also help secure our democracy.

Washington's is not the only quotation that comes to mind on this topic. To the President or member of Congress willing to take on these five issues, I feel compelled to offer the following warning in the voice of another great figure and a longtime personal hero of mine. Adam Smith worried in his day about the commercial barons he called "monopolists," but his cautions about taking them on apply equally well to any coalition of the powerful, including those who would organize to oppose these theses. Smith saw plainly the adversarial power an upright reformer would face, and he wrote, in 1776:

> The Member of Parliament who supports every proposal for strengthening this monopoly is sure to acquire not only a reputation of understanding trade, but great popularity and influence with an order of men whose numbers and wealth render them of great importance. If he opposes them, on the contrary, and still more if he has authority enough to be able to thwart them, neither the most acknowledged probity, nor the highest rank, nor the greatest public services can protect him from the most infamous abuse and detraction, from personal insults, nor sometimes from real danger, arising from the insolent outrage of furious and disappointed monopolists.[2]

Substitute any potent interest for monopolists, and Smith's warning still holds full force almost two and a half centuries later. I counter only that among those conflicts hazarding reputational detraction, abuse, insolent outrage, and conceivably even real danger are the fights most worthy of undertaking. For the leader who takes on any of the challenges that my five easy theses provide, there are at least these consolations: Adam Smith would have been proud of you, and a grateful nation will someday honor you.

Acknowledgments

There are so many people I ought to thank that I feel compelled to begin here by apologizing in advance to anyone who belongs on these pages and didn't make it. This book began as a discussion in a cloakroom with Robert Kuttner, a friend and fellow member of the Examiners Club in Boston. We talked about writing a book together. When we discovered that our views were similar but not congruent, he encouraged me to write this book on my own and introduced me to Ike Williams, who became my lawyer and agent. My author-brother Gene Stone strongly encouraged the project at about the same time, and he has become a key adviser at every phase. An old friend, economics professor Ben Friedman, urged the effort as well. Because I have terrible trouble starting work on a blank sheet or screen, I recruited professional help with the first of many drafts. I hired a terrific writer named Mike Bryan to interview me extensively by videoconference call, subject by subject, and then to transcribe and edit the interviews into rough text. While I doubt that a single sentence of that initial draft remains in the book by now, I have little confidence that I could have gotten started without Mike's help.

As I began to produce the next series of drafts, I turned to many experts for advice. Among those who read the whole manuscript and offered suggestions (but who do not necessarily agree with or endorse any of the positions I take) were Jack Beatty, David Ellwood, Stephen Kinzer, David Moss, Rebecca Henderson, Norman Rosenthal, Geoffrey Arnold, Tom Daschle, Raymond and Jaana Calamaro, and Clayton Yeutter. Then there were additional friends and friends of friends to whom I turned for expert advice on specific chapters. No one should assume that these readers, any more than the first batch, concurred with a single thought. Some, in fact, made their disagreements plain. Bob Pozen, Jim Roosevelt, and Alicia Munnell read and commented on the Fiscal Balance chapter and especially on issues surrounding Social Security. Janet Gornick, Christopher Houston, Carolyn Osteen, and Bob Lord made suggestions on the Inequality chapter, the three lawyers all concentrating on the pages about trusts. Michael Goldstein, Laura Perille, and Irvin Scott commented on the Education chapter. Alexis Pozen, Dr. Barbara Bierer, Dr. Robert Osteen, and Dr. Jonathan Quick provided expert commentary on the Health Care chapter. I received comments or help on the final chapter, dealing with Financial Sector Reform, from Alan Levithan, Steve Carlsen, and Paul Volcker.

There was no chance I could have done all the research, or just about any of the footnoting, by myself. Clémence Scouten and Daniel Tartakovsky pulled the long oars on those tasks. Clé helped with numerous other time-intensive chores at every stage as well. Next, I want to thank the team at Houghton Mifflin Harcourt. The company's board chairman, Larry Fish; the trade division publisher, Bruce Nichols; my editor, Alexander Littlefield; and the copy editor, Barbara Wood, all contradicted the conventional warnings I was given about author-publisher relationships. They were a professional joy to work with. I cannot at this stage thank the publicity team at Houghton Mifflin Harcourt nor the outside consultants I may employ to help market the book. They are unidentified as yet. If the book sells well enough to get a second printing, this space will go to them.

And, of course, the most important supporter of this project and of its author — intellectually, emotionally, and in every other way — was my wife, Cathleen Douglas Stone. Even Cathy, though, cannot be held responsible for any errors. Those would be mine.

Notes

1. Fiscal Balance

1. Office of Management and Budget, Table 1.1, "Summary of Receipts, Outlays, and Surpluses or Deficits (–): 1789–2019," Whitehouse.gov, whitehouse.gov/omb/budget/historicals, accessed December 29, 2014.
2. Ibid.
3. Ibid.
4. TreasuryDirect, "The Debt to the Penny and Who Holds It," Treasury Direct.gov, http://www.treasurydirect.gov/NP/debt/current, accessed June 13, 2015.
5. Kate Rogers, "Sticker Shock: U.S. Debt Is $123K per Working American," FoxBusiness.com, October 17, 2013, http://www.foxbusiness.com/personal-finance/2013/10/17/sticker-shock-us-debt-bill-is-123k-per-working-american/, accessed December 29, 2014.
6. U.S. Department of the Treasury, "Major Foreign Holders of Treasury Securities," http://www.treasury.gov/ticdata/Publish/mfh.txt, accessed June 13, 2015.
7. Congressional Budget Office, *The 2014 Long-Term Budget Outlook*, July 2014, Figure 1-1, "Federal Debt Held by the Public," https://www.cbo.gov/sites/default/files/45471-Long-TermBudgetOutlook_7-29.pdf, accessed June 13, 2015.
8. See note 1 for federal spending data showing approximately $3.5 trillion in outlays in 2012. State and local expenditures in that year totaled $3.2

trillion. See Jeffrey L. Barnett, Cindy L. Sheckells, Scott Peterson, and Elizabeth M. Tydings, "2012 Census of Governments: Finance — State and Local Government Summary Report," Census.gov, December 17, 2014, http://www2.census.gov/govs/local/summary_report.pdf, accessed December 29, 2014.

9. Author's calculations. Underlying data from Congressional Budget Office, "The Budget and Economic Outlook: 2014 to 2024," CBO.gov, https://www.cbo.gov/publication/45010; and Medicaid data from Congressional Budget Office, "Medicaid — Baseline Projections," April 2014 Baseline, CBO.gov, https://www.cbo.gov/publication/44204, accessed June 13, 2015.
10. Jacob Lew, Thomas Perez, Sylvia Burwell, Carolyn Colvin, Charles P. Blahous III, and Robert Reischauer, "The 2014 Annual Report of the Board of Trustees of the Federal Old-Age and Survivors Insurance and Federal Disability Insurance Trust Funds," SSA.gov, http://www.ssa.gov/oact/tr/2014/tr2014.pdf, accessed December 29, 2014.
11. "Big Oil's Misbegotten Tax Gusher: Why They Don't Need $70 Billion from Taxpayers Amid Record Profits," AmericanProgress.org, May 5, 2011, https://www.americanprogress.org/issues/tax-reform/news/2011/05/05/9663/big-oils-misbegotten-tax-gusher/, accessed January 2, 2015.
12. Environmental Working Group, "2012 Farm Subsidy Database," Ewr .org, http://farm.ewg.org/, accessed April 10, 2015.
13. William McBride, "A Brief History of Tax Expenditures," TaxFoundation.org, August 22, 2013, http://taxfoundation.org/article/brief-history-tax-expenditures, accessed December 29, 2014.
14. Sean Lowry, "Itemized Tax Deductions for Individuals: Data Analysis," *Congressional Research Services Report to Congress,* February 12, 2014, 2–3, http://www.fas.org/sgp/crs/misc/R43012.pdf, accessed December 29, 2014.
15. Bruce Bartlett, "The Sacrosanct Mortgage Interest Deduction," *New York Times,* August 6, 2013, http://economix.blogs.nytimes.com//2013/08/06/the-sacrosanct-mortgage-interest-deduction/, accessed December 29, 2014.
16. U.S. Congress, Joint Committee on Taxation, "Estimates of Federal Tax Expenditures for Fiscal Years 2011–2015," January 2012, https://www.jct.gov/publications.html?func=startdown&id=4385, accessed June 14, 2015.

17. According to my calculations, the average federal deficit from 1989 to 2014 was about $366 billion. See note 1.
18. U.S. Department of Commerce, U.S. Census Bureau, "2010 Census Shows Second Highest Homeownership Rate on Record Despite Largest Decrease Since 1940," U.S. Census Bureau Newsroom Archive, October 6, 2011, https://www.census.gov/newsroom/releases/archives/2010_census/cb11-cn188.html, accessed January 27, 2015.
19. Benjamin H. Harris and Daniel Baneman, "Who Itemizes Deductions?," *Tax Notes,* January 17, 2011, http://www.taxpolicycenter.org/UploadedPDF/1001486-Who-Itemizes-Deductions.pdf, accessed December 29, 2014.
20. Anthony Randazzo and Dean Stansel, "Mortgage Interest Deduction Saves Middle Class Taxpayers All of $51/Month," *Forbes,* December 18, 2013, http://www.forbes.com/sites/realspin/2013/12/18/mortgage-interest-deduction-saves-middle-class-taxpayers-all-of-51month/, accessed December 29, 2014.
21. Steven C. Bourassa, Donald R. Haurin, Patric H. Hendershott, and Martin Hoesli, "Mortgage Interest Deductions and Homeownership: An International Survey," Swiss Finance Institute, Research Paper Series No. 12-06, March 13, 2013, http://papers.ssrn.com/sol3/papers.cfm?abstract_id=2002865, accessed June 14, 2015.
22. James Surowiecki, "The Debt Economy," *The New Yorker,* November 23, 2009, http://www.newyorker.com/magazine/2009/11/23/the-debt-economy, accessed December 29, 2014.
23. Alvin C. Warren Jr., "The Corporate Interest Deduction: A Policy Evaluation," *Yale Law Journal* 83 (1974): 1585.
24. Bob Pozen and Lucas W. Goodman, "Capping the Deductibility of Corporate Interest Expense," *Tax Notes* 137 (2012), http://papers.ssrn.com/sol3/papers.cfm?abstract_id=2190966, accessed April 10, 2015.
25. This calculated number is derived from the Pozen and Goodman article (ibid.) and was confirmed with Pozen subject to its underlying assumptions.
26. Gillian Tan, "Debt Rises in Leveraged Buyouts Despite Warnings," *Wall Street Journal,* May 20, 2014, http://www.wsj.com/articles/SB10001424052702304422704579574184101045614, accessed December 29, 2014.
27. Ibid.
28. See note 10.
29. See note 10, Figure IV.B3.

30. Commission to Strengthen Social Security, Report of the President's Commission, "Strengthening Social Security and Creating Personal Wealth for All Americans," http://govinfo.library.unt.edu/csss/reports/Final_report.pdf, accessed January 27, 2015.
31. National Commission on Fiscal Responsibility and Reform, "The Moment of Truth," December 2010, http://www.fiscalcommission.gov/sites/fiscalcommission.gov/files/documents/TheMomentofTruth12_1_2010.pdf, accessed January 27, 2015.
32. "Committee Reports and Initial Passage," 1935 Congressional Debates on Social Security, http://www.ssa.gov/history/tally.html, accessed December 29, 2014.
33. "Historical Background and Development of Social Security," citing 1939 Report of the Social Security Board, SSA.gov, http://www.ssa.gov/history/briefhistory3.html, accessed December 29, 2014.
34. "Administrative Expenses as a Percentage of Total Expenditures, 1957–2014," ssa.gov, http://www.ssa.gov/oact/STATS/admin.html, accessed December 29, 2014.
35. "Social Security Basic Facts," SSA.gov, April 2, 2014, http://www.ssa.gov/news/press/basicfact.html, accessed December 29, 2014.
36. "Fact Sheet, Social Security: 2014 Social Security Changes," SSA.gov, http://www.ssa.gov/pressoffice/factsheets/colafacts2014.pdf, accessed December 29, 2014.
37. See note 33, at "Trust Funds."
38. "Life Expectancy for Social Security," SSA.gov, http://www.ssa.gov/history/lifeexpect.html, accessed December 29, 2014.
39. *2014 OASDIA Trustees Report,* Table V.A4, "Cohort Life Expectancy," http://www.socialsecurity.gov/OACT/TR/2014/lr5a4.html, accessed December 29, 2014.
40. See note 38.
41. See note 39.
42. See note 38.
43. See note 39.
44. "Live Births, Birth Rates, and Fertility Rates, by Race: United States, 1909–2003," CDC.gov, http://www.cdc.gov/nchs/data/statab/natfinal2003.annvol1_01.pdf, accessed December 29, 2014.
45. Ibid.
46. Ibid.
47. D'Vera Cohn and Paul Taylor, "Baby Boomers Approach 65 — Glumly,"

Pew Research Center, December 20, 2010, http://www.pewsocialtrends.org/2010/12/20/baby-boomers-approach-65-glumly/, accessed June 16, 2015.

48. James A. Dorn, "The Real Costs of Social Security," Cato Institute, August 20, 2010, http://www.cato.org/publications/commentary/real-costs-social-security, accessed April 12, 2015.
49. Table IV.B2, "Covered Workers and Beneficiaries, Calendar Years 1945–2085," SSA.gov, http://www.socialsecurity.gov/OACT/tr/2010/lr4b2.html, accessed June 16, 2015.
50. Ibid.
51. Ibid.
52. "Benefits Planner: Maximum Taxable Earnings (1937–2015)," SSA.gov, http://www.ssa.gov/planners/maxtax.htm, accessed December 29, 2014.
53. Tax Policy Center, "Historical Social Security Tax Rates," January 20, 2015, http://www.taxpolicycenter.org/taxfacts/content/pdf/ssrate_historical.pdf, accessed June 16, 2015.
54. "Full Retirement Age: If You Were Born in 1960 or Later," SSA.gov, http://www.ssa.gov/retirement/1960.html, accessed December 29, 2014.
55. "Cost-of-Living Adjustments," SSA.gov, http://www.ssa.gov/oact/cola/colaseries.html, accessed December 29, 2014.
56. The statistics apply to a two-earner couple, each making $44,800 in 2013 constant dollars. The 2015 lifetime Social Security benefits are about $601,000, 33 percent higher than the 1990 benefits of $455,000 and 66 percent higher than the 1970 benefits of $360,000. See C. Eugene Steuerle and Caleb Quakenbush, "Social Security and Medicare Taxes and Benefits over a Lifetime: 2013 Update," November 2013, Urban Institute, http://www.urban.org/sites/default/files/alfresco/publication-pdfs/412945-Social-Security-and-Medicare-Taxes-and-Benefits-over-a-Lifetime.PDF, accessed June 16, 2015.
57. Martin Feldstein and Andrew Samwick, "The Transition Path in Privatizing Social Security," in *Privatizing Social Security,* ed. Martin Feldstein, 256–8, http://www.nber.org/chapters/c6251.pdf, accessed January 27, 2015.
58. Nicole Woo, Janelle Jones, and John Schmitt, "Raising the Social Security Payroll Tax: How Many Workers Would Pay More?," Center for Economic and Policy Research, http://www.cepr.net/documents/publications/ss-2013-01.pdf, accessed December 29, 2014.

59. See Option 18 under “Revenues” in “Options for Reducing the Deficit: 2014–2023,” Congressional Budget Office, November 13, 2013, https://www.cbo.gov/budget-options/2013/44811, accessed June 16, 2015.
60. The additional expected years of life left for whites compared to blacks is 4.3 at birth but only 1.3 at age sixty-five and 0.9 at age seventy. See Elizabeth Arias, “United States Life Tables, 2009,” *National Vital Statistics Reports* 62, no. 7 (January 6, 2014), http://www.cdc.gov/nchs/data/nvsr/nvsr62/nvsr62_07.pdf, accessed June 16, 2015.
61. “This Baby Could Live to Be 142 Years Old,” *Time*, February 23, 2015.
62. Social Security Administration (Office of the Chief Actuary), “Provisions Affecting Retirement Age,” provision C2.5, September 18, 2014, http://www.ssa.gov/oact/solvency/provisions/charts/chart_run249.pdf, accessed June 16, 2015.
63. Lyndon B. Johnson, “Remarks with President Truman at the Signing in Independence of the Medicare Bill,” Social Security History: Lyndon B. Johnson, SSA.gov, July 30, 1965, http://www.ssa.gov/history/lbjstmts.html, accessed December 29, 2014.
64. Philip Rucker, “Sen. DeMint of S.C. Is Voice of Opposition to Health-Care Reform,” *Washington Post*, July 28, 2009, http://www.washingtonpost.com/wp-dyn/content/article/2009/07/27/AR2009072703066_2.html, accessed December 29, 2014.
65. “Policy Basics: Where Do Our Federal Tax Dollars Go?,” Center on Budget and Policy Priorities, March 31, 2014, http://www.cbpp.org/cms/?fa=view&id=1258, accessed December 29, 2014.
66. Walter E. Williams, “Washington’s Lies,” Foundation for Economic Education, September 22, 2010, http://fee.org/freeman/detail/washingtons-lies, accessed December 29, 2014.
67. See note 53.
68. “Social Security History: History of SSA During the Johnson Administration,” SSA.gov, http://www.ssa.gov/history/ssa/lbjmedicare3.html#21, accessed December 29, 2014.
69. “Part B Costs,” Medicare.gov, http://www.medicare.gov/your-medicare-costs/part-b-costs/part-b-costs.html, accessed December 29, 2014.
70. “The Facts on Medicare Spending and Financing,” Henry J. Kaiser Family Foundation, July 28, 2014, http://kff.org/medicare/fact-sheet/medicare-spending-and-financing-fact-sheet/, accessed December 29, 2014.
71. Ibid.

72. See Option 8 in "Options for Reducing the Deficit: 2015–2024," Congressional Budget Office, November 20, 2014, https://www.cbo.gov/budget-options/2014, accessed June 16, 2015.
73. Dennis Cauchon, "Federal Retirement Plans Almost as Costly as Social Security," *USA Today*, September 29, 2011, http://usatoday30.usatoday.com/news/washington/story/2011-10-11/federal-retirement-pension-benefits/50592474/1, accessed December 29, 2014.
74. Ibid. The representative quoted is Jim Cooper (D-TN).

2. Inequality

1. From 2009 to 2012, 91 percent of income gains went to the top 1 percent of earners. See Emmanuel Saez, "Striking It Richer: The Evolution of Top Incomes in the United States (Updated with 2014 Preliminary Estimates)," June 25, 2015, http://eml.berkeley.edu/~saez/saez-UStopincomes-2014.pdf, accessed June 30, 2015.
2. Heidi Shierholz and Lawrence Mishel, "A Decade of Flat Wages: The Key Barrier to Shared Prosperity and a Rising Middle Class," Economic Policy Institute, August 21, 2013, http://www.epi.org/publication/a-decade-of-flat-wages-the-key-barrier-to-shared-prosperity-and-a-rising-middle-class/, accessed July 10, 2015.
3. See note 1, Figure 1.
4. Richard Fry and Paul Taylor, "A Rise in Wealth for the Wealthy; Declines for the Lower 93%," Pew Research Center, April 23, 2013, http://www.pewsocialtrends.org/2013/04/23/a-rise-in-wealth-for-the-wealthydeclines-for-the-lower-93/, accessed July 9, 2015.
5. Drew DeSilver, "For Most Workers, Real Wages Have Barely Budged for Decades," Pew Research Center, October 9, 2014, http://www.pewresearch.org/fact-tank/2014/10/09/for-most-workers-real-wages-have-barely-budged-for-decades/, accessed January 14, 2015.
6. Arloc Sherman and Chad Stone, "Income Gaps Between Very Rich and Everyone Else More Than Tripled in Last Three Decades, New Data Show," Center on Budget and Policy Priorities, June 25, 2010, http://www.cbpp.org/cms/?fa=view&id=3220, accessed April 11, 2015.
7. See note 1, Figure 1.
8. See note 1, Figure 2.
9. Congressional Budget Office, "Trends in the Distribution of Household Income Between 1979 and 2007," CBO.gov, October 25, 2011, Figure

2, https://www.cbo.gov/publication/42729, accessed January 14, 2015.

10. Lawrence Mishel and Alyssa Davis, "CEO Pay Continues to Rise as Typical Workers Are Paid Less," Economic Policy Institute, EPI.org, Issue Brief 380, June 12, 2014, http://s1.epi.org/files/2014/ceo-pay-continues-to-rise.pdf, accessed July 3, 2015.
11. This quotation is often attributed to Ambrose Bierce but the documentation may be unreliable.
12. Alan Dunn, "Average America vs. the One Percent," *Forbes,* March 21, 2012, http://www.forbes.com/sites/moneywisewomen/2012/03/21/average-america-vs-the-one-percent/, accessed July 14, 2015. One can join the upper 1 percent with only seven to eight times the median income, but the mean income of this group is much higher.
13. Robert Gebeloff and Shaila Dewan, "Measuring the Top 1% by Wealth, Not Income," *New York Times,* January 17, 2012, http://economix.blogs.nytimes.com/2012/01/17/measuring-the-top-1-by-wealth-not-income/, accessed April 11, 2015.
14. The average net worth of a family in the top 0.01 percent is $371 million. Since there are about sixteen thousand such families, their combined net worth is about $5.96 trillion. See Emmanuel Saez and Gabriel Zucman, "Wealth Inequality in the United States Since 1913: Evidence from Capitalized Income Tax Data," National Bureau of Economic Research, Working Paper No. 20625, October 2014, Table 1, http://www.nber.org/papers/w20625.pdf, accessed July 5, 2015.
15. "Adult" refers to people at age forty. See Richard V. Reeves and Isabel V. Sawhill, "Equality of Opportunity: Definitions, Trends, and Interventions," Federal Reserve Bank of Boston, October 10, 2014, https://www.bostonfed.org/inequality2014/papers/reeves-sawhill.pdf, accessed July 7, 2015.
16. Facundo Alvaredo, Anthony B. Atkinson, Thomas Piketty, and Emmanuel Saez, "The Top 1 Percent in International and Historical Perspective," *Journal of Economic Perspectives* 27, no. 3 (Summer 2013): 3–20, http://eml.berkeley.edu/~saez/alvaredo-atkinson-piketty-saezJEP13top1percent.pdf, accessed January 14, 2015.
17. Robert M. Adams, "Consolidation and Merger Activity in the United States Banking Industry from 2000 Through 2010," Federal Reserve Board, August 8, 2012, http://www.federalreserve.gov/pubs/feds/2012/201251/index.html, accessed January 27, 2015.

18. Their market share rose from 39.9 percent in 1993 to 63.8 percent in 2013. See U.S. Department of Agriculture, Economic Research Service, Ers .usda.gov, May 11, 2015, http://www.ers.usda.gov/topics/food-markets -prices/retailing-wholesaling/retail-trends.aspx, accessed July 5, 2015.
19. Mark J. Perry, "Fortune 500 Firms in 1955 vs. 2014; 89% Are Gone, and We're All Better Off Because of That Dynamic 'Creative Destruction,'" American Enterprise Institute, AEIdeas, August 18, 2014, http://www .aei.org/publication/fortune-500-firms-in-1955-vs-2014-89-are-gone -and-were-all-better-off-because-of-that-dynamic-creative-destruction/, accessed July 6, 2015.
20. U.S. Securities and Exchange Commission, "Annual Staff Report Relating to the Use of Data Collected from Private Fund Systemic Risk Reports," Sec.gov, August 25, 2014, http://www.sec.gov/reportspubs/ special-studies/im-private-fund-annual-report-081514.pdf, accessed January 14, 2015.
21. Lobbying Database, Center for Responsive Politics, Opensecrets.org, http://www.opensecrets.org/lobby/, accessed April 13, 2015.
22. Eamon Javers, "Inside Obama's Bank CEOs Meeting," *Politico*, April 3, 2009, http://www.politico.com/news/stories/0409/20871.html, accessed January 14, 2015.
23. Joseph Stiglitz, *The Price of Inequality: How Today's Divided Society Endangers Our Future* (New York: Norton, 2013).
24. Peter Coy, "An Immodest Proposal: A Global Tax on the Superrich," *Bloomberg Business*, April 10, 2014, http://www.businessweek.com/ar ticles/2014-04-10/thomas-pikettys-global-tax-on-capital-may-not-be-a -crazy-idea, accessed January 27, 2015.
25. The combined aggregate value of two of the largest asset types, publicly traded shares and homes, is around $50 trillion. See Cory Hopkins, "Combined Value of U.S. Homes to Top $25 Trillion in 2013," Zillow .com, December 19, 2013, http://www.zillow.com/blog/value-us-homes -to-top-25-trillion-141142/, accessed July 12, 2015; and Central Intelligence Agency, "Market Value of Publicly Traded Shares," *The World Factbook 2013–14*, https://www.cia.gov/library/publications/the-world -factbook/rankorder/2200rank.html, accessed July 12, 2015. Share ownership is more concentrated than homeownership. Appreciation of these two categories alone would be over $2.5 trillion annually at 5 percent and $5 trillion annually at 10 percent, respectively.
26. Internal Revenue Service, Statistics of Income (SOI) Division, Estate Tax

Data Tables, Table 1, "Estate Tax Returns Filed in 2013, by Tax Status and Size of Gross Estate," November 12, 2014, http://www.irs.gov/uac/SOI-Tax-Stats-Estate-Tax-Statistics-Filing-Year-Table-1, accessed July 5, 2015.

27. Chye-Ching Huang and Brandon DeBot, "Ten Facts You Should Know About the Federal Estate Tax," Center on Budget and Policy Priorities, March 23, 2015, http://www.cbpp.org/research/ten-facts-you-should-know-about-the-federal-estate-tax, accessed July 5, 2015.
28. Congressional Budget Office, "The Budget and Economic Outlook: 2015 to 2025," CBO.gov, January 26, 2015, Table 4-1, "Revenues Projected in CBO's Baseline," https://www.cbo.gov/publication/49892, accessed July 5, 2015.
29. See note 14.
30. Kerry A. Dolan and Luisa Kroll, eds., "Forbes 400: The Richest People in America 2014," *Forbes,* September 29, 2014, http://www.forbes.com/forbes-400/, accessed April 11, 2015.

3. Education

1. Three entries for China have been omitted from the original OECD listing. If included, and depending on how the three entries are weighted, China would rank at the top — in either first or second place. See OECD, "Programme for International Student Assessment (PISA): Results from PISA 2012, United States," http://www.oecd.org/pisa/keyfindings/PISA-2012-results-US.pdf, accessed July 18, 2015.
2. OECD, "Indicator C2: How Do Early Childhood Education Systems Differ Around the World?," in *Education at a Glance 2014: OECD Indicators,* OECD Publishing, Chart C2. 1, "Enrolment Rates at Age 3 in Early Childhood Education (2005 and 2012)," http://www.oecd.org/edu/EAG2014-Indicator%20C2%20(eng).pdf, accessed July 18, 2015.
3. Common Core State Standards Initiative, "Development Process," http://www.corestandards.org/about-the-standards/development-process/, accessed January 22, 2015.
4. For data on gross state product, see U.S. Department of Commerce, Bureau of Economic Analysis, "Broad Growth Across States in 2014," News Release, June 10, 2015, http://www.bea.gov/newsreleases/regional/gdp_state/gsp_newsrelease.htm, accessed July 18, 2015. For data on state spending on education, see U.S. Department of Commerce, U.S. Census

Bureau, "2012 Census of Governments: State & Local Finances," http://www.census.gov/govs/local/, accessed July 18, 2015.

5. U.S. Department of Commerce, U.S. Census Bureau, *Public Education Finances 2013,* 2013 Annual Survey of School System Finances, June 2015, Table 8, "Per Pupil Amounts for Current Spending of Public Elementary-Secondary School Systems by State: Fiscal Year 2013," http://www.census.gov/govs/school/, accessed July 18, 2015.
6. "Rankings & Estimates 2013–14: Rankings of the States 2013 and Estimates of School Statistics 2014," Nea.org, March 2014, https://www.nea.org/assets/docs/NEA-Rankings-and-Estimates-2013-2014.pdf, accessed April 12, 2015.
7. U.S. Department of Commerce, U.S. Census Bureau, *Public Education Finances 2013,* 2013 Annual Survey of School System Finances, June 2015, Table 18, "Per Pupil Amounts for Current Spending of Public Elementary-Secondary School Systems in the United States by Enrollment: Fiscal Year 2013," http://www.census.gov/govs/school/, accessed July 18, 2015.
8. Bruce D. Baker, David G. Sciarra, and Danielle Farrie, *Is School Funding Fair? A National Report Card,* Fourth Edition Education Law Center, Spring 2015, http://www.schoolfundingfairness.org/National_Report_Card_2015.pdf, accessed July 18, 2015.
9. Michael Leachman and Chris Mai, "Most States Funding Schools Less Than Before the Recession," Center on Budget and Policy Priorities, May 20, 2014, http://www.cbpp.org/research/most-states-funding-schools-less-than-before-the-recession, accessed January 22, 2015.
10. Ibid.
11. Ibid.
12. The particular category referred to is twenty-five-to-thirty-four-year-old non-students. See *Education at a Glance 2014: OECD Indicators,* OECD Publishing, Table A4.4, "Educational Mobility Among Non-Students, by Age Group and Parents' Educational Attainment (2012)," http://www.oecd.org/edu/Education-at-a-Glance-2014.pdf, accessed July 18, 2015.
13. U.S. Department of Labor, Bureau of Labor Statistics, "College Enrollment and Work Activity of 2014 High School Graduates," BLS.gov, April 16, 2015, http://www.bls.gov/news.release/hsgec.nr0.htm, accessed July 18, 2015.
14. About 56 percent of first-time degree-seeking students who entered

college in fall 2007 had completed a degree within six years. See Doug Shapiro, Afet Dundar, Mary Ziskin, Xin Yuan, and Autumn Harrell, *Completing College: A National View of Student Attainment Rates—Fall 2007 Cohort,* Signature Report No. 6, National Student Clearinghouse Research Center, December 15, 2013, http://nscresearchcenter.org/wp-content/uploads/NSC_Signature_Report_6.pdf, accessed July 18, 2015.

15. American Institute for Economic Research, "The Cost of Living Calculator," https://www.aier.org/cost-living-calculator, accessed January 18, 2015.
16. William J. Baumol, *The Cost Disease* (New Haven: Yale University Press, 2012). This source reports that the increase has been 250 percent since the early 1980s. The text extrapolates backward to estimate change since 1978. An excerpt from the book can be found at http://yalepress.yale.edu/yupbooks/excerpts/Baumol_excerpt.pdf.
17. Digest of Education Statistics, Table 320, "Average Undergraduate Tuition and Fees and Room and Board Rates Charged for Full-Time Students in Degree-Granting Institutions, by Type and Control of Institution: 1964–65 Through 2006–07," National Center for Education Statistics, http://nces.ed.gov/programs/digest/d07/tables/dt07_320.asp, accessed April 13, 2015.
18. CollegeBoard, "Average Published Undergraduate Charges by Sector, 2014–15," CollegeBoard.org, http://trends.collegeboard.org/college-pricing/figures-tables/average-published-undergraduate-charges-sector-2014-15, accessed January 18, 2015.
19. The median household income in 2013 was $51,939. See Carmen DeNavas-Walt and Bernadette Proctor, Current Population Reports, "Income and Poverty in the United States: 2013," U.S. Census Bureau, September 2014, http://www.census.gov/content/dam/Census/library/publications/2014/demo/p60-249.pdf, accessed January 22, 2015.
20. Columbia University, "FAQs," Columbia University Undergraduate Admissions, https://undergrad.admissions.columbia.edu/ask/faq/topic/381, accessed July 21, 2015.
21. Harvard University, "Tuition and Expenses," Harvard.edu, https://college.harvard.edu/financial-aid/how-aid-works/cost-attendance, accessed January 18, 2015.
22. Brown University, "Tuition & Fees," Brown.edu, http://www.brown.edu/academics/gradschool/courses-manual/tuition-fees, accessed January 18, 2015.

23. Harvard University, "Financial Aid," Harvard.edu, https://college.harvard.edu/financial-aid, accessed January 18, 2015.
24. Brown University, "Facts About Financial Aid," Brown.edu, http://www.brown.edu/about/facts/financial-aid, accessed January 18, 2015.
25. See note 18.
26. Costs rose from about $28,500 to about $31,200. See CollegeBoard, "Tuition and Fees and Room and Board over Time, 2004–05 to 2014–15," CollegeBoard.org, http://trends.collegeboard.org/college-pricing/figures-tables/tuition-fees-room-board-time-2004-05-2014-15, accessed July 19, 2015.
27. Ibid. Costs rose from about $7,800 to about $9,100 over the six-year period, an increase of about 17 percent.
28. Project on Student Debt, "Student Debt and the Class of 2013," Institute for College Access & Success, November 2014, 18, http://ticas.org/sites/default/files/legacy/fckfiles/pub/classof2013.pdf, accessed July 20, 2015.
29. Ibid.
30. Outstanding student loan balances rose to nearly $1.2 trillion at the end of 2014 from about $500 billion in 2006. For 2006 data, see Meta Brown, Andrew Haughwout, Donghoon Lee, Joelle Scally, and Wilbert van der Klaauw, "Measuring Student Debt and Its Performance," Staff Report No. 668, Federal Reserve Bank of New York, April 2014, http://www.newyorkfed.org/research/staff_reports/sr668.pdf, accessed July 21, 2015. For 2014 data, see "Quarterly Report on Household Debt and Credit," Federal Reserve Bank of New York, http://www.newyorkfed.org/householdcredit/2014-q4/data/pdf/HHDC_2014Q4.pdf, accessed July 21, 2015.
31. "Quarterly Report on Household Debt and Credit." In terms of total household debt, student loans were 10 percent, auto loans were 8 percent, and credit card loans were 6 percent.
32. U.S. Department of Labor, Bureau of Labor Statistics, "Youth Employment and Unemployment, July 2014," Bls.gov, August 19, 2014, http://www.bls.gov/opub/ted/2014/ted_20140819.htm, accessed July 21, 2015; U.S. Department of Labor, Bureau of Labor Statistics, "Employment Situation Summary," Bls.gov, July 2, 2015, http://www.bls.gov/news.release/empsit.nr0.htm, accessed July 21, 2015; and U.S. Department of Labor, Bureau of Labor Statistics, "Databases, Tables & Calculators by Subject," Bls.org, http://data.bls.gov/timeseries/LNU04000000?years_option=all_

years&periods_option=specific_periods&periods=Annual+Data, accessed January 22, 2015.

33. U.S. Department of Education, "Federal Student Aid," Studentaid.ed.gov, https://studentaid.ed.gov/types/loans/interest-rates, accessed July 21, 2015.
34. Marco Rubio, "Rubio Comments on Obama's Student Loan Announcement," Rubio.Senate.gov, http://www.rubio.senate.gov/public/index.cfm/press-releases?ID=1eb3a4c8-64cd-41b2-aff8-d0669234a159, accessed January 22, 2015.
35. Louis Lavelle, "College ROI: What We Found," *Bloomberg BusinessWeek,* April 9, 2012, http://www.businessweek.com/articles/2012-04-09/college-roi-what-we-found, accessed January 22, 2015.
36. Ibid.
37. "Boston's Education Pipeline: A Report Card," Boston Indicators Project, 104, http://www.bostonindicators.org/~/media/Files/IndicatorsReports/Reports/Indicator%20Reports/Education%20Pipeline.pdf, accessed January 25, 2015.
38. Melissa Roderick, Jenny Nagaoka, and Elaine Allensworth, "From High School to the Future: A First Look at Chicago Public School Graduates' College Enrollment, College Preparation, and Graduation from Four-Year Colleges, Report Highlights," University of Chicago Consortium on Chicago School Research, April 2006, http://ccsr.uchicago.edu/downloads/p82mini.pdf, accessed January 22, 2015.
39. William C. Symonds, Robert B. Schwartz, and Ronald Ferguson, *Pathways to Prosperity: Meeting the Challenge of Preparing Young Americans for the 21st Century,* report issued by the Pathways to Prosperity Project, Harvard Graduate School of Education, February 2011, 10.
40. Robert Reich, "Back to College, the Only Gateway to the Middle Class," Robert Reich's blog, http://robertreich.org/post/96377869820, accessed January 22, 2015.
41. Eoghan Harris, "German-Style Apprenticeship Is What Our Youth Need," *Independent,* http://www.independent.ie/opinion/columnists/eoghan-harris/germanstyle-apprenticeship-system-is-what-our-youth-need-29507676.html, accessed January 25, 2015.
42. Ibid.
43. William James, "The Moral Equivalent of War" (1910), Constitution.org, http://www.constitution.org/wj/meow.htm, accessed January 25, 2015.

44. Joseph M. Speakman, "Into the Woods: The First Year of the Civilian Conservation Corps," *Prologue Magazine* 38, no. 3 (Fall 2006), National Archives, http://www.archives.gov/publications/prologue/2006/fall/ccc.html, accessed January 25, 2015.
45. Peace Corps, "1960's," Peacecorps.gov, http://www.peacecorps.gov/about/history/decades/1960/, accessed January 25, 2015.
46. Lyndon B. Johnson, "Remarks at the University of Kentucky," February 22, 1965, http://www.presidency.ucsb.edu/ws/index.php?pid=27438.
47. Harris Wofford, "The Politics of Service: How a Nation Got Behind AmeriCorps," Brookings, Fall 2002, http://www.brookings.edu/research/articles/2002/09/fall-civilsociety-wofford, accessed January 23, 2015.
48. America's Promise Alliance, http://www.americaspromise.org/our-history, accessed January 23, 2015.
49. "USA Freedom Corp: Strengthening Service to Meet Community Needs," White House, Bush Record, http://georgewbush-whitehouse.archives.gov/infocus/bushrecord/factsheets/needs.html, accessed January 23, 2015.
50. American Society of Civil Engineers, "2013 Report Card for America's Infrastructure: Overview: Executive Summary," Infrastructurereportcard.org, http://www.infrastructurereportcard.org/a/#p/overview/executive-summary, accessed January 23, 2015.
51. American Society of Civil Engineers, "2013 Report Card for America's Infrastructure," Infrastructurereportcard.org, http://infrastructurereportcard.org/a/#p/home, accessed July 21, 2015.
52. U.S. Department of Transportation, Federal Highway Administration, "The Quotable Interstate," Fhwa.dot.gov, http://www.fhwa.dot.gov/interstate/quotable.cfm, accessed April 12, 2015.
53. Conor Friedersdorf, "The Case Against Universal National Service," *The Atlantic,* June 26, 2013, http://www.theatlantic.com/politics/archive/2013/06/the-case-against-universal-national-service/277230/, accessed January 23, 2015.
54. Bruce Chapman, "A Bad Idea Whose Time Is Past," Brookings, Fall 2002, http://www.brookings.edu/research/articles/2002/09/fall-civilsociety-chapman, accessed January 23, 2015.
55. Richard A. Posner, "Universal National Service," Becker-Posner blog, September 23, 2007, http://www.becker-posner-blog.com/2007/09/universal-national-service--posner.html, accessed January 23, 2015.

56. Ibid.
57. The social cost of about 125,000 members is estimated to be about $2 billion, or around $16,000 per member. See Clive Belfield, "The Economic Value of National Service," Franklin Project of the Aspen Institute, September 2013, 1.
58. Ibid.
59. Ibid.

4. Health Care

1. Institute of Medicine, "Report Brief: U.S. Health in International Perspective: Shorter Lives, Poorer Health," Iom.edu, January 9, 2013, http://iom.edu/Reports/2013/US-Health-in-International-Perspective-Shorter-Lives-Poorer-Health/Report-Brief010913, accessed January 26, 2015.
2. World Health Organization, "Life Expectancy, Data by Country," Who.int, http://apps.who.int/gho/data/view.main.680?lang=en, accessed January 26, 2015; World Health Organization, "Probability of Dying per 1000 Live Births, Data by Country," http://apps.who.int/gho/data/view.main.CM1320R?lang=en, accessed July 22, 2015; and World Health Organization, "Maternal Mortality Ratio, Data by Country," http://apps.who.int/gho/data/view.main.1390, accessed July 24, 2015.
3. K. Davis, K. Stremikis, C. Schoen, and D. Squires, "Mirror, Mirror on the Wall, 2014 Update: How the U.S. Health Care System Compares Internationally," Commonwealth Fund, June 2014, http://www.commonwealthfund.org/publications/fund-reports/2014/jun/mirror-mirror, accessed January 26, 2015.
4. World Health Organization, "Life Expectancy, Data by Country," Who.int, http://apps.who.int/gho/data/view.main.680?lang=en, accessed July 22, 2015.
5. Central Intelligence Agency, *The World Factbook,* Cia.gov, https://www.cia.gov/library/publications/the-world-factbook/fields/2177.html, accessed January 26, 2015. Some have suggested that the elements of the discrepancies may arise from gun deaths, car accidents, or different ways to quantify infant mortality, but the basic fact of a comparison unfavorable to the United States is seldom challenged.
6. See note 1.
7. Centers for Medicare & Medicaid Services, "NHE Fact Sheet, Historical NHE, 2013," Cms.gov, http://www.cms.gov/Research-Statistics-Data

-and-Systems/Statistics-Trends-and-Reports/NationalHealthExpend Data/NHE-Fact-Sheet.html, accessed January 26, 2015.

8. OECD, "Compare Your Country: Health Profile," Compareyourcountry .org, http://www.oecd.org/els/health-systems/oecd-health-statistics -2014-frequently-requested-data.htm, accessed April 12, 2015.
9. Ibid.
10. Sean Keegan et al., "National Health Expenditure Projections, 2014–24: Spending Growth Faster Than Recent Trends," *HealthAffairs*, no. 8, July 28, 2015, http://content.healthaffairs.org/content/early/2015/07/15/ hlthaff.2015.0600.full.pdf, accessed August 2, 2015.
11. Barack Obama, "Remarks by the President at the Opening of the White House Forum on Health Reform," White House, https://www.white house.gov/the-press-office/remarks-president-opening-white-house -forum-health-reform, accessed January 26, 2015.
12. International Federation of Health Plans, "2012 Comparative Price Report," http://hushp.harvard.edu/sites/default/files/downloadable_files/ IFHP%202012%20Comparative%20Price%20Report.pdf, accessed January 26, 2015.
13. Sara Thomas, Daniel Bachman, Abhijit Khuperkar, and Guarav Vadnerkar, "Dig Deep: Impacts and Implications of Rising Out-of-Pocket Health Care Costs," Deloitte, https://www2.deloitte.com/content/dam/ Deloitte/us/Documents/life-sciences-health-care/us-lchs-dig-deep -hidden-costs-112414.pdf, accessed January 26, 2015.
14. George I. Kowalczyk, Mark S. Freeland, and Katharine R. Levit, "Using Marginal Analysis to Evaluate Health Spending Trends," *Health Care Finance Review Journal* 10, no. 2 (Winter 1988): 123–29, Table 3, http://www.ncbi.nlm.nih.gov/pmc/articles/PMC4192920/table/t3 -hcfr-10-2-123/, accessed August 1, 2015. Also see Stan Liebowitz, "Why Health Care Costs Too Much," Cato Policy Analysis No. 211, June 1994, http://www.cato.org/pubs/pas/pa211.html, accessed January 29, 2015.
15. Linda J. Bilmes, "The Financial Legacy of Iraq and Afghanistan: How Wartime Spending Decisions Will Constrain Future National Security Budgets," HKS Faculty Research Working Paper Series RWP13-006, March 2013, https://research.hks.harvard.edu/publications/working papers/citation.aspx?PubId=8956, accessed July 22, 2015.
16. World Bank, "Health Expenditure, Public (% of Total Health Expenditure)," http://data.worldbank.org/indicator/SH.XPD.PUBL, accessed July 24, 2015.

17. "Department of Finance Publishes Fiscal Year 2016 Tentative Assessment Roll," NYC Finance press release, http://www1.nyc.gov/assets/finance/downloads/pdf/press_release/press_release_2016_tent_assess_roll.pdf, accessed July 22, 2015. The tax valuations actually used in New York City are lower, by abatement or otherwise, than the city's own market value assessments, the values cited in the text.
18. OECD, Health Statistics 2014, "How Does the United States Compare?," OECD.org, http://www.oecd.org/unitedstates/Briefing-Note-UNITED-STATES-2014.pdf, accessed April 12, 2015.
19. OECD, Health Statistics 2014, "How Does Norway Compare?," OECD.org, http://www.oecd.org/els/health-systems/Briefing-Note-NORWAY-2014.pdf, accessed April 12, 2015.
20. World Bank, "GNI per Capita, Atlas Method (Current US$)," http://data.worldbank.org/indicator/NY.GNP.PCAP.CD, accessed August 2, 2015.
21. OECD, Health Statistics 2014, "How Does Japan Compare?," OECD.org, http://www.oecd.org/els/health-systems/Briefing-Note-JAPAN-2014.pdf, accessed July 23, 2015.
22. OECD (2012), U.S. health care system from an international perspective, Released on June 28, 2012, http://www.oecd.org/health/healthdata, Paris; http://www.oecd.org/unitedstates/HealthSpendingInUSA_HealthData2012.pdf.
23. U.S. Department of Labor, Bureau of Labor Statistics, "Consumer Expenditure Survey, 2014," Bls.org, Table A, http://www.bls.gov/news.release/cesan.nr0.htm, accessed January 26, 2015.
24. U.S. Department of Labor, Bureau of Labor Statistics, "Occupational Outlook Handbook: Physicians and Surgeons," January 2014, http://www.bls.gov/ooh/healthcare/physicians-and-surgeons.htm#tab-5, accessed August 2, 2015.
25. David M. Cutler and Dan P. Ly, "The (Paper) Work of Medicine: Understanding International Medical Costs," *Journal of Economic Perspectives* 25, no. 2 (Spring 2011): 3–25, Table 2, http://pubs.aeaweb.org/doi/pdfplus/10.1257/jep.25.2.3, accessed August 2, 2015.
26. Ibid.
27. Esther Hing and Susan M. Schappert, "Generalist and Specialty Physicians: Supply and Access, 2009–2010," CDC.org, http://www.cdc.gov/nchs/data/databriefs/db105.htm#number), accessed July 24, 2015.
28. OECD, "Health at a Glance 2011: OECD Indicators," OECD Publishing, November 2011, Figure 4.1.1, http://www.oecd-ilibrary.org/sites/

health_glance-2011-en/04/01/g4-01-01.html?itemId=/content/chapter/health_glance-2011-29-en&_csp_=785dba4abcba409e00e41ac61cf308b1, accessed July 24, 2015.

29. All references to Dr. Gawande's research in the following paragraphs are from Atul Gawande, "The Cost Conundrum," *The New Yorker,* June 1, 2009, http://www.newyorker.com/magazine/2009/06/01/the-cost-conundrum, accessed January 25, 2015.
30. Atul Gawande, "Overkill," *The New Yorker,* May 11, 2015, http://www.newyorker.com/magazine/2015/05/11/overkill-atul-gawande, accessed July 23, 2015.
31. Gardiner Harris, "Hospital Savings: Salaries for Doctors, Not Fees," *New York Times,* July 24, 2009, http://www.nytimes.com/2009/07/25/health/policy/25doctors.html, accessed January 25, 2015. The senator was Charles Schumer (D-NY).
32. Ibid.
33. See note 27.
34. OECD, "Government at a Glance 2011: Doctors' and Nurses' Salaries," OECD Publishing, June 2011, http://dx.doi.org/10.1787/gov_glance-2011-32-en, accessed July 24, 2015.
35. Paywizard, "Nurses in the United States Earn 8 Times More Than in Russia," Paywizard.org, http://www.paywizard.org/main/salary/global-wage-comparison, accessed January 29, 2015.
36. Lynn Feldman, "Managing the Cost of Diagnosis," *Managed Care,* May 2009, http://www.managedcaremag.com/archives/0905/0905.diagnosis.html, accessed January 26, 2015.
37. For an estimate that waste in diagnostic testing amounts to $210 billion (quite possibly more than one-third of all testing expenses), see the Doctors for America website, Dr. Sachin D. Shah, "Cutting the Waste in Medicine," September 10, 2012, http://www.drsforamerica.org/blog/cutting-the-waste-in-medicine, accessed July 25, 2015.
38. See "Choosing Wisely," http://www.choosingwisely.org, accessed August 2, 2015.
39. See note 36.
40. Emad Rizk, "Molecular Diagnostic Testing Presents $5 Billion Conundrum, *Managed Care,* April 2009, http://www.managedcaremag.com/archives/0904/0904.moleculartesting.html, accessed January 16, 2015.
41. "MRI Cost and MRI Procedures Information," New Choice Health, http://www.newchoicehealth.com/mri-cost, accessed January 26, 2015.

The International Federation of Health Plans in a 2013 report places the average cost of an MRI in the United States at $1,145. That study contains interesting comparisons of cost in the United States and five other countries on a number of other procedures and drugs. The United States has the highest costs in all of the rankings.

42. OECD, "46. Magnetic Resonance Imaging (MRI) Exams, Total per 1000 Population," OECD Publishing, http://www.oecd-ilibrary.org/social-issues-migration-health/magnetic-resonance-imaging-mri-exams-total_mri-exam-total-table-en, accessed January 25, 2015.
43. "Getting an MRI Head Scan," Medtronic, http://www.medtronic.com/patients/essential-tremor/living-with/mri-scan/, accessed January 26, 2015.
44. Tara Haelle, "Putting Tests to the Test: Many Medical Procedures Prove Unnecessary — and Risky," *Scientific American,* March 5, 2013, http://www.scientificamerican.com/article/medical-procedures-prove-unnecessary/, accessed January 26, 2015.
45. H. Gilbert Welch, *Should I Be Tested for Cancer?* (Oakland: University of California Press, 2006).
46. For today's normal standard, see American Heart Association, http://www.heart.org/HEARTORG/Conditions/HighBloodPressure/AboutHighBloodPressure/Understanding-Blood-Pressure-Readings_UCM_301764_Article.jsp, accessed July 25, 2015. For an older standard, see H. Gilbert Welch, MD, MPH, Lisa M. Schwartz, MD, MS, and Steven Woloshin, MD, MS, "Changing the Rules," *Dartmouth Medicine,* Winter 2010.
47. Michael B. Rothberg et al., "The Cost of Defensive Medicine on 3 Hospital Medicine Services," *JAMA Internal Medicine* 174, no. 11 (November 2014): 1967–68, http://archinte.jamanetwork.com/article.aspx?articleid=1904758, accessed July 23, 2015.
48. Centers for Disease Control and Prevention, FastStats, "Health Expenditures," Cdc.gov, http://www.cdc.gov/nchs/fastats/health-expenditures.htm, accessed January 26, 2015.
49. Simon King, "The Best Selling Drugs Since 1996 — Why AbbVie's Humira Is Set to Eclipse Pfizer's Lipitor," *Forbes,* July 15, 2013, http://www.forbes.com/sites/simonking/2013/07/15/the-best-selling-drugs-since-1996-why-abbvies-humira-is-set-to-eclipse-pfizers-lipitor/, accessed January 26, 2015.
50. Doctors Without Borders, "Countries Must Fix Critical Access to Medi-

cines Flaws in the Trans-Pacific Trade Pact," May 7, 2013, http://www.doctorswithoutborders.org/news-stories/press-release/countries-must-fix-critical-access-medicines-flaws-trans-pacific-trade, accessed January 26, 2015.

51. Experts in Chronic Myeloid Leukemia, "The Price of Drugs for Chronic Myeloid Leukemia (CML) Is a Reflection of the Unsustainable Prices of Cancer Drugs: From the Perspective of a Large Group of CML Experts," *Blood* 121, no. 22 (May 30, 2013), http://www.bloodjournal.org/content/121/22/4439#ref-2, accessed January 26, 2015.
52. Ibid.
53. Kaustubh Kulkarni and Suchitra Mohanty, "Novartis Loses Landmark India Patent Case on Glivec," Reuters, April 2, 2013, http://in.reuters.com/article/2013/04/01/india-drugs-patent-novartis-glivec-idINDEE93000920130401, accessed July 24, 2015. The drug is generally marketed as Gleevec in the United States and Glivec internationally.
54. Ibid.
55. Lena Groeger, "Big Pharma's Big Fines," ProPublica, February 24, 2014, http://projects.propublica.org/graphics/bigpharma, accessed January 26, 2014.
56. Lena Groeger, Charles Ornstein, Mike Tigas, and Ryann Grochowski Jones, "Dollars for Docs: How Industry Dollars Reach Your Doctors," ProPublica, July 1, 2015, https://projects.propublica.org/docdollars/, accessed July 24, 2015.
57. Ibid.
58. Craig W. Lindsey, "The Top Prescription Drugs of 2011 in the United States: Antipsychotics and Antidepressants Once Again Lead CNS Therapeutics," *ACS Chemical Neuroscience* 3, no. 8 (September 2012): 630–31, http://pubs.acs.org/doi/abs/10.1021/cn3000923, accessed August 2, 2015.
59. Wenjun Zhong et al., "Age and Sex Patterns of Drug Prescribing in a Defined American Population," *Mayo Clinic Proceedings* 88, no. 7 (June 2013): 697–707, http://www.mayoclinicproceedings.org/article/S0025-6196(13)00357-1/pdf, accessed August 2, 2015.
60. Ethan Rome, "Big Pharma Pockets $711 Billion in Profits by Robbing Seniors, Taxpayers," *Huffington Post*, April 8, 2013, http://www.huffingtonpost.com/ethan-rome/big-pharma-pockets-711-bi_b_3034525.html, accessed January 26, 2015.

61. Wendell Potter, "Docs, Drug Companies, Insurers Drive Up Medicare Costs," Center for Public Integrity, August 25, 2014, http://www.publicintegrity.org/2014/08/25/15345/docs-drug-companies-insurers-drive-medicare-costs, accessed January 26, 2015.
62. Federal Trade Commission, "FTC Chairman Leibowitz: Eliminating Pay-for-Delay Pharmaceutical Settlements Would Save Consumers $3.5 Billion Annually," FTC News Release, June 23, 2009, https://www.ftc.gov/news-events/press-releases/2009/06/ftc-chairman-leibowitz-eliminating-pay-delay-pharmaceutical, accessed January 26, 2015.
63. "Persuading the Prescribers: Pharmaceutical Industry Marketing and Its Influence on Physicians and Patients," Pew Charitable Trusts Fact Sheet, November 11, 2013, http://www.pewtrusts.org/en/research-and-analysis/fact-sheets/2013/11/11/persuading-the-prescribers-pharmaceutical-industry-marketing-and-its-influence-on-physicians-and-patients, accessed July 24, 2015.
64. *60 Minutes,* "The Cost of Dying," CBSnews.com, November 19, 2009, http://www.cbsnews.com/news/the-cost-of-dying/, accessed January 26, 2015.
65. Reed Abelson, "Weighing Medical Costs of End-of-Life Care," *New York Times,* December 22, 2009, http://www.nytimes.com/2009/12/23/health/23ucla.html?, accessed January 26, 2015.
66. Michael Bell, "Why 5% of Patients Create 50% of Health Care Costs," *Forbes,* January 10, 2013, http://www.forbes.com/sites/michaelbell/2013/01/10/why-5-of-patients-create-50-of-health-care-costs/, accessed July 24, 2015.
67. Baohui Zhang et al., "Health Care Costs in the Last Week of Life: Associations with End of Life Conversations," *Archives of Internal Medicine* 169, no. 5 (March 9, 2009): 480–88, http://www.ncbi.nlm.nih.gov/pmc/articles/PMC2862687/, accessed January 28, 2015.
68. Ibid.
69. See note 65.
70. John E. Wennberg, *Tracking the Care of Patients with Severe Chronic Illness: The Dartmouth Atlas of Health Care 2008,* Dartmouth Institute for Health Policy and Clinical Practice Center for Health Policy Research, 2008, http://www.dartmouthatlas.org/downloads/atlases/2008_Chronic_Care_Atlas.pdf, accessed August 2, 2015.
71. Jonathan Skinner and Elliott S. Fisher, "Reflections on Geographic

Variations in U.S. Health Care," Dartmouth Institute for Health Policy and Clinical Practice Center for Health Policy Research, March 31, 2010, updated May 12, 2010, http://www.dartmouthatlas.org/downloads/press/Skinner_Fisher_DA_05_10.pdf, accessed August 3, 2015.

72. Atul Gawande, *Being Mortal* (New York: Metropolitan Books, 2014), 178.
73. Ibid., 177.
74. Ibid., 6, 192.
75. Stephanie Armour and Louise Radnofsky, "End-of-Life Talk Proposed as New Medicare Benefit," *Wall Street Journal,* July 8, 2015, http://www.wsj.com/articles/government-proposes-to-pay-health-providers-for-end-of-life-discussions-1436396400, accessed October 12, 2015.
76. Lara C. Pullen, "New End-of-Life Discussion Codes a Step Toward Reimbursement?," Medscape.com, http://www.medscape.com/view article/832017, accessed July 24, 2015.
77. Institute of Medicine, "Dying in America — Improving Quality and Honoring Individual Preferences Near the End of Life," Iom.edu, http://www.iom.edu/Reports/2014/Dying-In-America-Improving-Quality-and-Honoring-Individual-Preferences-Near-the-End-of-Life/Report%20Brief.aspx, accessed April 12, 2015.
78. Pam Belluck, "Panel Urges Overhauling Health Care at End of Life," *New York Times,* September 17, 2014, http://www.nytimes.com/2014/09/18/science/end-of-life-care-needs-sweeping-overhaul-panel-says.html, accessed January 26, 2015.
79. Alvin Tran, "We're No. 1, Not in a Good Way: Highest Hospital Administrative Costs," WBUR, September 8, 2014, http://commonhealth.wbur.org/2014/09/us-highest-hospital-administrative-costs, accessed January 28, 2015.
80. Ibid.
81. Ibid.
82. Steffie Woolhandler, Terry Campbell, and David U. Himmelstein, "Costs of Health Care Administration in the United States and Canada," *New England Journal of Medicine* 349 (August 21, 2003): 768–75, http://www.nejm.org/doi/full/10.1056/NEJMsa022033, accessed January 28, 2015.
83. Jeffrey Pfeffer, "The Reason Health Care Is So Expensive: Insurance Companies," *Bloomberg Business,* April 10, 2013, http://www.bloomberg.com/bw/articles/2013-04-10/the-reason-health-care-is-so-expensive-insurance-companies, accessed April 12, 2015.

84. *2014 Annual Report of the Boards of Trustees of the Federal Hospital Insurance and Federal Supplemental Medical Insurance Trust Funds,* July 28, 2014, 85, http://www.cms.gov/Research-Statistics-Data-and-Systems/Statistics-Trends-and-Reports/ReportsTrustFunds/downloads/tr2014.pdf, accessed January 28, 2015.
85. Henry J. Kaiser Family Foundation, "Explaining Health Care Reform: Medical Loss Ratio," February 29, 2012, http://kff.org/health-reform/fact-sheet/explaining-health-care-reform-medical-loss-ratio-mlr/, accessed January 28, 2015.
86. Margaret A. Hamburg, "Celebrating 30 Years of Easier Access to Cost-Saving Generic Drugs," FDA Voice, September 24, 2014, http://blogs.fda.gov/fdavoice/index.php/2014/09/celebrating-30-years-of-easier-access-to-cost-saving-generic-drugs/, accessed July 24, 2015.
87. Steffie Woolhandler and David Himmelstein, "Why Canadian Hospitals Outperform U.S. Hospitals," *HealthAffairs,* December 14, 2014, http://sph.cuny.edu/2014/12/14/why-canadian-hospitals-outperform-u-s-hospitals/, accessed January 28, 2015.
88. See the Liebowitz source in note 14.
89. Nathaniel Weixel, "New CBO Report Projects Long-Term Decrease in Medicare Spending Growth," *Bloomberg BNA,* http://www.bna.com/new-cbo-report-n17179894686/, accessed January 29, 2015. Also see Congressional Budget Office, "An Update to the Budget and Economic Outlook: 2014 to 2024," August 2014, http://www.cbo.gov/sites/default/files/cbofiles/attachments/45653-OutlookUpdate_2014_Aug.pdf, accessed August 2, 2015.
90. PBS, "Sick Around the World," *Frontline,* http://www.pbs.org/wgbh/pages/frontline/sickaroundtheworld/, accessed January 29, 2015.
91. Ibid.
92. Ibid.
93. Ibid.
94. Ibid.
95. Sharon Willcox et al., "Measuring and Reducing Waiting Times: A Cross-National Comparison of Strategies," *HealthAffairs* 26, no. 4 (July 2007): 1078–87, http://content.healthaffairs.org/content/26/4/1078.full, accessed July 24, 2015.
96. Cited, with attribution, by Congressional Budget Office Director Peter Orszag at the Health Reform Summit of the Committee on Finance, U.S.

Senate, "Opportunities to Increase Efficiency in Health Care," June 16, 2008, 3, http://www.cbo.gov/sites/default/files/06-16-healthsummit.pdf, accessed August 4, 2015.

5. Financial Sector Reform

1. Franklin D. Roosevelt, "Fireside Chat 6: On Moving Forward to Greater Freedom and Greater Security," Franklin D. Roosevelt Presidential Library and Museum, September 20, 1934, http://docs.fdrlibrary.marist.edu/093034.html, accessed August 15, 2015.
2. U.S. Department of Commerce, U.S. Census Bureau, *Historical Statistics of the United States: Colonial Times to 1970, Part 1,* Washington, DC, September 1975, "Series D. 85-86. Unemployment: 1890–1970," http://www2.census.gov/prod2/statcomp/documents/CT1970p1-05.pdf, accessed January 25, 2015.
3. Ibid.
4. See data for 1929–33 in U.S. Department of Commerce, Bureau of Economic Analysis, National Income and Product Accounts Tables, BEA.gov, Table 1.1.5, "Gross Domestic Product," http://www.bea.gov/iTable/iTableHtml.cfm?reqid=9&step=3&isuri=1&904=1929&903=5&906=a&905=1933&910=x&911=0, accessed August 15, 2015.
5. Federal Deposit Insurance Corporation, "A Brief History of Deposit Insurance in the United States," FDIC.gov, September 1998, Table 5, "Commercial Bank Suspensions, 1921–1933," https://www.fdic.gov/bank/historical/brief/brhist.pdf, accessed August 15, 2015.
6. For the current regulation, see 220.12 Supplement, "Margin Requirements," in Fed. Reg. T 12 CFR 220, Federal Reserve Board, *Regulations,* http://www.federalreserve.gov/bankinforeg/reglisting.htm#T, accessed August 15, 2015. For history, see New York Stock Exchange Market Data, "FRB Initial Margin Requirements — Percent of Total Value Required to Purchase Stock," NYXData.com, http://www.nyxdata.com/nysedata/asp/factbook/viewer_edition.asp?mode=table&key=52&category=8, accessed January 25, 2015.
7. Federal Deposit Insurance Corporation, "Historical Timeline," FDIC.gov, https://www.fdic.gov/about/history/timeline/1930s.html, accessed January 25, 2015.
8. A. W. Jones, "History of the Firm," http://www.awjones.com/historyofthefirm.html, accessed January 25, 2015.

9. Ibid.
10. "Hedge Fund Industry, Assets Under Management," BarclayHedge, http://www.barclayhedge.com/research/indices/ghs/mum/Hedge_Fund.html, accessed January 31, 2015.
11. Ibid.
12. Ibid.
13. *Goldstein v. SEC*, 451 F.3d 873 (D.C. Cir. 2006).
14. A valid comparison with hedge fund performance over a long time span would require comparing the composite fund results with a portfolio matching the S&P and then leveraged with debt to the same degree as the fund index.
15. The S&P 500 has outperformed hedge funds for a decade. See "Going Nowhere Fast," *The Economist*, December 22, 2012, http://www.economist.com/news/finance-and-economics/21568741-hedge-funds-have-had-another-lousy-year-cap-disappointing-decade-going, accessed August 15, 2015.
16. Federal Deposit Insurance Corporation, "Commercial Bank Reports, Historical Statistics on Banking," FDIC.gov, Table CB02, "Changes in Number of Institutions: FDIC-Insured Commercial Banks," https://www2.fdic.gov/hsob/HSOBRpt.asp, accessed August 15, 2015.
17. See "The Three Hundred Largest Banks in the United States, Listed in Order of Amount of Deposits on Dec. 31, 1949," in John Porter, *Moody's Manual of Investments* (New York: Moody's Investor Service, 1950).
18. Erik Holm, "Ranking the Biggest U.S. Banks: A New (Old) Entrant in Top 5," *Wall Street Journal*, December 10, 2014, http://blogs.wsj.com/moneybeat/2014/12/10/ranking-the-biggest-u-s-banks-a-new-old-entrant-in-top-5/, accessed July 27, 2015.
19. See note 17.
20. See note 18.
21. Hubert P. Janicki and Edward Simpson Prescott, "Changes in Size Distribution of U.S. Banks: 1960–2005," Federal Reserve Bank of Richmond, https://www.richmondfed.org/publications/research/economic_quarterly/2006/fall/pdf/janicki_prescott.pdf, accessed January 31, 2015.
22. The top ten banks have about $10 trillion in assets out of about $15 trillion in assets for all banks. For data on the top ten banks, see note 277. For data on total assets, see H.8 Statistical Release, "Selected Assets and Liabilities of Commercial Banks in the United States," Federal Reserve

Board, August 14, 2015, http://www.federalreserve.gov/releases/h8/current/h8.pdf, accessed August 15, 2015.

23. See note 21.
24. Connecticut Department of Banking, "Bank Geographic Structure," http://www.ct.gov/dob/cwp/view.asp?a=2235&q=297892, accessed April 13, 2015.
25. Ronald A. Wirtz, "Loosening the Strings of Regulation," Federal Reserve Bank of Minneapolis, November 1, 2004, https://www.minneapolisfed.org/publications/fedgazette/loosening-the-strings-of-regulation, accessed January 25, 2015.
26. Ibid.
27. Matthew Sherman, "A Short History of Financial Deregulation in the United States," Center for Economic and Policy Research, July 2009, http://www.cepr.net/documents/publications/dereg-timeline-2009-07.pdf, accessed July 27, 2015.
28. Center for Responsive Politics, "Top Industries," Opensecrets.org, https://www.opensecrets.org/lobby/top.php?indexType=i&showYear=2014, accessed January 25, 2015.
29. Ibid.
30. Center for Responsive Politics, "Ranked Sectors," Opensecrets.org, https://www.opensecrets.org/lobby/top.php?showYear=a&indexType=c, accessed January 25, 2015.
31. U.S. Congress, House Committee on Oversight and Government Reform, "The Financial Crisis and the Role of Federal Regulators," 110th Cong., 2d Sess. (Washington, DC: GPO, 2008), statement of Alan Greenspan, former chairman of the Federal Reserve, http://www.gpo.gov/fdsys/pkg/CHRG-110hhrg55764/html/CHRG-110hhrg55764.htm, accessed August 15, 2015.
32. "The Safe Banking Act: A Summary Background and FAQ," Demos.org, April 22, 2010, http://www.demos.org/publication/safe-banking-act-summary-background-and-faq, accessed January 25, 2015.
33. Thomas Hoenig, "Global Banking: A Failure of Structural Integrity," FDIC, December 13, 2013, https://www.fdic.gov/news/news/speeches/spdec1313.html, accessed July 27, 2015.
34. Daniel K. Tarullo, "Financial Stability Regulation," Federal Reserve Board, October 10, 2012, http://www.federalreserve.gov/newsevents/speech/tarullo20121010a.htm, accessed August 15, 2015.

35. Richard W. Fisher, "Remarks at the SW Graduate School of Banking," Federal Reserve Bank of Dallas, June 3, 2010, http://www.dallasfed.org/news/speeches/fisher/2010/fs100603.cfm, accessed January 25, 2015.
36. Simon Johnson, "The Debate on Bank Size Is Over," *New York Times*, March 28, 2013, http://economix.blogs.nytimes.com/2013/03/28/the-debate-on-bank-size-is-over/, accessed January 25, 2015.
37. Jamie Dunkley and Andrew Hough, "Banks Warn 'Hostility Will Push Us' Abroad After King Attack," *Telegraph*, March 12, 2012, http://www.telegraph.co.uk/finance/newsbysector/banksandfinance/9138630/Banks-warn-hostility-will-push-us-abroad-after-King-attack.html, accessed January 25, 2015.
38. Mervyn King, "Bank of England Governor Mervyn King's speech to the Lord Mayor's Banquet," *The Guardian*, June 18, 2009, http://www.theguardian.com/business/2009/jun/18/bank-of-england-mervyn-king, accessed January 25, 2015.
39. Leo Melamed, "Milton Friedman's 1971 Feasibility Paper," LeoMelamed.com, http://www.leomelamed.com/articles/12-71FriedmanCato.html, accessed January 31, 2015.
40. "Futures/Futures Exchanges/History," GoldAvenue, http://info.goldavenue.com/info_site/in_glos/in_glos_futures.html, accessed April 13, 2015.
41. Don Chance, "A Brief History of Derivatives," in *Essays in Derivatives: Risk-Transfer Tools and Topics Made Easy* (Hoboken, NJ: John Wiley & Sons, 2008), http://onlinelibrary.wiley.com/doi/10.1002/9781118266885.ch2/summary/, accessed August 15, 2015.
42. Will Acworth, "2014 Annual Global Futures and Options Volume," *Futures Industry Magazine*, March 9, 2015, https://fimag.fia.org/articles/2014-fia-annual-global-futures-and-options-volume-gains-north-america-and-europe-offset, accessed April 13, 2015.
43. U.S. Commodity Futures Trading Commission, "History of the CFTC," CFTC.gov, http://www.cftc.gov/about/historyofthecftc/index.htm, accessed January 31, 2015.
44. Scot Warren, "Innovate to Advance: 30 Years of S&P 500 Futures," *Open Markets*, May 4, 2012, http://openmarkets.cmegroup.com/3215/innovate-to-advance-30-years-of-sp-500-futures, accessed July 30, 2015.
45. Baker Library Historical Collections, Harvard Business School, "Federal National Mortgage Association," http://www.library.hbs.edu/hc/

lehman/company.html?company=federal_national_mortgage_association, accessed January 13, 2015.

46. Ibid.
47. Efraim Benmelech and Jennifer Dlugosz, "The Credit Rating Crisis," Chapter 3 in *NBER Macroeconomics Annual 2009* 24, National Bureau of Economic Research (Chicago: University of Chicago Press, 2010), http://www.nber.org/chapters/c11794.pdf, accessed July 28, 2015.
48. Office of the Comptroller of the Currency, "OCC's Quarterly Report on Bank Trading and Derivatives Activities, First Quarter 2015," OCC.gov, http://www.occ.gov/topics/capital-markets/financial-markets/trading/derivatives/dq115.pdf, accessed January 31, 2015.
49. If estimates are correct about the worldwide notional value of derivatives, that total runs to more like twenty times the world's GNP. The aggregate GNP of the world was about $75 trillion in 2013, according to Central Intelligence Agency, *The World Factbook,* 2013, https://www.cia.gov/library/publications/the-world-factbook/geos/xx.html, accessed January 31, 2015; and the World Bank, World Development Indicators Database, July 1, 2015, http://databank.worldbank.org/data/download/GDP.pdf, accessed July 27, 2015.
50. The equity capital of JPMorgan Chase was $236 billion in 2015 and $215 billion at Citigroup. For each, see "Balance Sheet," March 31, 2015, Yahoo! Finance, http://finance.yahoo.com/q/bs?s=C; and Yahoo! Finance, http://finance.yahoo.com/q/bs?s=JPM, accessed August 17, 2015. The notional value of open derivatives positions at the former was $56 trillion, and at the latter $53 trillion, according to the OCC website. It can easily be argued that these leverage ratios and position sizes provide a mixed benefit at best for the owners of the banks — their shareholders. Because public-equity markets are fickle and not reliably wise, I hesitate to use market prices at any point in time to prove an argument. At times, though, they do seem to speak clearly. Shares in JPMorgan and Citigroup, where derivatives trading is most dominant, sell as of July 25, 2015, at 1.2 times book value and .95 times book value, respectively, while Wells Fargo carries a market worth almost 1.8 times its book value. The two larger banks sell for eight to twelve times trailing earnings, while Wells Fargo fetches fourteen times earnings. The most obvious difference is the scale of open derivatives positions. Wells Fargo holds open positions at only about one-tenth the scale of JPMorgan's. The smaller, and more traditional, of these banks is now the most valu-

able bank in the world, with a market value $42 billion greater than Morgan's. While such conclusions are necessarily conjectural, a reasonable guess is that shareholders believe the value of the traditional bank will be less vulnerable to the next storm. See Emily Glazer, "Wells Fargo & Co. Is the Earth's Most Valuable Bank," *Wall Street Journal*, July 22, 2015. The Office of the Comptroller of the Currency employs a different but confirmatory risk index. Rather than notional value, it publishes a ratio with a derived measure of derivatives, Credit Exposure, as the numerator and regulatory defined Risk-Based Capital as the denominator. It computes a ratio of 182 times capital for Citi and 229 for JPMorgan. See note 48.

51. "US Loan-to-Deposit Ratio the Lowest in 30 Years and Falling," Sober Look, October 6, 2013, http://soberlook.com/2013/10/us-loan-to-deposit-ratio-lowest-in-30.html, accessed July 27, 2015. See also Steven W. Carlsen, "Relative Performance of Banking and Insurance Through the Financial Crisis," ETD Collection for Fordham University, January 1, 2013, http://fordham.bepress.com/dissertations/AAI3588206, accessed August 15, 2015.
52. Ruth King, "Loan-to-Deposit Ratio Moves in the Right Direction for Banks," Market Realist, June 17, 2015, http://marketrealist.com/2015/06/loan-deposit-ratio-moves-right-direction-banks/, accessed July 27, 2015; and the Carlsen source in note 51.
53. See the Carlsen source in note 51.
54. Berkshire Hathaway Inc., "2002 Annual Report, 15, http://www.berkshirehathaway.com/2002ar/2002ar.pdf, accessed July 27, 2015.
55. Descriptions and timing of events related in this paragraph are from Federal Reserve Bank of St. Louis, "The Financial Crisis: Full Timeline," StLouisFed.org, https://www.stlouisfed.org/financial-crisis/full-timeline, accessed July 30, 2015.
56. Ibid.
57. Ibid.
58. Jesse Bricker et al., "Changes in U.S. Family Finances from 2010 to 2013: Evidence from the Survey of Consumer Finances," *Federal Reserve Bulletin* 100, no. 4 (September 2014), Figure 2, "Change in Median and Mean Family Net Worth, 2007–13 Surveys," http://www.federalreserve.gov/pubs/bulletin/2014/pdf/scf14.pdf, accessed January 31, 2015.
59. See data for 2008–15 in U.S. Department of Commerce, Bureau of Economic Analysis, "National Income and Product Accounts Tables,"

BEA.gov, Table 1.1.3, "Real Gross Domestic Product, Quantity Indexes," http://www.bea.gov/iTable/iTable.cfm?ReqID=9&step=1#reqid=9&step=3&isuri=1&904=2006&903=3&906=a&905=2015&910=x&911=0, accessed July 27, 2015.

60. International Monetary Fund, "IMF Urges Countries to Redouble Growth Drive, Revive MDGs," IMF.org, September 20, 2010, http://www.imf.org/external/pubs/ft/survey/so/2010/NEW092010A.htm, accessed January 31, 2015.
61. U.S. Department of Labor, Bureau of Labor Statistics, "Labor Force Statistics from the Current Population Survey," BLS.gov, http://data.bls.gov/timeseries/LNS14000000, accessed January 31, 2015.
62. Federal Reserve Bank of St. Louis and U.S. Office of Management and Budget, "Federal Debt: Total Public Debt as Percent of Gross Domestic Product [GFDEGDQ188S]," https://research.stlouisfed.org/fred2/series/GFDEGDQ188S/, accessed January 31, 2015.
63. Michiyo Nakamoto and David Wighton, "Citigroup Chief Stays Bullish on Buy-outs," *Financial Times,* July 9, 2007, http://www.ft.com/cms/s/0/80e2987a-2e50-11dc-821c-0000779fd2ac.html, accessed July 27, 2015.
64. Timothy Geithner, *Stress Test: Reflections on Financial Crises* (New York: Crown Publishers, 2014).
65. Graeme Wearden, "Sir Mervyn King: Don't Demonise Bankers," *The Guardian,* May 19, 2013, http://www.theguardian.com/business/2013/may/19/mervyn-king-dont-demonise-bankers, accessed January 31, 2015.
66. Stephen Gandel, "By Every Measure, the Big Banks Are Bigger," *Fortune,* September 13, 2013, http://fortune.com/2013/09/13/by-every-measure-the-big-banks-are-bigger/, accessed January 31, 2015.
67. Mayra Rodríguez Valladares, "Derivatives Markets Growing Again, with Few New Protections," *New York Times,* May 13, 2014, http://dealbook.nytimes.com/2014/05/13/derivatives-markets-growing-again-with-few-new-protections/, accessed January 31, 2015.
68. Al Lewis, "The Coming Financial Crisis," *Wall Street Journal,* March 30 2014, http://www.wsj.com/articles/SB10001424052702303325204579465610191507216, accessed January 31, 2015.
69. U.S. Department of Commerce, U.S. Census Bureau, "2010 Census Shows Second Highest Homeownership Rate on Record Despite Largest Decrease Since 1940," *U.S. Census Bureau Newsroom Archive,* October 6, 2011, https://www.census.gov/newsroom/releases/archives/2010_census/cb11-cn188.html, accessed January 31, 2015.

70. Ibid.
71. Ibid.
72. See, for instance, Benjamin Landy, "How the Financial Sector Consumed America's Economic Growth," Century Foundation, February 25, 2013, http://www.tcf.org/blog/detail/graph-how-the-financial-sector-consumed-americas-economic-growth, accessed August 15, 2015; Jordan Weissman, "How Wall Street Devoured Corporate America," *The Atlantic,* March 5, 2013, http://www.theatlantic.com/business/archive/2013/03/how-wall-street-devoured-corporate-america/273732/, accessed January 31, 2015; and Thomas Philippon, "Why Has the U.S. Financial Sector Grown So Much? The Role of Corporate Finance," Working Paper No. 13405, National Bureau of Economic Research, September 2007, http://www.nber.org/papers/w13405, accessed July 26, 2015.
73. Thomas Philippon, "Has the US Finance Industry Become Less Efficient? On the Theory and Measurement of Financial Intermediation," *American Economic Review* 105, no. 4 (April 2015): 1408–38, http://dx.doi.org/10.1257/aer.20120578, accessed August 16, 2015.
74. U.S. Department of Commerce, Bureau of Economic Analysis, "National Income and Product Accounts Tables," BEA.gov, Table 6.16A, "Corporate Profits by Industry," http://www.bea.gov/iTable/iTableHtml.cfm?reqid=9&step=3&isuri=1&903=236, accessed August 15, 2015.
75. Ibid., Table 6.16D, "Corporate Profits by Industry," http://www.bea.gov/iTable/iTable.cfm?ReqID=9&step=1#reqid=9&step=3&isuri=1&903=239, accessed August 16, 2015. Also see Benjamin M. Friedman, "Is Our Financial System Serving Us Well?," *Daedalus* 139, no. 4 (Fall 2010): 9–21, http://www.mitpressjournals.org/doi/abs/10.1162/DAED_a_00038, accessed August 15, 2015; and Benjamin M. Friedman, "Overmighty Finance Levies a Tithe on Growth," *Financial Times,* August 26, 2009, http://www.ft.com/intl/cms/s/0/2de2b29a-9271-11de-b63b-00144feabdc0.html, accessed July 25, 2015.
76. Michael Mandel, "A Bad Decade for Nonfinancial Profits," *Bloomberg Business,* Econochat, March 4, 2009, http://www.businessweek.com/the_thread/economicsunbound/archives/2009/03/a_bad_decade_fo.html, accessed January 31, 2015.
77. See Richard Henderson, "Industry Output and Employment Projections to 2022," Monthly Labor Review, BLS.gov, December 2013, Table 1, "Employment by Major Industry Sector, 2002, 2012, and Projected 2022,"

http://www.bls.gov/opub/mlr/2013/article/industry-employment-and-output-projections-to-2022-1.htm, accessed August 16, 2015.

78. As this chapter was being completed, the Federal Reserve Board of Governors announced new rules that would move somewhat in this direction. The affected banks will consider the step larger than this author, but the direction is commendable. See Federal Reserve Board press release, July 20, 2015, http://www.federalreserve.gov/newsevents/press/bcreg/20150720a.htm, accessed August 16, 2015.
79. This approach was first suggested to me by Steven W. Carlsen, PhD. See note 51.

A Concluding Remark

1. George Washington, in a letter of September 24, 1776, to the President of the Continental Congress, often referred to as "On Recruiting and Maintaining an Army." The letter is reprinted in full on the website American History, http://www.let.rug.nl/usa/presidents/george-washington/on-recruiting-and-maintaining-an-army-1776.php, accessed July 22, 2015.
2. Adam Smith, *An Inquiry into the Nature and Causes of the Wealth of Nations* (1776), Book IV, Chapter II.

Index

Page numbers in italics indicate figures.